Out
of the
Ashes

Between 2005 and 2008, Tim Albone was based in Afghanistan where he wrote for *The Times* and *Sunday Times*. He has also reported from Iraq, Pakistan, Yemen, Ethiopia and India.

In 2008 he was shortlisted for the Bayeux Calvados award for war correspondents.

Out of the Ashes, the film, premiered at the Edinburgh International Film Festival, also won the Special Jury Prize at the Peace and Sport Awards in Monaco and it was shown on the BBC in February 2011.

Out of the Ashes is Tim's first book.

Out
of the
Ashes

The extraordinary rise and rise
of the Afghanistan cricket team

Tim Albone

To Dad, I miss you.

To Mum, Charlie, Liz and Victoria, I love you.

2 4 6 8 10 9 7 5 3 1

First published in 2011 by Virgin Books, an imprint of Ebury Publishing
A Random House Group Company

The Random House Group Limited Reg. No. 954009

Addresses for companies within the Random House Group can be found at
www.randomhouse.co.uk

A CIP catalogue record for this book is available from the British Library

The Random House Group Limited supports The Forest Stewardship
Council [FSC], the leading international forest certification organisation.
All our titles that are printed on Greenpeace-approved FSC-certified
paper carry the FSC logo. Our paper procurement policy can be found at
www.rbooks.co.uk/environment

Mixed Sources
Product group from well-managed
forests and other controlled sources
www.fsc.org Cert no. TT-COC-2139
© 1996 Forest Stewardship Council

Printed and bound in Great Britain
by CPI Mackays, Chatham, ME5 8TD.

ISBN 9780753522479

To buy books by your favourite authors and register for offers,
visit www.rbooks.co.uk

Contents

Foreword

The best books about sport are, of course, about more than just sport and *Out of the Ashes* fits perfectly into this genre. It is, in turn, a story about despair, initially, and then hope; about dreams that, by any standards, appear impossible and about how the drive, dedication and, occasionally, the downright madness of one man on a mission can inspire others.

The game through which these dreams are achieved is cricket and on the sub-continent, I suppose, it could only be cricket. But elsewhere there have been similar stories of how sport, especially, has the capacity to carry disadvantaged people far beyond the limitations imposed by others. The sporting success of African Americans, pre the Civil Rights' movement, being a perfect example.

Afghanistan summons up pictures of bombs and devastation, of invasions and repression, but in even the most depressed places a sort of normality exists; people find ways of carrying on and work hard to recreate the kinds of activities that mark us out as creative human beings. For

Taj Malik, a man who the Australians would definitely describe as a 'tragic', this normality involved cricket.

I wasn't surprised reading about the latent enthusiasm for cricket in Afghanistan. After all, it is just over the border from Pakistan, where some of the most outrageously gifted cricketers of the modern game have come from, sprouting up from the most unlikely circumstances and often with minimal facilities save a tape-ball and god-given talent.

More than that, on my last tour as an England player in 2000 we had travelled along the Khyber Pass, where we were able to look upon Kabul before the latest devastation rained down. On our way back, we stopped in at a road-side bazaar and wandering through the shops, we were amazed at the level of recognition that these mountain people had of English cricketers from far away. Taj Malik was clearly onto a good thing.

Malik is the central character in this tale, the man who had the dream initially of producing, firstly, a cricket team but not just any old cricket team; a team that might make the world sit up and take notice. With no money, no facilities and no infrastructure and out of an annihilated country, he did just that. Malik's dream of reaching the World Cup proper didn't quite come off, but Afghanistan did reach the finals of the World Twenty20 competition, which, in many ways, suits the 'smaller' cricketing nations much better.

This is the story of that journey. It is a story that illuminates a level of the game that is often hidden from view. One of the policies of the International Cricket Council in the last few years has been to try and broaden cricket's narrow base. Currently, there are a handful of full Test-playing nations, most of whom are concentrated in an area that is rife with violence and corruption. It makes for a vulnerable game that is international only in name.

The flowering of cricket in Afghanistan, then, is not just important from the perspective of giving meaning, hope and a focus to a people and a country that has suffered appallingly, it is part of a wider narrative of cricket striving for a truly international voice. China, America – you name it – cricket is attempting to put down roots. Why not? It is, after all, a wonderful game. Just ask Taj Malik and his players what it has done for them.

Mike Atherton

Introduction

I remember the email clearly. It came from my editor at *The Times* in October 2005, asking me if I'd do a piece on the Afghan cricket team. Cricket, I thought, in this place? It seemed ridiculous but I was assured that *The Economist* had just done a piece on cricket in Afghanistan so it must be true. In fact, England were due to play a Test in neighbouring Pakistan (in the days when it was still safe enough for international teams to travel there), so it would make a timely piece. I was just starting out and desperate for work. An email from an editor offering me work (rather than me pleading for it) was a welcome turnaround.

I'd arrived in Afghanistan in August 2005, having left my job on a local paper in Somerset, with designs on becoming a foreign correspondent. I ended up staying for over two and a half years and writing for *The Times* and *The Sunday Times*, amongst others. The cricket piece was just one of the many I wrote, but something struck a chord.

The two and a half years I spent in Afghanistan were the most amazing, exciting, terrifying, exhilarating years of my life. I had been caught in a roadside bomb while travelling with Canadian troops, chased by a mob who, according to Tahir, my giggling translator, wanted to skin me alive, was shot at while on an army patrol with British troops and almost fell off the side of a cliff when the car I was driving in skidded on ice and performed a 360-degree turn on a single track road. I lived in a house where electricity came on for an hour or two every few days, where the pipes froze in winter and heating was a wood-burning stove in the corner of the room. My guard (who also doubled as a gardener and handyman) was in his seventies and grew his own hashish in the garden, where he chain-smoked.

In Afghanistan I also drank more cups of green tea than I imagined possible, laughed more than I had ever laughed before, hiked in the mountains on the border with China for two weeks with Yaks and – after some gentle persuasion from the blonde, female French photographer I was travelling with – got some American soldiers to let me fire an automatic grenade launcher at a bare hillside (I have to confess it was great fun!).

Afghanistan got under my skin. I, like so many others, fell in love with the place. When I left at the end of 2007, I had a few months off in India but decided I wanted to make a documentary on the country I had fallen for. I was fed up of writing about war and death, the country was so much more than that. I wanted to do a film that showed the other side of the country. The beauty, the madness, the humour, the resilience, the enterprise, the humanity and the people. Most Afghans hate how war defines them to the rest of the world. I wanted to do something that got away from the war. Of course war is always there but it is not the totality of the story, it is a part of the sum.

When I thought about what I wanted to film I kept coming back to cricket. The team, who didn't allow its pathetic facilities, lack of money or lack of training to dim it's hope and enthusiasm, had touched a nerve with me. I've always been a sucker for the underdog. I'd supported Cameroon over England at the 1990 World Cup, cried during the film *Cool Runnings* and loved watching Kenya get to the semi-finals of the 2003 Cricket World Cup.

When I heard the Afghan team was trying to go to the World Cup, and its first qualifier was in Jersey, I knew I had to follow it. The project started as a film, which was broadcast by the BBC, but also became this book. There was so much I couldn't get in the film that needed telling. How could a war-ravaged country like Afghanistan play a sport more associated with the British village green? And by what absurd twist of fate had they ended up playing their first World Cup qualifier in the Channel Islands? I dare you to imagine somewhere more diametrically opposed to Afghanistan than quaint, peaceful, parochial Jersey.

Initially most people thought I was crazy. They couldn't understand why I was heading back to Afghanistan to cover cricket! The team didn't think I was mad; the players knew they had a story worth telling and they welcomed me with open arms (literally, I have never been hugged so much in my life). They let me into their lives, invited me to their homes, took me on the team bus and didn't kick me out of the changing rooms during team talks. Taj Malik, and then Kabir Khan, made me feel like I was part of the team. I was lucky in that I was never made to feel like an interloper, an intruder or an outsider. I wonder if any other national teams would have made a stranger feel so welcome and almost part of the team? I wonder if I would have been so trusting if the tables were turned?

There are so many people who can claim to have played a part in setting up cricket in Afghanistan. If anything I have written doesn't tally with your own recollection, I can only apologise. I spoke to as many people as possible and got as many different points of view and tried to steer the middle course. If nothing else, I hope you will enjoy reading about your team and what they have achieved.

Spending time with the Afghan team was an inspiration for me. I realised that the human mind is a wonderful thing: if you truly believe in something and never give up, you can achieve far more than you've ever dreamed. The world would be a better place if we all had a bit more of the spirit of the Afghan team in us.

Tim Albone

Chapter 1

The Incredible Journey

THE BORDER BETWEEN AFGHANISTAN AND PAKISTAN, DECEMBER 2001

It is an encounter unlike any other. Thousands of Taliban fighters are fleeing the unlikely alliance of US bombers, Special Forces and ragtag Afghan militia that is thundering down through Afghanistan from the north. The fighters slip away on dirt trails and mountain passes pausing, perhaps, to gaze at Taj Malik Alam, who is travelling in the other direction towards the chaos.

As Taj – carrying only a spare change of clothes, a cricket bat and ball – crosses into Afghanistan from Pakistan, he contemplates the scene: distant bombs shake the earth, the Taliban, ousted from power less than three months before, are scattered throughout the countryside and Al-Qaeda, which funded the Taliban regime, though broken and in retreat, are still a present danger. Many of the Taliban's feared Arab and foreign fighters are roaming the hills, seeking revenge. Taj is terrified of coming across them and those fears only intensify as the jagged, snow-capped peaks of the White Mountains loom into view. He will have to pass underneath their shadow on his way to Kabul. Below them lie the Tora Bora caves, a complex underground labyrinth, under the control of Islamists. Despite dropping tens, if not hundreds, of thousands of pounds of bombs, the Americans have been unable to flush out the fighters. It is rumoured that Osama bin Laden is hiding there. Most of the country is still lawless and, in mid-December, as Taj makes his journey he is aware that the country is in a state of flux. Kabul, the capital, had only been captured on 13 November; Kunduz, in the north, wasn't taken until the end of November and Kandahar, the spiritual home-land of the Taliban, has only been wrested from Taliban control days before.

The Allied forces have a mission that, history tells us, no one has ever successfully carried out before – to try to bring peace and stability to Afghanistan.

Taj Malik Alam has his own, and some would say equally futile, mission: he wants to assemble an Afghan cricket team and, because he doesn't lack ambition or belief, take it to the Cricket World Cup. He's dreamt of this day since he was a child. As an Afghan, who has been forced by war to live his life in exile, this return couldn't come soon enough.

Taj is full of energy; he always seems to be moving. If he has to sit still he fidgets and talks incessantly. He laughs easily and when his laughter comes it is shrill and urgent. He has a charm and, despite being overweight and balding, when he smiles it reveals, creased with laughter lines, a handsome, kind and open face.

For this journey he has grown a scraggly beard and swapped his usual tracksuit for traditional robes. As he crosses the border, as well as feeling nervous he feels a surge of positive energy. He is home. And finally he feels; if the Allied invasion is successful, Afghanistan might see peace – something that Taj, who was born in 1975, has never known.

For the past 16 years he has been forced to live as a refugee in Pakistan. His earliest memories are of Soviet helicopters scouring the skies, of brave men with nothing but Kalashnikovs taking on one of the strongest armies in the world, of victory celebrations in Peshawar when the Red Army pulled out and of disappointment when the country was consumed by civil war. He pauses to look up at the towering, snow-capped mountains that mark the eastern border of his homeland and his mind flashes to an event three months earlier that shook the world and changed his destiny and that of his country forever.

On 11 September 2001, 19 suicide bombers flew planes, loaded with civilians, into targets across the east coast of America. As the Twin Towers fell and thousands lost their lives, Afghanistan's history took another unlikely and bloody turn. George W Bush, the American president, declared war on international terrorists and the country that housed them: that country was Afghanistan.

He announced – on 7 October, the day that the American Air Force launched their bombing raids – that America would not falter in its quest for peace and freedom. The Taliban had been issued with a list of demands – close down terrorist cells and return all foreign hostages – neither of these demands was met and now, in response to 9/11 and for the security of the Western world, Bush was launching war. As well as the fighter planes, Bush and Britain sent in Special Forces, soldiers who linked up with the anti-Taliban Northern Alliance to attack Taliban positions.

Before 9/11 Afghanistan largely survived on the largesse of terrorists. Without Al-Qaeda, Taliban Afghanistan couldn't have existed: they were the main funders of the regime. How it had got to that stage reads like a thriller: it is a story steeped in intrigue, betrayal, religious fundamentalism and blood. Afghanistan's history had rarely been peaceful but the last 30 years leading up to 2001 had been particularly bloody.

Until this point Taj's life has been a tough one marked by exile, war and poverty, but he wouldn't change it for anything. All these factors have combined to bring him an unexpected gift – cricket.

He has spent over half his life in the vast Kacha Gari refugee camp in Pakistan. Here, along with tens of thousands of other Afghans, he sheltered from the war that was ravaging his country. The camp, on the edge of the sprawling western Pakistani city of Peshawar, was, at its height in the 1980s and 1990s, a mini-city. More than that, it was a state in exile. Beside the mud huts, where the poor lived, stood the palatial houses of Afghan tribal chiefs and the elite. For most, including Taj, daily life was a struggle. His first year in the camp was incredibly tough. Even today, the family home is little more than a mud hut with a tin roof and had only three rooms; it had no electricity or water. After a year the water and electricity came but as his family increased (by 2001 he had eight brothers and three sisters), the rooms became more cramped. Taj's parents have one room, all the boys share one and all the girls the other. There is very little privacy.

The family has no kitchen to speak of, and is forced to cook on a small gas cooker, often in the dark as the electricity supply, when it comes, is unreliable. The water supply is not clean enough to drink: they have to boil it and drink it as tea, which, like all Afghans, they drink by the gallon.

There is no sewerage system, and human waste, as well as rubbish, collects in puddles and piles in the dirt tracks that pass for roads. Unsurprisingly, disease is rife. As a child Taj had malaria several times as well as typhoid.

Like many of the children who grew up in the refugee camps, Taj's father was a fighter who made trips into Afghanistan to battle the Soviets. He rose to the rank of commander, which eventually brought Taj's family a level of privilege and relative wealth. He was considered a freedom fighter. The family ate well, never went hungry and had enough money to live. However, after the Soviet withdrawal and the subsequent civil war, the family struggled.

Although Taj's father had no hesitation in fighting the Soviets, he believed it was his moral and religious duty, he had no inclination to kill his fellow Afghans. As a result the family's income and prestige was dissipated, and they once more struggled for money and food.

Although they continued to live a life of poverty, for his family and thousands like them, the camp allowed a freedom Afghanistan didn't: people could walk around without having to worry about bombs and violence, the children could go to school and, of great importance to Taj, they could also play cricket. It was his hope that with the American invasion he could return home and take the sport with him. He wanted to see children playing cricket in Afghanistan like he had done as a boy in Pakistan; he wanted to take the game to his homeland.

Taj had fallen in love with cricket early in his stay in Pakistan. In 1987, two years after he had arrived in the country on the back of a donkey with his family and all the possessions they could carry, the cricket World Cup was held in India and Pakistan. He was 12 years old, and in the way of boys that age the world over he fell in love deeply and quickly with the sport. His family was too poor to own a TV but he couldn't fail to notice the game. Pakistan was cricket crazy before the tournament, but in 1987 it reached endemic proportions. Every teahouse and every shop was showing live games on TV, every radio was switched to the commentary, and on every patch of land kids were re-enacting catches, wickets and sixes from games they had seen. In Peshawar the excitement hit fever pitch when on 17 October, England and Sri Lanka came to town, the only World Cup game to be staged in the city. Across the border in Afghanistan, the Mujahideen were waging war. They used Peshawar as a staging post for attacks and came to the city to recuperate, raise funds and spend time with their families. The city was less than 70 miles from the nearest Soviet base inside Afghanistan and it was here that England were playing.

It is not difficult for Taj to explain why he loves cricket. It is, he says, the game of kings. For a young Afghan refugee, with no television, very little education and isolated from the world at large, cricket is a window. Although he had heard about England before cricket, and England soon became his favourite team, countries like New Zealand and Zimbabwe were new to him. Other places were even more obscure and it took him a while to figure out what and where the West Indies were. But Taj immersed himself in the subject, showing the type of commitment and doggedness that would serve him well later in life. Pretty soon he had learnt about all the grounds and players from the ten Test nations.

Almost as soon as Taj started watching cricket he started playing it, though this was not without problems. As he couldn't afford any equipment, he started playing with a stick and plastic bags wrapped up to make a ball. There was no flat ground on which to play as the refugee camp was on rutted, dusty scrubland, and to make matters worse, his father, who dreamed of Taj getting the education war and poverty had denied him, forbade him from playing the game. Taj would have to wait until his father was away fighting in Afghanistan, then he could play cricket to his heart's content.

Taj was not alone in his love for the bat and ball. His elder brother, Sayed, head of the family during their father's lengthy absences, and younger brothers Karim and Hasti were also keen cricketers. Together, the four brothers would skip school to go out and play the game. It didn't do them much good. When their father returned from fighting and heard tales of their cricket playing he beat the brothers. He was uneducated and illiterate and wanted more for his boys than the life he had. Neighbours called the boys wasters and gangsters and, as they grew older, said it would be hard for them to find brides if all they did was play cricket.

The brothers were poor but canny, and soon found ways, through cricket, to make money. One day, like many others, Taj had skived off school to play and had persuaded his brothers and friends to do the same. They only had one old bat and it broke. As they were despairing they saw a funeral procession go by – the pitch was next to a graveyard. Taj came up with a plan: he persuaded the players to join the mourning, aware that often those that attended funerals were given a small financial gift. Taj and the players did their part, crying and sobbing when needed and when the funeral came to an end each of them was given 20 rupees (about 15 pence). It wasn't much, but when they combined their money it was enough to buy two brand new bats.

It wasn't long before Taj had set up a team in the refugee camp. He named it the Afghan Cricket Club. Made up exclusively of Afghan refugees, they became very good. The club would take the best Afghan players from the camps and challenge other teams from across Peshawar to games of tennis-ball cricket. And they would play for money. Often the bets would be for 3,000 rupees (just over £20 today, but then a fortune to the boys). More often than not, the team only had a few hundred rupees between them, but they were certain they would win so they would bet high. With their winnings they would buy bats and more tennis balls (wrapping them in gaffer tape to add extra weight and dull the bounce). Eventually they could even afford to lay a concrete pitch in a graveyard outside their house, and this became the first home of the Afghan Cricket Club.

From the start the team showed an amazing passion and zeal for the game; they also showed they hated to lose. During one local competition they had bought a big cup to give to the winners, which they assumed would be their team, but things didn't go according to plan and they lost in the final. The brothers swapped the large cup for a smaller cup they found at home and presented it to the winning team, keeping the big trophy for themselves. Inevitably a fight broke out, but they never gave up the bigger cup. By way of justification the brothers laughed; they were the better team and they had deserved to win, they just got unlucky. Taj likes to say that lose is not a word in his dictionary; it is something unknown to him.

Their obsession with the game grew, and soon they did little else but play. Their father eventually tired of breaking their equipment and beating them and eased up on them, tolerating their endless games. They no longer had to hide their cricket equipment on the roof of the house, lie about their whereabouts or sneak out behind his back. But he and those around them still thought they were crazy. They had given up their education for a sport. Not only that but a foreign sport. Although the brothers weren't educated – Taj claims to have done one year of university, but Hasti could barely write and Karim happily confessed to having very few interests outside of cricket – they were street smart. Hasti had a natural flair for business: he was often the one who organised the games and the betting syndicates. Taj would organise the brothers – he would hold training sessions, sort out the kit and equipment and very early took on the role of coach. Karim was always the most talented – he could hit the hardest, bowl the best and would combine this with some kamikaze wicketkeeping, diving across hard earth to take spectacular catches. Between them the three brothers formed the backbone of the Afghan Cricket Club, a team of refugees, playing with tennis balls or plastic bags in a refugee camp in Pakistan.

Throughout their childhood they had only one dream: it seemed an impossible one but it was to represent their country in an international cricket match. Taj was determined to make it happen. This book tells the story of Taj and his team's incredible journey from refugees to international cricketing stars.

Chapter 2

Grand Designs

AFGHANISTAN, 2001

After making it across the border to the eastern city of Jalalabad, Taj has to hole up in an anti-Taliban military base. It is basic – a few buildings with no windows, covered in bullet holes and surrounded by concertina wire – and it is cold because there is no heating, but at least he feels safe. At night he can hear bombs dropping in the distance, by day he hears tales of murder and destruction from soldiers who have returned from the frontlines. Despite this, Taj knows that if he is to realise his dream of establishing cricket in his beloved Afghanistan, he needs to make it to Kabul. Getting there is not going to be easy; although the journey is only a hundred miles, public transport is non-existent. The only option to move about the country is by private minivan.

The owners load their vehicles with people wanting to make the journey and charge them a few pounds for the privilege. Passengers are crammed in, three men sharing a seat is not uncommon. Women in burqas take the back seat and very often the boot where they fight for space with chickens and other livestock. Aside from the risks of bandits, Talibs and foreign fighters, the road itself poses many dangers to overloaded vehicles of dubious safety; at one point it winds its way through a gorge with a drop on one side of hundreds of feet.

Despite his concerns, Taj plucks up his courage, buys a seat and makes the dangerous journey to the capital. As the minibus winds its way to Kabul, Taj sees the destruction wreaked on his country – piles of rubble where houses once stood, and burnt-out cars and tanks litter the roadside – but his spirits are lifted by the sheer beauty of the scenery. After years in a dusty, dirty and claustrophobic refugee camp, the contrast is stark. Way below the mountain road he can see a fast-flowing river and above him jagged snow-capped mountain peaks. The temperature is dropping and the air is cool. The sky is perfectly clear. The air is fresh, a pleasant change from home where the air is full of the smells of humans living on top of each other. But while the countryside is beautiful, it is also deadly; Afghanistan is one of the most mined countries in the world and the side of the road is littered with deadly ordnance.

The catalogue of destruction shocks Taj. Villages that once thrived alongside the road have been laid to waste; although people are returning, it is a far cry from the bustling scenes Taj remembers from his childhood. Houses have been bombed out, mosques gutted and shops looted. War has also taken its toll on the road. A journey that had once taken three hours takes seven. The road is a ribbon of torn-up tarmac, potholes and rocks. Bombs, rockets, the heavy tracks of tanks and years of wear and tear have destroyed the asphalt, which had originally been laid in the 1960s. At that time Afghanistan was relatively peaceful. It was a stop-off point on the hippie trail, and America and the Soviet Union both vied for influence, building roads, schools and airports to curry favour and win support from the local population. Hippies would spend months at a time living in the hills of Afghanistan, smoking hashish, eating kebabs and swimming in the rivers. They came from all over Europe and America and were normally wealthy and taking a break before or after university. Today the only foreigners are troops, journalists and a smattering of brave aid workers.

When Taj finally arrives in Kabul it is early afternoon and the city is awakening from its Taliban slumber: barbers have returned, music shops have opened and women are out on the streets. The infrastructure is still non-existent: there is no electricity, no traffic lights, no rubbish collection, no mobile phone network and no functioning police force or army, the only security is provided by armed fighters from the anti-Taliban Northern Alliance. But changes are afoot. An interim government is in place and there is an air of optimism in the city for the first time in over 20 years.

Taj has no time to lose. He intends to set up a meeting with the head of the Afghan Olympic Committee. It might seem bizarre that Afghanistan, with its history of turmoil, even has an Olympic Committee. But the association has a long, if unsuccessful, history. It was formed in the early 1930s, when Afghanistan was a monarchy, and the nation entered its first Olympics in 1936. It has missed only five since, including the 1984 Los Angeles games when it was part of the Soviet-led boycott. In 2001, Afghanistan has yet to win an Olympic medal. Although cricket is not an Olympic sport, Taj needs the committee's permission to press forward with his plans for the formation of an Afghan cricket team, as it is the only body in the country that can approve such a venture.

It isn't easy setting up the meeting. In post-Taliban Kabul, getting anything done is hard. When it comes to sports, it's even harder and when it is a sport very few people have any knowledge of, let alone passion for, it is harder still. There are no mobile telephones, the landline network cuts in and out, and it's difficult to get hold of the telephone numbers of people or institutions you might want to contact anyway. The government is only just finding its feet. It wasn't even clear when Taj arrived who was in charge of sports in the city. He has met a representative of the committee and got him to agree to support the project, but when the former wrestling champion Anwar Jagdalek returns from exile to retake the position as head of the committee – a post he had occupied after the Soviets were ousted from Afghanistan – Taj has to start again.

Despite this setback, Jagdalek's appointment is a stroke of luck for Taj. Jagdalek is famous throughout Afghanistan for his courage and ferocity in the wrestling ring and on the battlefield. He was regarded as a courageous and shrewd fighter and his reputation drew a following of Hezb-e-Islami Mujahideen fighters during the 1980s jihad against the Soviets. Although Taj is too young to have fought in that conflict – despite his claim that as a young boy he fired a rocket-propelled grenade at a Soviet helicopter and missed – his father had fought alongside Jagdalek, and in a country where nepotism is still alive and can open doors, he is certain this will help smooth his passage.

With this in mind, before he goes into the meeting he enlists the aid of a distant relative called Bashir, who is also related to Jagdalek. Blood is thicker than water and this might help persuade Jagdalek, who Taj has heard is sceptical, of the country's need for a national cricket team. But Taj has another card to play: he is armed with the knowledge that both his father and his mother grew up in the same village as Jagdalek. Taj feels that he is in a strong position.

Despite all this, the meeting doesn't start well. Jagdalek doesn't like cricket. Worse still, Taj is intimidated by his powerful rock-like physique. His head seems to grow out of his sloped shoulders, his eyes tell you everything you need to know, this is a man who has seen war and has very likely killed people. His nose is flattened and crooked, the result of many breaks. His voice is deep and booming. He isn't a man you would mess with and he has no time for niceties. 'Cricket isn't Afghan,' he tells Taj rather abruptly. But Taj hasn't come all this way to be dismissed so lightly and attempts to talk him around. Cricket is the game of gentlemen, he says; it encourages players to follow rules, to live structured lives. Jagdalek pauses for a moment, impressed with this argument. Then Taj plays his trump card. There is, he argues, no better platform on which to show the outside world a different perspective of Afghanistan than the cricket pitch.

It works, and Taj leaves the meeting with a letter affirming the Afghan government's approval of his plans to form the Afghan national cricket team. Despite this, the odds are still stacked against him. For cricket to grow he has to overcome huge obstacles. Not least is that most Afghans know little about cricket and those that do largely don't care for it. Dari speakers dominate the interim government and most of the refugees that fled to Pakistan and learnt cricket are Pashtu speakers. The Dari speakers are suspicious of cricket as they feel it is a Pakistani game. Although Pakistan has housed millions of Afghan refugees, most Afghans view their neighbours with suspicion and with good reason. Pakistan has long cast a nefarious shadow over Afghanistan: they supported the Taliban and are generally seen to want to destabilise the country.

On top of this Taj has no money (the Afghan government has none to give), no pitch in Kabul (the nearest one is in Peshawar), no squad, no kit and very few balls and bats. Afghan cricket is, according to Taj, starting with less than zero facilities. And it appears that Taj has a rival. A man called Allah Dad Noori has similar plans for an Afghan team. The son of a foreign currency dealer, like Taj, he learnt the game in Peshawar refugee camps. Under the Taliban regime, he had returned to Kabul in 1995 and set up something called the Afghan Cricket Federation.

Contrary to common misconception, the Taliban never totally banned sports; they just introduced strict rules for players and fans. Sportsmen (women, of course, couldn't play) had to wear long trousers (they once shaved the heads of a touring Pakistani football team for wearing shorts), wear beards (at the 2000 Olympics the only Afghan entrant, a boxer, was disqualified for having a beard: under Olympic rules all boxers must be clean shaven) and stop for prayer. The Taliban also issued edicts for crowd behaviour, apart from shouts of 'Allah Akbar' (God is great), no cheering was allowed. Cricket, where players dress in long trousers and where the crowd very rarely gets too excited was, as far as sports go, Taliban-friendly. Still, Allah Dad – who is tall, slim, with a narrow face, hair styled in curtains and a neatly trimmed beard – had to do some wrangling before finally persuading the regime to support the federation.

In June 2001 Allah Dad had also registered the Afghan Cricket Federation (ACF) with the world's governing body, the International Cricket Council (ICC). The ICC, it seemed, was one of the few sports governing bodies that had allowed the Taliban to register a team – unlike the Olympic Committee, which banned the Taliban-endorsed teams in 1999 due to its treatment of women.

Although the Taliban regime has now fallen, he still feels he is the head of Afghan cricket and doesn't take kindly to Taj muscling in on his territory. For his part, Taj feels his team of Afghan exiles is the real team and doesn't like the idea of anyone else claiming to have started cricket in

Afghanistan before him. The two completely contrasting characters – Allah Dad is quiet, calculating and reserved, Taj is vivacious, passionate and bombastic – are left in a quandary. They hate each other, but they also need each other.

If Taj wants to get any help from the outside world he needs Allah Dad. Allah Dad is also stuck. Taj has now taken control of the Afghan side of the operation and he can't do anything about it. He is worried that an immediate return to Afghanistan – he went back to Peshawar after the US-led invasion – would lead to a prison sentence. Although he has no connection with the Taliban regime other than through cricket, he is concerned that he might get caught up in the anti-Taliban witch-hunt that is sweeping through the country. His brother-in-law – who had set up the meeting with the Taliban that enabled him to establish cricket – has just been arrested and sent to Guantanamo Bay, accused of smuggling gold and buying surface to air missiles for Al-Qaeda. Allah Dad knows that all Taj would have to do to get him out of the picture and take control of cricket is to accuse him of a deeper involvement with the Taliban movement.

In the months that follow the fall of the Taliban, Taj and Allah Dad come to an uneasy truce. But they start by fighting, long and hard, over who should head up the federation. Someone even floats the idea of deciding it through a cricket match, with each bringing their own team and the winner taking the position. Though the winner-takes-all match doesn't take place, as usual in Afghanistan it is family members who sort things out. Hasti Gul and Karim,

Taj's younger brothers, and Khaliq Dad, the younger brother of Allah Dad, are cricket players and they all want a strong team. They know that for this to happen their brothers will have to get on. Hasti and Karim also want Taj in a coaching role. He has coached them all their lives and they can't think of anyone better to continue coaching them. In the end Taj agrees that he doesn't want to be an administrator, so he lets Allah Dad have the presidency and takes the role of coach.

In early 2002, Allah Dad takes the risk of moving back to Kabul, and he and Taj quickly agree that their first priority is to get some money. The government has none to give, of course, but during the Taliban regime Allah Dad had toiled hard to establish cricket in the country with little success. In 1998 his luck changed. He was playing a game of cricket on some land in central Kabul when he was spotted by William Reeve. Genial like a headmaster, bespectacled and utterly fearless, Reeve was the BBC correspondent at the time. Reeve is an old Afghan hand, he was there during the civil war and the Taliban time and survived numerous hairy moments, including having grenades lobbed over his wall, bombs going off outside his compound and in 2001, as the Americans were bombing strategic targets across the country, a 2000lb American bomb, landing in the compound next to his, knocking a wall onto him live on air. Before 1998 he had never seen a game of cricket being played in Kabul.

Reeve wasn't a huge cricket fan but he had a good nose for a quirky story and wrote a piece for radio on the cricket he witnessed in Taliban-controlled Afghanistan. The news was also translated and broadcast on local Afghan radio, which at the time was listened to by over 60 per cent of the population.

Showing a canny understanding of the Western media, Allah Dad arranged a six-team tournament, one of the first of its kind in Kabul, and named it the BBC Cup. He figured if he named a tournament after the organisation they'd have to cover it.

Not only did they cover it but Reeve also provided the cup.

An editor from *Wisden*, the cricket almanac, heard one of Reeve's pieces on the radio. The story goes he was so impressed that cricket was flourishing in unheard of corners of the world that he decided he would encourage the Afghan cricketers to try to join the ICC. He planned to fax them an application form, only he had no idea how to get a fax to Kabul. He didn't have a correspondent in Afghanistan but he did have one in Sri Lanka so he faxed him the application form; it was, after all, closer to Kabul than London. Presumably he also had correspondents in India and Pakistan (both closer to Kabul than Sri Lanka) and it is unclear why he didn't fax it to them. The writer had no idea how to get an application form from Colombo to Kabul so he passed it to the ambassador for the UAE in Sri Lanka, which was closer still. He faxed it to his colleague in Islamabad who passed it to the Taliban ambassador to Pakistan (one of only three countries to recognise the Taliban regime) and he then took it back to Kabul and handed it to the cricketers.

In November 1998, Reeve took Stuart Bentham, a British businessman who was one of the founding partners of the first private sector telephone networks in the country, on a walking tour of Kabul and introduced him to Allah Dad. Bentham was so touched by the passion the team showed, like the refugees in Peshawar they were playing with sticks and plastic bags, that he persuaded Marylebone Cricket Club to donate some equipment. The world-famous MCC is one of the oldest cricket clubs in the world and is responsible for guarding the laws of the game. The club also has a mission to broaden the appeal of cricket across the world. It seemed natural that they should donate some 'whites' to Afghanistan – the first proper kit the Afghans had ever owned.

Bentham had also helped Allah Dad fill out the forms, sent by *Wisden* via Sri Lanka, to get the Afghan Cricket Federation registered with the ICC. After Bentham had given them equipment and helped them join the ICC, Khalaq Dad, Allah Dad's younger brother who ran a carpet shop and would go on to play for the national team, made Bentham a special carpet. On the carpet were some wickets, a cricket ball and bat with the names of the Afghan federation members on it and Bentham's own name. They also gave him a carpet to give to the MCC.

*

When Taj and Allah Dad are looking around for funding and support, they immediately think of contacting the newly re-opened British embassy. The British, after all, love cricket. The only problem is they have no idea who to contact. They think about knocking on the door of the embassy but fear they might be mistaken for suicide bombers and shot. Then one day, out of the blue, a message comes through the Olympic Committee. They are requested to report to the British embassy and ask for a Major Andrew Banks.

In early 2002, Major Banks has been seconded to the British embassy in Kabul for six months. As a major in the military police, he is put in charge of the troops who guard the embassy and the ambassador. Banks has to contend with potential Taliban attacks, suicide bombs and the day-to-day safety of the ambassador. These are not his only concerns, though. One thing that troubles him deeply is that he will be away from England during the cricket season and, though he never travels without his cricket bat, he is worried about how he'll get his fix.

He has seen children playing cricket in the streets of Kabul and has read a newspaper article about cricket in the country. He's even heard about the formation of a national team and so decides to investigate. Banks works with an Afghan translator and he asks him to make some enquiries. The first step is explaining to the translator what cricket is. Banks isn't hopeful but he thinks it's worth a shot.

After a few days the translator comes back, having made contact with the Olympic Committee. They have, he says, just authorised a national cricket team. They tell the translator that their cricket representatives will be at the embassy shortly.

Taj and Allah Dad are nervous before the meeting, they know the English love cricket but they have never met a British soldier before. They wonder what he will be like, whether he'll be friendly and sympathetic. They decide to take along Khalil Khan, a friend of theirs who speaks good English, comes from a wealthy family and who is acting as their marketing manager.

The British embassy in Kabul sits on a hill high above the capital in Karte Parwan, a north-western suburb that provides a good defensive location. Kabul had been through many changes since the embassy opened in the 1920s. Lord Curzon, the former Viceroy of India, declared that its ambassador would be the best-housed man in Asia and had designed an embassy accordingly. He had constructed a grand stucco building, set in 24 acres, with arches, clean lines and carefully manicured lawns. Up until the late 1970s the embassy held the best parties in Kabul, some said in Asia. Revellers would play croquet on the lawn, dance on the sprung dance floor, swim in the pool and drink gin and tonics in wicker chairs. It even had a private squash court for those who wanted to exercise. In the 1980s, during the Soviet-era, the British kept a skeleton staff, but by 1989, as civil war descended, the mission pulled out, leaving the compound to the ravages of war. It was late 2001 before another British ambassador hoisted the Union flag over the grounds – and by then the main building had collapsed, fire had gutted another and the gardens had been left to overgrow. As a result the former hospital compound became the embassy's focal building. It was basic, with the emphasis placed on beefing up security rather than restoring the aesthetic. British troops have secured it with blast walls, barbed wire and barricades, which ring the compound.

When Taj, Allah Dad and Khalil Khan arrive at the embassy, Banks gets a bemused phone call from one of his soldiers on the main gate. His boys, as he calls the troops under his command, can't believe the men in front of them are Afghan cricketers. They think it's a wind-up. But it isn't. Banks instructs them to let the cricketers in.

When Banks meets them, he is surprised by what he sees. They don't look like cricketers. Taj has worn a suit for the occasion but won't stop talking, Allah Dad, neat in his traditional dress, is shrewd and intelligent, while Khalil Khan is clearly the wheeler-dealer. Though in his early twenties, he looks about 15 and is dressed in a pair of tight stonewashed jeans and a figure hugging T-shirt. His hair is mussed in the best boy-band style, he is clean-shaven and sports a pair of enormous shades low down on his nose. Banks quickly nicknames them the 'three amigos'.

To the 'three amigos', Banks appears to have the demeanour and physique of the archetypal British military officer. His short, brown hair is styled in a side-parting, his straight back, wiry physique and no-nonsense manner and the clear, precise, clipped way he speaks all mark him out as the classic officer type. Yet unlike many soldiers, when Banks smiles it is warm and easy. His kind, open eyes seem unaffected by the soldiering he has done.

Emboldened by Banks' kind manner and obvious love of cricket, the three immediately launch into a tirade of complaints: the government don't support them, they have no money, there is nowhere to train apart from a half-length concrete pitch, they have no equipment and they have no kit. As they talk, the Afghan cricketers quickly realise Banks could make a real difference. For his part, Banks sees the chance to do something to nurture his favourite sport in a country destroyed by war. It is not often, he thinks, you can come to a country and in six months make a real, tangible difference. He now sees his chance. He isn't sure he can win government support or find the team somewhere to train but he thinks he might be able to help them get equipment and kit. None of them know it yet, but Banks is set to become a key ally of Afghanistan's fledgling cricket administration.

Every night after 6 p.m. the embassy compound locks down, meaning no traffic is allowed in or out. The gates are bolted and sentries posted. Once Banks has finished writing up the day's reports, unless anything important happens, he is free. He sets about his new task immediately. He speaks to the ambassador and gets permission to use the Internet, telephone and fax machine. Afghanistan is three and a half hours ahead of England so while it is evening in Afghanistan, it is still daytime in Europe. Banks has a window of opportunity where he can still catch people at their desks. His first job is to get some donations for the Afghan team.

He begins by contacting all of the 18 first-class English county sides asking for help. Half of them don't respond, fail to help or promise kit that never arrives. The rest provide all kinds of equipment, including Hampshire who send their full, season-old, one-day strip. The English Cricket Board donates a number of artificial grass wickets that can be laid on top of gravel or concrete and he also receives promises of bats, balls, gloves and helmets. He never expected such a positive reaction.

But now a new problem arises. How will he get the kit from England to Kabul? Although Kabul has a post office – which sells 30-year-old postcards depicting Kabul when it was still known as the Paris of Central Asia – no post from abroad ever seems to arrive. You can get items sent by private courier but, as Banks is doing the job pro bono, he can't afford the expensive fees. He has one final option: a friend of his is a soldier in the Royal Logistics Corp (RLC), who, as luck would have it, is responsible for organising military equipment being sent into Afghanistan. The RLC are responsible for loading up all the equipment the army needs – weapons, clothing, kitchen goods, food, bedding and housing products – onto massive Hercules C-130 transport planes. The RAF then flies the cargo into Kabul. Banks manages to persuade his friend to load the cricket equipment on the planes, which he then collects from the military side of Kabul International Airport. When the equipment is handed to Taj and Allah Dad they can't believe what they see. There are bats, balls, shirts, trousers, hats and pads. The equipment is second-hand but in good condition, and the two have never seen so much of it.

Already Banks has helped Allah Dad and Taj achieve far more than they ever dreamed. Although the two men are very different and hated each other at first, the pair has bonded through their blind faith that Afghan cricket will succeed. The arrival of the equipment has finally provided some concrete proof that the game might just take root and flourish in its new home.

Although most of the British embassy staff prefer football, Banks quickly finds an ally in a diplomat named Steve Brooking, who is also a keen cricketer. With his sandy hair and strong, athletic build Brooking is more action hero than desk-bound diplomat. He has a reputation as one of the most knowledgeable and fearless operators in Kabul. He is cut from the same cloth as the young officers who ventured into Afghanistan in the 19th century to partake in the 'Great Game', the shadowy struggle for influence that Victorian Britain and Tsarist Russia waged over Central Asia. In 2002 he is awarded the Order of the British Empire for work in Afghanistan after the invasion.

His curiosity piqued by the notion of local cricket, Brooking wanders down to the Chaman-i-Hozori, which rather optimistically means Military Parade Ground, where Taj and his colleagues play their regular pick-up games. It's a wide expanse of dusty wasteland that stands in the shadow of the Olympic Stadium. The Olympic Stadium sounds grand but it isn't. There is no formal seating, just depressing slabs of grey concrete terraces. Splashes of red paint have been added to try and inject some joy but the paint is flaking. The terraces are ringed with a fence. After years of Taliban neglect the pitch has no grass. It was here the Taliban would execute adulterous women;

the bloodstains have gone but an air of menace still hangs over the stadium.

Brooking is a good cricketer; he played for university and school and was a member of MCC. He joins in the games but often with little success. It doesn't help that locals umpire the games, and they lik e nothing more than sending the Brit interloper back to the embassy with as few runs as possible. Some of the umpiring decisions, he says, are 'a bit suspect'. But he is impressed by the talent he sees among some of the players.

Brooking and Taj strike up a friendship that quickly develops as they while away hours discussing tactics and plans for the future over tea after the games. Brooking, who is based permanently in Afghanistan, helps Taj put the artificial wickets donated by the MCC into local schools. In March 2002 the diplomat organises Afghanistan's first 'international' against a team made up of foreign peace-keepers from the International Security Assistance Force (ISAF) and diplomats.

Before the game with the peacekeepers can take place, Taj and Allah Dad organise a hasty trial. They need to get their team together. They hold the trial on a patch of land in the upmarket suburb of Wazir Akbar Khan. It is here that most of the embassies have their compounds. Many left during the Taliban time but are now returning. The patch of earth where the trial is held is owned by the United Arab Emirates and overlooked by the heavily guarded Bulgarian embassy. The ground is uneven, there is no grass wicket, it's concrete, and the outfield is dust not grass.

Allah Dad knows the ground well; this is where he played during the Taliban regime. He has invited some of the players he knew from the Taliban team and Taj has invited players he knows from the refugee camp. In total there are only 25 players. Most Afghans who play cricket still live in Pakistan, getting the word out is difficult, the journey dangerous and after selection they only have a game against the peacekeepers to look forward to.

Already certain to be in the starting line-up are two players Taj knows very well: his brothers Karim Saddiq and Hasti Gul. Karim, a wicketkeeper and a top-order batsman, is the star and undoubtedly Taj's favourite of the two brothers. He is squat, about five foot five, and tough looking. Taj calls him 'the Hero'. He has pockmarked skin and when he scowls, which happens when he is concentrating, he looks vicious, but as soon as he smiles his face is transformed into a charming and rather handsome one. He is, according to Taj an incredible talent, but also a temperamental livewire. He smokes, chews tobacco (often while playing) and likes to check out girls. When he is upset, normally if he has batted badly and is out cheaply, he sulks, removes himself from the company of other players and buries himself in his mobile phone, watching videos, sending texts and making calls. When he has batted well or is in a good mood, he tells jokes, dictates conversations and, despite his stature, dominates whatever room he is in. If he is happy he is bumptious, bellicose and loud.

When Karim walks he barrels along, his shoulders, which are pulled back to push out his chest, move up and down with his legs, which are spread as far apart as possible. Karim is a maverick, a rebel and one of a kind. He is incredibly loyal to his family, if not always his teammates. As a big hitter Taj has persuaded him to bowl off-breaks and he has agreed to give it a try.

Hasti is a middle-order batsman and medium-pace bowler. Unlike his brother, his temperament is much more even and if there is one thing that marks him out it is the fact that he is a joker. There are always jokers in any team but only one can unanimously claim to be 'the Joker' and that is Hasti. He constantly plays practical jokes, impersonates just about everyone he meets and, mischievously, loves to swear. He speaks with a lisp, which makes the impersonations all the more impressive. Hasti is also a shrewd businessman. He has no education and can barely write, but has always supported himself financially. During the civil war he ran household products from Pakistan into Afghanistan, selling them at a huge profit. The trips were dangerous and one day, stepping off a bus, he was caught in the crossfire of a gunfight. He says that he took a bullet in the chest, blacked out and the next thing he knew he was in a hospital. Hasti survived, but still has a scar on his chest and one below his shoulders. It was months before he could play cricket again.

However, there are other players who stand out during practice, in particular a batsman Raees Ahmadzai, a potential all-rounder Nowroz Mangal, and a fast bowler Dawlat Ahmadzai. In addition the team will include Allah Dad and his brother Khaliq Dad. Taj will act as coach.

As the match draws near, the main problem Taj faces is that his players have only just started playing with a leather ball. Amazingly, for many of them the match against the ISAF will be the first in which they have bowled with and batted against a hard leather ball. They have only ever played with a tennis ball wrapped in gaffer tape and Taj is worried how the players will react. Facing a makeshift ball is a very different experience from facing a leather one.

In the event, he needn't have worried as the Afghans skittle the ISAF out for a meagre 56 runs. Things are looking good for the home team, but then, after four years of drought, the heavens open and the pitch is deluged with rain – in classic English style 'rain stops play'. When play finally resumes, the Afghans chase down the score in four overs, Karim hits a quick-fire 40. Their opponents are humbled. The Afghans have dealt with the hard ball. They are presented with more kit, and finally Taj starts to realise that perhaps this can work.

As spring gives way to summer and Banks can see Afghan cricket growing, he feels the team are still missing something very important. Many village teams in England turn up for games in blazers and ties. Certainly no self-respecting international side would be without them. Although Taj and Allah Dad occasionally wear suits, they are in the minority. Most of the players wear the baggy shalwar kameez; not only is it the traditional Afghan dress, it is all they own. Banks knows that if the players are going to be taken seriously they will have to look the part. A blazer and tie would be a good start.

The Afghan government has still to provide any financial support for cricket. They have allowed the creation of the federation but haven't provided an office, a phone, any money or equipment; so there is certainly no money for sartorial improvements. But with Brooking's help, Banks persuades the ambassador to dip into the discretionary fund, a pot of money for low-level projects, to find the cash for team blazers.

He puts Taj in charge of getting them. It is a mistake. Taj, or the local tailor he recruits, have never worn, made or even seen a blazer before. The results, though not terrible, are not likely to appear in *Vogue*. They are forest green, with the Afghan cricket symbol – some wickets in front of a rising sun surrounded by a wreath – hand-sewn on the breast pocket. But they are ill fitting and the stitching is clumsy and clearly visible. Banks is a perfectionist and, after seeing this first foray into menswear production, decides he will take control of the ties.

He contacts companies in England and asks them if they would be interested in producing and donating some ties to the Afghan national cricket team. His first call is to Tie Rack. Unbelievably, within five minutes he has the boss on the phone and hears him agreeing to send 30 ties, free of charge, to the Afghans. The ties will be silk with thick diagonal black, red and green stripes (the colours of the Afghan flag). On the bottom of the tie is the Afghan cricket logo.

When they arrive Taj and Allah Dad confess that, although they have on occasion worn a suit, they have never tied a tie before. Banks lets them into a secret and shows them the old schoolboy trick of sliding them on and off without totally undoing them.

And then in one of those odd serendipitous moments that every good story needs, Banks hears that the British ambassador is due to meet Hamid Karzai, the Afghan president. The ambassador doesn't like cricket but Banks persuades him to wear an Afghan cricket tie to the meeting and to take one, as a gift, for the president.

Karzai loves the tie. The present proves so popular that the defence minister, also at the meeting, wonders why he can't have one. The ambassador ends up taking his tie off and giving it to the defence minister.

Banks is convinced that the gift to Karzai represents a major turning point for Afghan cricket. Suddenly the ACF is taken seriously; promises are made of an office and land for a training academy. Banks attributes this to the fact that, behind the Americans, the British are the major player in Afghanistan.

But Taj and Allah Dad still have no money. The government has pledged support but, unsurprisingly in post-Taliban Afghanistan, funding a cricket team is at the bottom of a very long list of projects that need money. There are roads to build, hospitals to construct, teachers to train and a police and army to recruit and train. The 'three amigos' are still working with no salary and although they have grand plans – setting up an academy, building a stadium and touring foreign countries – they have to find ways to finance it all.

Their first thought is to try and get a government minister

on their side. Sherzada Massoud is an advisor to President Karzai on tribal affairs and one of the few Pashtuns in the interim government. With a common language and culture he seems like an ideal choice.

Massoud has hands as big as wicketkeeper's gloves, a broad smile, a bushy beard and a full head of hair. He dyes his beard and hair jet black to cover the grey. He wears a turban or a pakoul hat and dresses in smart, neatly pressed shalwar kameez, with a Western suit jacket over the top. Often he drapes a green and purple striped silk Afghan cape over his shoulders. If the outfit wasn't enough, you can tell he is important because he has a driver and an armed bodyguard.

Mr Massoud is influential and has the ear of the president but there is one problem – he is not a cricket fan; worse still he admits to not even knowing what the game is. He prefers volleyball. But Taj, who leads the charge to recruit Massoud, is not to be put off. He chases the minister day and night telling him about cricket and his plans to take a team abroad, reiterating how the game could change negative perceptions of Afghanistan. Finally, perhaps exhausted by Taj's enthusiasm, Massoud sets Taj a task. He tells Taj if he can bring a thousand cricketers to his office, he will support the team, put their case forward and act as their president. Taj doesn't manage to gather a thousand cricketers, he is only able to get a few hundred together, but Massoud is sufficiently impressed by the number of men gathered before him that he relents and agrees to be their president.

He claims that he has decided to support cricket as he

can see how popular it is with the youth. As his armed bodyguard stands behind him, and without a hint of irony, he says that sport is the messenger of peace. As Massoud speaks he joins his hands together touching the fingertips of one hand to the other and flexing them. He has the slow, measured speaking manner of a seasoned politician; he wants you to hear what he says and to take in every word. The cynic might argue that Massoud supports cricket for the promise of perks, for as soon as the team starts travelling abroad Taj has promised him he can join them.

With Massoud installed as President, Taj and Allah Dad dole out a plethora of titles to themselves. Taj becomes Secretary General and Coach and Allah Dad Executive Vice President, Founder and Captain. For the time being at least everyone seems happy.

It's hard to appreciate the risks Taj has taken in going to Kabul, and not just to his personal safety. He had no money and little support and risked ridicule at every turn. If he had failed to establish cricket, he would have had to return to Peshawar with his tail between his legs. As much as anything he wanted to show his father and his neighbours that those years spent playing cricket, when he should have been at school or working, were not wasted. He still does; he still wants to show that he can become someone.

Taj didn't have an education, so stood by and watched as his more studious peers left the refugee camp for university scholarships in Egypt and across the Middle East. He always hoped cricket might open doors for him but when Afghanistan was mired in civil war he had, briefly, left cricket to pursue another career – acting. He always wanted his life to count for something and he thought perhaps he could become a famous actor – Kacha Gari's first. Although many Pashtu films were filmed in Peshawar, he had bigger aspirations. He wanted to act in Urdu cinema. These films were shown all over Pakistan and as Taj spoke Urdu he thought the larger the potential audience, the better.

One day in his twenties, he had gathered together as much money as he could and bought a bus ticket to Lahore and Lollywood, the heart of the Pakistani film industry, seven hours away, near the border with India.

But he never made it as an actor; he claims he was shocked by the excess and artificiality of the acting world. He thought those involved were swindlers. The women, he said, wore too much make-up and weren't anywhere near as attractive as they appeared on screen. The men were not as strong or muscled and their beards not as thick.

It is perhaps more likely that Taj was not offered any parts and didn't get the break he needed. Still, this failure had marked him, and he decided cricket was the way to make something of his life and now Kabul was liberated he had his chance. He wasn't going to let it slip.

Taj had grand designs from the start. He wanted Afghanistan to play on the international stage, he wanted them to be on television and he wanted to be a famous coach. Although the foundations had been marked out and cricket had been established in Kabul, there was still a long way to go.

Chapter 3

The First Team

KABUL, MAY 2003

Taj now has official backing, some equipment, blazers and ties but he knows that if he wants cricket to grow, he is missing one vital ingredient: a team. He has an idea of some of the players he wants to pick for the squad, having grown up playing with many of them in Peshawar, but he also knows that he needs some fresh talent.

Together with Allah Dad, Taj decides to hold a trial in Kabul. Allah Dad held a trial in Peshawar 2001 and another was held in Kabul before the game against the ISAF. This year – to try and discover as many players as possible – the trial will take the form of a regional 40-over tournament and Taj will pick players for the incipient national squad, which is to include under-19 and under-17 teams, based on their performances in the matches.

They have decided to hold the tournament in Kabul for a number of different reasons. Even though most of the teams have provincial names and some of the players live in these provinces, most of talent has come to Kabul from Peshawar. The players generally play for the province of their, or their parents', birth although there are no fast and hard rules. The tournament is also being held in the Afghan capital out of a sense of national pride; although the cricketers have been exiled by war and the chaos it brought in its wake, they want it to be clear that the team picked from this trial is going to represent Afghanistan. Taj and Allah Dad want the players to show their love of their country. They want the world to know that they are Afghans and proud of it.

They also want to showcase the sport to their fellow countrymen. The country still knows little of cricket: most Afghans who weren't exiled in Pakistan are completely ignorant of the game and its development. An even bigger problem is the government, which despite supporting cricket on paper still views the sport with suspicion. Although Hamid Karzai, the interim president, is a Pashtu, the majority of the government is not. They have been drawn from the anti-Taliban Northern Alliance and are mainly ethnic Tajiks. Their suspicious reaction to cricket is rooted in the fact that they see it as a Pakistani sport and the Pakistanis supported the Taliban, who they fought against. Added to this all of the players, at least initially, are Pashtu and many don't speak very good Dari, the language of the new political elite.

Taj and Allah Dad are also hoping that the tournament will inspire and enthuse young and old in Afghanistan – across tribal barriers – as they were inspired in their childhood by this peculiar but compelling game. They want cricket to become a unifying bond in daily life.

On the playing side, Taj has a few ideas about what he needs to round out his squad. He has a lot of seam bowlers, although he is still in search of a really fast one, but his most pressing need is for a spin bowler. Unearthing an effective spinner is something he's always struggled with. Afghans, he says, only like to bowl fast. They think the faster you can bowl, the more manly you are. It's easy to measure pace bowling, the faster the ball the stronger you are; with spin quality is harder to determine. Taj has tried to persuade some of his batsman to take up spin. The hard hitters who bat high up the order have, he feels, already proved their manliness and might be persuaded to adopt the most artful form of bowling. After all, they have got nothing left to prove and won't lose face. He's had some luck with his brother Karim but needs to persuade others.

In terms of batting, Taj is hoping he can persuade the batsmen to calm down. The cricket they play in the refugee camps is limited overs and the outfields are very rough, which means the Afghan batsmen like to hit big. They rarely play for singles – preferring to try to keep the ball in the air and clear the boundary. Taj knows that, if they are going to play internationals, he will need a classy batsman who can hold the innings together. One who has a calm measured approach to the game and doesn't try to hit every ball for six.

Teams have been invited from all over Afghanistan: from Khost in the east; from Kandahar, the Taliban heartland in the south; from Parwan, the province just to the north of the capital and from Kabul itself. There are also a number of academies represented, these are mostly private teams set up by a benefactor, although the name is misleading as they are very unstructured. Taj has decided to play for one based in Kabul. To make up the numbers the ISAF team has also been invited. This is partly because the Afghans want to show them how strong they are, but also because Taj and Allah Dad hope the soldiers might be able to provide some organisational assistance. In total there are 14 teams, divided into two groups.

The tournament, like the federation itself, is a triumph of sheer willpower rather than precision planning. How all the teams came together in Kabul on the correct days and with the correct number of players remains a bit of a mystery, even to those involved.

The matches all take place on the Chaman-i-Hozori. The only flat patch of land on the cricket ground is a concrete wicket that was laid in a hurry. The outfield is nothing but heavily rutted bare earth. It is covered in rubbish and, when a breeze blows, a heavy coating of dust and plastic bags are blown up into the air. The burnt-out shell of a Soviet helicopter, its fuselage littered with bullet holes, lies just outside the boundary. Nearby, on a raised patch of earth, is a downed twin-propeller plane, cracked down the middle of its body. They are remnants of the country's years of war.

The few sprigs of grass that had managed to take hold have been chewed back by sheep that sometimes graze on the patch. The pitch, if you can call it that, is bordered on one side by one of the city's busiest roads. The smoke from the traffic, the sound of car horns, the noise from hawkers trying to sell their wares, the pleas from beggars pleading for money and the general chaos of Kabul make it an inauspicious place to play cricket. But this is the only venue available and it is here, after they have chased off the football players, that they are holding the Afghan cricket trials or, as they are called after the sponsorship has been agreed, the First Olympia Lube Oil Cricket Tournament. It is in this ramshackle venue that the first Afghan national cricket team will be selected.

The tournament opens with Taj's academy playing the ISAF. The ISAF are chasing 151 in their 40 overs but are bowled out for 140.

There is one standout player in the first game: Asghar Stanikzai, who scores an unbeaten 65 and takes five wickets. He is the first player drafted into the Afghan national cricket squad, alongside Taj's brothers Karim and Hasti Gul.

Asghar, soon to be nicknamed 'the Dandy', has long, floppy hair that covers his eyes and which he sometimes colours with henna to give it a red tint. He always wears traditional Afghan clothes but often they have chintzy embroidery added to the cuffs and collar; and he wears a skullcap littered with brightly coloured jewels. The lopsided grin, big nose and long face give him more than a passing resemblance to the actor Adrien Brody.

Asghar plays his cricket with style; his favourite shot is the flick and his batting is very wristy, making him an elegant and smooth player. Unlike most Afghan cricket players, he comes from a wealthy family. His father, who owns a large modern house in one of Peshawar's most expensive districts, is a gem dealer. Although quick to make jokes and laugh, Asghar takes his cricket seriously and plays with a freedom, style and elegance reminiscent of his favourite cricketer, the Pakistan Test player Ramiz Raja.

As the tournament progresses, Taj and Allah Dad remark on the general standard of play – it's much higher than they anticipated – although quite a few of the players are already known to them, the new players offer a wealth of fresh talent, which is exactly what they're looking for.

The tournament also draws Samiullah 'the Model' Shinwari, as good in the field, at least in Taj's eyes, as the Australian legend Mark Waugh. Sami, who bowls leg-breaks, is also handy with the bat, idolises Shane Warne and copies his movements when bowling. When he celebrates a wicket he thrusts one arm in the air, his feet rooted to the spot; when he bowls badly he crosses his arms lifting one arm up to rest his chin on his hand, shaking his head from side to side and exhaling.

Sami, as everyone likes to call him, lives in a tumbling old house in Peshawar. He never really knew his father who, before he passed away, was a Holy Man in Saudi Arabia but he is pretty sure he wouldn't approve of him playing cricket. Sami styles his hair with gel and wears Western clothes: stonewashed jeans and tight garish T-shirts. He says that when his cricketing days are over he dreams of being a male model or a Bollywood actor. He is handsome and rugged-looking, although his jug ears might be a problem.

Another certainty for the squad is Khaliq Dad, a fast bowler. He is tall and pacy and once played for the Pakistan under-17s but was dropped when they discovered he was Afghan. He lacks accuracy, but his quickness and the fact that Allah Dad is his brother sees him chosen for a place.

Then there is Raees Ahmadzai, 'the Elder Statesman', one of Taj's oldest friends. The two have played cricket together all their lives. Taj has Raees marked down as the captain. He is tough, uncompromising and driven. Like Taj, Raees is desperately poor and has had a hard life. The rumour goes that Raees once broke up rocks with a pickaxe to sell them and make money to buy cricket equipment. He looks older than the other players and his face is heavily lined.

Another possible captain is Nowroz Mangal, also known as 'Mr Calm'. He played on the Taliban team with Allah Dad. Nowroz is an opening batsman and is another with movie-star good looks – high cheekbones and an easy smile. His back is ramrod straight and although quiet and softly spoken, he projects a calm authority. He oozes class and carries himself with dignity. He rarely loses his temper, stands just under six feet tall, slim with a neatly trimmed beard.

Nowroz learnt cricket in Pakistan but has spent most of his life in Khost, an eastern province that borders Pakistan. He lived there throughout the Taliban regime.

Midway through the tournament, Taj is pleased with

the players he has selected but he's thinking big. He knows that if his team is going to compete on the international stage he needs more players. Still required are a fast bowler (although Taj has a few to choose from, he feels he needs a really world-class one) and a classy all-rounder. He soon finds them in the form of Hamid Hassan and Mohammad Nabi.

Both Taj and Allah Dad have seen Nabi before but Hamid is totally new. Hamid, 'the Young Pretender', is overweight, but not as heavy as he used to be: a year before he weighed 17 stone. He has never bowled with a hard ball before but when he does he is quick and accurate, reaching speeds of up to 90 mph. Considering he has only played cricket for a few years, his natural ability is astounding.

Taj's brother, Hasti had seen him playing tennis-ball cricket in Peshawar and persuaded him to come along to the tournament. Hamid is tall, over six foot, and only 17. He had to sneak out of the house against his father's wishes and was missing his final school exams to be here. It is his first time in Afghanistan and he has only turned up because Hasti has persuaded him he is good enough to play for the national team. How Hasti knows this when he has only seen him play with a tennis ball is unclear. Although Hasti often gives Taj his thoughts, he is in no position to decide who plays in the national team. Hamid has taken a huge risk in coming. If he doesn't make it and isn't considered good enough for the team he is unsure what he will do.

Hamid has a joke he plays on people – when he shakes

their hands he keeps squeezing. He is strong for his age and often leaves adults squealing with pain. Despite his size he is still very much a boy. Although both Taj and Allah Dad agree that he has incredible talent, he does not make the main squad but is put into the junior team. Hamid is disappointed but Hasti reassures him that he bowled very well and if he carries on progressing in the way he is before long he'll be promoted to the full squad.

Nabi, 'the All-Rounder', is 18 and is a classy player with bat and ball. He is as tall as Hamid but slimmer, with the body of a sportsman. Despite being only a year older than Hamid, Nabi is considered mature enough and talented enough for the senior team.

Another great find is a fast bowler called Sharpour Zadran. He is the tallest person many of the players have ever seen, he stands over six foot five and all his features are large. He wears his hair long and looks like an action hero from the 1980s. Sharpour is quiet and when he speaks, he stutters and stumbles – his tongue is too big for his mouth.

The final of the competition is between Khost and the Pir Baba Cricket Academy. On the day, Nowroz – Mr Calm – lives up to his reputation, hitting an unbeaten 75 and following that up with four wickets to win the match for Khost. It proves a fitting end to the tournament, which has given both Taj and Allah Dad a lot to think about.

With their differences settled, at least for the present, Taj and Allah Dad are convinced that they have the makings of a good team. What they need now are some testing opponents. They have to start making noises to the international cricket organisations to move up the ladder and, luckily, one thing they have in common, it is that they can both make a nuisance out of themselves. Nothing can discourage them and the two play off each other in the way most double acts do. Allah Dad stresses that he wants to use cricket to get fighters away from guns: he is serious and sombre. Taj talks in grand terms: he wants to show the world a different side to Afghanistan and he wants Afghanistan in the World Cup.

In 2003, there is a feeling of optimism in the country, which has been largely peaceful since the ousting of the Taliban two years before. The ACF uses this feeling of goodwill to its advantage, claiming the country is safer than at any time in the last 25 years. Though it has been registered with the ICC since 2001, the ACF has had little or no contact with the sport's governing body. Instead it turn its attentions to the Asian Cricket Council (ACC), who it hopes will more readily understand its problems. The ACF persuades the ACC, who immediately accepts their registration, to send a representative to review the status of cricket in the country.

On 7 August, Iqbal Sikander, a development officer from the ACC, arrives in Kabul and is introduced to the Afghan cricketers. Sikander is a former World Cup-winner with Pakistan so he knows the game at the highest level. His week-long visit is intended as a fact-finding mission on behalf of both the ACC and the ICC to see what they can do to help. He will assess what Afghan cricket needs, how the organisations can help develop it and identify areas that need urgent attention.

Sikander has no idea what cricket in Afghanistan will be like, he has no idea about the conditions and no idea who the people involved are. For him it is a journey into the unknown. He also has no idea what to expect from the players – he's never seen an Afghan play cricket. In turn, Taj hopes that the visit will lead to increased funding, fixtures with other Asian nations and invitations to enter regional ACC tournaments through which his players can get much needed international experience. His arrival marks a big day for Afghan cricket.

But Sikander knows talent when he sees it and is at once impressed by what he finds in Afghanistan. Taj and Allah Dad arrange for him to watch the national team train and he describes what he sees as 'tremendous'.

He is even more impressed because the ability he sees in the players is natural – it hasn't been developed through coaching or through having any cricketing facilities worthy of the name. The conditions for cricket in Afghanistan would from an outsider's point of view work against rather than for the encouragement of talent. And it's not only the lack of facilities.

Afghanistan doesn't have a trained coach, there are no qualified umpires and the league system is virtually non-existent. The national team has only just been formed and there is no development programme and no equipment. Although there are around 350 clubs, and cricket is being played in at least 12 of the 34 provinces, most play with tennis balls and there is virtually no organisation. There are no grass pitches, no academy and no training programme. Sikander realises that if cricket is to grow plans need to be made quickly. The current crop of players is extremely gifted and that mustn't be allowed to go to waste. It is unprecedented that a nation with so much potential could just emerge as if from nowhere; but, of course, war has isolated Afghanistan from the cricket world at large.

To have a chance to build on the talent harvested from the refugee camps in Pakistan, Sikander realises that the ACC has to move quickly. He immediately recommends that Afghanistan be given the support and funding necessary to develop and encourage cricket in the country.

He crams a lot into his visit. He meets Sherzada Massoud, President of the ACF, and Anwar Jagdalek, who as well as heading the Olympic Committee is also the Mayor of Kabul. At each meeting the patter from Taj, Allah Dad and Sikander is the same, the federation needs help, support and money.

Sikander's meeting with Jagdalek goes smoothly and this is significant. In his dual roles controlling sport and the city of Kabul, Jagdalek has the power to make things happen. Although he had initially been so sceptical of cricket, Jagdalek is grateful to the ACC and ICC for coming to Afghanistan. He assures Sikander that he will help find some land for an academy and a cricket ground. The following day a meeting is arranged with the Vice President of Afghanistan, Hadayat Amin Arslan.

The Afghan Cricket Federation rolls out the red carpet. Arslan, who claims to have played cricket in his college days, agrees that the government will build a pavilion at the ground.

Sikander leaves the meeting elated. His trip to Kabul has gone better than he could have hoped for. On his final day in Kabul he holds a press conference to announce the developments.

Sikander reports back to the ACC and ICC and a decision is quickly taken to invest US$10,000 in the cricket ground, and somewhere between US$30,000 to US$40,000 into the ACF for the development of an academy. An injection of funds rarely happens this quickly but the ACC is excited about Afghanistan.

Everything is in place for Afghanistan to have their first ground and academy only a year and a half after the Taliban had been ousted and Taj arrived in the capital. The good news continues. Afghanistan are invited to participate in the ACC Trophy in 2004. The tournament is designed to give associate and affiliate nations (those outside of Test cricket) experience of playing one-day cricket. Associate nations, such as Hong Kong, Malaysia, UAE and Singapore, are countries where cricket is firmly established. Affiliate nations, such as Afghanistan, are countries that play by the international rules governing cricket, but are new to the international fraternity. The tournament will also help decide regional rankings for Asian teams.

Arrangements have to be made immediately. With travel

comes the need for administrative help and the logistical headaches that any international team encounters. A huge stumbling block for the ACF is in obtaining passports for the players. None of the players has one. Although there are border posts between Afghanistan and Pakistan, people are rarely stopped and if they are they pay a small bribe and are let through.

Filling in the passport application forms is a fiasco. A significant complication is that most of the players don't know when they were born. In Afghanistan the average life expectancy is in the early forties and child mortality is one of the highest in the world. To combat this parents have lots of children, often in quick succession. The birthdays of each child aren't recorded and, in Afghan culture, aren't important. There are no birth certificates and birthdays are not celebrated in the same way they are in the West, in fact they aren't marked at all. With each passing year the memory of when the child was born fades further. To complicate things even more the Afghans have a different calendar. Often by the time they reach early adulthood, and their parents have five or six other children, they have only a vague recollection of when they were born. Sometimes they remember who was in power; sometimes a major event in history jogs the memory. Just as often they have absolutely no idea.

Most of the players have trouble compiling the necessary information. Nowroz is at a slight advantage when it comes to remembering his birthday; his name means New Year as he was born on the Afghan New Year. New Year usually falls on 22 March yet in his passport Nowroz's birthday is marked as 28 November 1984. His is not the only discrepancy. Hasti and Karim, Taj's brothers, who although they share the same mother, are according to their government-issued Afghan passports, born only 48 days apart! Hasti's birthday is on 1 January 1984, Karim's on 18 February 1984.

At best the passport dates seem to be guesstimates and at worst widely inaccurate. Raees 'the Elder Statesman' for example, claims he was born in 1980, is registered as being born in 1984, but looks at least ten years older. Still, the passports are officially approved and they seem to work. The team makes it to Malaysia for the 2004 ACC Trophy.

When the players set off for Malaysia it is the first time any of them has ever been on a plane. Travelling only between Afghanistan and Pakistan, they have had no need for travel documents. Clutching their new passports, with the ink still metaphorically wet, they fly away from home for the first time in their lives. When they land at Dubai Airport, they are awestruck. They have never seen travelators before and stumble along, unable to find their balance, all the while gazing at the brightly lit shops and restaurants. The players have a day in Dubai to acclimatise and it throws up more firsts. At the hotel the players are astonished to see women in bikinis. They are too shy to approach the girls, but can't believe they lie by the pool wearing so little in front of men. Most of the guests are Russian sun seekers so, even if the players weren't crippled by shyness, conversation would have been impossible.

Some of the players speak English, but none knows any Russian. They are content to watch from the shadows and wonder about the new world they are fast discovering.

The next morning when they board the plane to Kuala Lumpur, the players can't stop smiling. They chat to anyone and everyone often in Urdu, the lingua franca of the Asian subcontinent where many in Dubai come from, or broken English. It seems like a dream and one they never thought would happen. There have been promises of trips before, and they have all fallen through, but this time they are really going.

The tournament sees 18 teams contesting 50-over matches. The Afghans will play three group games. Their first-ever international is against Oman, and following that are fixtures against Hong Kong and Bahrain.

Nowroz scores a century on his and the country's international debut, and Nabi takes three for 26. Despite this Oman win the match by four wickets. In their next match, against Hong Kong, they lose by 12 runs with Raees top scoring with 60. Against Bahrain, however, Karim scores a century and the Afghans win by eight wickets.

Despite losing twice they reach the quarter-finals. Here they face Kuwait where Nowroz again performs well – hitting 63 and taking four for 27 – but they lose by 49 runs. However, the tournament is not over. The team has a fifth-place play-off against the hosts Malaysia. Afghanistan wins by three wickets, with Nowroz finishing top of the bowling figures, taking two wickets for seven runs.

Behind the scenes, though, things have not gone so well.

During the match against Bahrain, Hasti becomes aware of an altercation on the boundary between Taj and the tour manager, Rais Jaji. Rais is bad-mouthing the coach for not selecting his cousin for the match, instead choosing Karim simply because they are brothers. Hasti rushes over and punches Rais. Karim, who is wicket-keeping, runs from the pitch to join in the fight. Taj finally drags the two apart but not before the match referee has got involved. So much for messengers of peace. And the problems between Allah Dad, who is not performing well on the field, and Taj continue. With the bat Allah Dad only manages a top score of three and with the ball (he considers himself a bowler more than a batsman) he ships runs. He bowls ten overs in three matches, conceding 85 runs and taking only one wicket. This poor performance offers a means of resolving the conflict between the two of them, but also sets up the potential for further skirmishes in the future.

When the dust settles, however, Taj takes stock. By finishing fifth in the ACC Trophy the team has done well for its first tournament. The players have certainly not disgraced themselves and exceeded everyone's expectations. By forming the team and taking it to its first international tournament, Taj has achieved his first goal. When he arrived in Kabul from Peshawar in 2001 it seemed impossible that in three years he would have a team competing against other nations. People laughed at Taj and his bravado but he has gone some way to showing them he is a man to be taken seriously. But even Taj's biggest supporters are staggered by his next boast: he is, he says, going to take his rookie team to the World Cup. Before Taj can really start planning that, the Afghan Cricket Federation is thrown into chaos as his deteriorating relationship with Allah Dad comes to a head.

Chapter 4

A Giant Step

AFGHANISTAN, 2004

Shortly after the team returns from Malaysia, the whole thing falls apart. Taj and Massoud have had enough of Allah Dad and kick him out of the federation. No one is quite sure how this happens, and if they do, they are not talking. Rumours abound of corruption, bribes and power struggles.

One rumour is that Allah Dad has been told he can no longer be vice president and captain. The story doing the rounds is that he resigned as vice president, expecting to keep his place in the team, only to find he was immediately dropped from the squad. But the fact is that he has been sacked. For Allah Dad, who made his own attempt to set up Afghan cricket as far back as 1995 and has worked without a salary since, it is a bitter pill to swallow. He has seen his team get ACC approval, receive funding, go to their first tournament and then be unceremoniously ousted.

In the months after the tournament, immediately after Allah Dad is sacked, the Afghan Cricket Federation gets its academy. It is basic: four nets, one bowling machine and a patch of grubby earth about the size of a football pitch; but for refugees used to playing in a graveyard it is their equivalent of Lord's.

Allah Dad's removal signals a shift in the ACF it moves from the naivety and optimism of the early days to a more hardnosed professionalism. The first competition brought with it its first casualty. There were sure to be more.

As the team enjoys its newfound status and relative success in its first competition, Afghanistan is becoming more and more violent. By 2006 the peaceful honeymoon that initially welcomed refugees back to Afghanistan after the fall of the Taliban is well and truly over.

NATO had taken control of the ISAF in 2003. It is NATO's first mission outside Europe. Although the recovery is costing NATO billions of dollars a year, most of this goes on the military. That year Care, an international charity working in Afghanistan, estimated that the average Afghan received only US$42; in Bosnia (US$326) and Kosovo (US$288) it was significantly higher, despite the fact that Afghans were in desperate need of help. Their country was ruined and needed rebuilding. In Bosnia there was one peacekeeper per 113 people, in Kosovo one per 48 and in Afghanistan one per 5,380. Up until 2006, when NATO troop numbers increased, these troops were all based in the capital, Kabul.

In the summer of 2006 NATO forces, who until now have stuck to the major towns, move into the southern

Afghan provinces, previously only patrolled by small numbers of American troops, operating outside NATO command, and some highly trained Special Forces. The influx of troops brings a vicious response. One British military commander likens the process to kicking a hornet's nest. Dumped into the Taliban and drug lords' heartland, the NATO soldiers experience fierce fighting almost immediately. The British in Helmand and the Canadians in Kandahar bear the brunt of the violence. But it is not just in the south that violence is increasing. Suicide bombings, unheard of in Afghanistan before 2001, are happening with alarming regularity and there are reports of bloodshed throughout the rest of the country.

These incidents suggest that after a five-year hiatus, the Taliban have regrouped, rearmed and are ready for a fight. They have funded their resurgence with money from heroin production – 90 per cent of the heroin on the streets in the UK comes from Afghan poppies – and from donations from across the Arab world.

This, the international community says, wasn't meant to happen. After initially being welcomed they underestimated the needs of the country. Afghanistan is, in many places, like stepping back into the 16th century: most people can't read or write, there is no electricity, and there are few schools, few hospitals and no paved roads.

The international community underestimated the massive task of building the country from scratch. If they wanted to stop Afghans sliding back into the grip of fundamentalists, they needed to provide better opportunities for the populace but they had failed to do this. The world's governments, who in 2001 had been so keen to replace the Taliban regime, had become distracted by the war in Iraq. Afghanistan had become of secondary interest.

Thankfully for everyone involved, the cricket team is following the opposite trajectory to the rest of the country. As disaster after disaster befalls the nation and it descends into chaos, the cricket team keeps improving. In 2006 the Afghan team has more international tournaments to play. It starts the year with an ACC Middle East Cup appearance in Kuwait and Oman in February. Here the team reaches the final, after beating Kuwait and Saudi Arabia, but ultimately loses to Bahrain by three wickets.

In August the players head back to Malaysia for their second appearance in the ACC Trophy. This time they finish third after losing to Hong Kong in the semi-finals. The team loses largely because the game is shortened by rain and neither Taj nor the captain Raees are fully aware of the complex Duckworth-Lewis rule, which determines how many runs they need to win (the Duckworth-Lewis method is a complicated set of calculations implemented by the ICC in 1999 to allow a fair result in matches cut short by rain, bad light, and even sandstorms). Afghanistan don't bat with enough urgency and fall short by 18 runs.

It is in Malaysia that the team first hears they will be able to enter the World Cup qualifiers. It is announced that the ICC has decided that for the 2011 World Cup tournament, the winners of the new ICC Trophy will go into Division Three of the ICC Cricket League, the runners-up will go into Division Four and the third- and fourth-placed teams will go to Division Five. Division Five is the furthest point away from the World Cup. Only the top four teams of Division One will be given places at the World Cup itself, but for Afghanistan there is hope: successive promotions could see them do it. They don't hold back on celebrating, they truly believe they are going to make it. It strikes journalists and ICC officials as strange, especially as they haven't even managed to win this tournament, but the Afghan players are adamant they can do it.

Qualification for the World Cup has never been decided this way before so there is no precedent, but everyone else agrees it would be impossible. Afghanistan would have to win (or finish second) in Divisions Five, Four and Three. The only concession would be that if they did this they would skip Division Two and head straight into Division One (The World Cup Qualifier): from which four teams, out of 12, will get places in the competition proper. In previous years World Cup qualification had been decided through the knockout ICC Trophy. Participants for the ICC trophy included the top five non-Test nations plus seven other teams chosen arbitrarily by the ICC. The United States, for example, had been in the previous final 12-team tournament although they would now be in Division Five with Afghanistan. This is the first time a league system has been instigated and the first time any nation in the league could, theoretically at least, make it to the finals. The Afghans are ecstatic; they feel that now they are in control of their destiny. If World Cup qualification was still to be decided by the knockout ICC Trophy and Afghanistan were chosen, it would have been easier but there was no guarantee they would have been picked for the tournament; now they have been accepted and they know what they need to do.

Beating Nepal in the third-place play-off isn't enough to save Raees' job. Raees had been Taj's first choice as captain. Now though, Taj feels that he needs someone who he perhaps doesn't know so well, over whom he can wield more power. Raees' natural successor – someone both Taj and Allah Dad had spotted as having leadership ability at the trials – is Nowroz. Nowroz, the one with the movie-star good looks, had to face down his parents to get here. They tried to stop him playing cricket and wanted him to become a doctor, but he was not academic. He once tried to become a mechanic when he was very poor and fed up with cricket, but was told he wasn't intelligent enough. That's not to say he is stupid, but it is definitely on the cricket pitch that he is at his strongest and all the players on the team look up to him. One look from Nowroz is often enough to silence dissent. While Taj huffs and puffs, talks, laughs, cries and invests all his emotions in cricket, Nowroz is more stand-offish, a calmer foil to his coach's exuberant behaviour.

Nowroz's story is remarkable. His cricket career was almost cut short by his father's insistence that he quit the game after September 2001. So Taj went to Khost, a journey of about seven hours, to talk to Nowroz's father to persuade him to allow his son to continue to play. At the time Nowroz was just a competent batsman and part-time bowler, but Taj had plans for him.

Taj stayed overnight, begging Nowroz's father to allow his son to continue playing cricket, explaining that it was a wonderful game and that one day Nowroz would captain his country. Taj negotiated for the whole night and finally got his way. After the 2006 ACC trophy in Malaysia, Nowroz was rewarded with a present of land and a tractor donated by a local businessman. His family finally saw Taj's point. It had been a risk for Taj though – if Nowroz or Afghanistan had failed, it would have been a heavy burden for him to bear.

Since then, Nowroz has never looked back. Today, cricket fills his every waking moment. He has been dreaming about cricket and what it can bring to Afghanistan. He genuinely and passionately believes that cricket can help improve the fortunes of Afghanistan. It is a lofty aim but it is one shared by all the players.

The first tournament under the new captain is the ACC Twenty20 Cup and he wins it – well almost. The tournament is being held in Kuwait where there is a huge Afghan population and thousands turn up to see the team play.

Afghanistan reach the final where they play Oman, one of the most powerful teams in the region and the team that beat them in their first-ever international match. After 20 overs the teams are tied on 157, but somehow the Afghans have miscalculated and their fans flood onto the pitch thinking they have won. Normally in Twenty20 draws a bowl-out is instigated to decide the winner – a bit like a penalty shootout in football – but the Afghan fans have ruined the wicket. The Afghans are convinced they have won. Although the match is declared a draw, the team and their fans refuse to accept the decision. The team somehow manages to leave the ground and Kuwait with the winners' trophy. Remarkably nobody at the ICC or ACC seems to notice that the cup is missing.

Results on the pitch mean the Afghans are starting to make waves in the cricket community; their near victory in Kuwait earns them some attention on cricket websites. One man who hears about them is Mark Scrase-Dickins, a former soldier and foreign office employee, who has been to Afghanistan a number of times. He has become increasingly interested in Afghan cricket and is impressed when he sees the national team in the nets on a trip to Kabul.

Back in England, as a member of the MCC, he decides to raise the issue of the Afghan cricket team at an MCC general meeting. When the floor is opened to general members, Mr Scrase-Dickins gets to his feet and asks the MCC what they are doing to support the Afghan cricket team? As soon as he asks the question, jaws drop: many members of the MCC didn't even know there was an Afghan cricket team, but the very next day he receives a phone call and is asked what the MCC can do to help.

The MCC hierarchy has some knowledge of the Afghans; they had after all given Stuart Bentham some kit to take out. Now, they tell Scrase-Dickins, they want to do more. Led by their president, Robin Marlar, who in his previous life as a journalist had been instrumental in getting Bangladesh accepted as a Test nation, the MCC set about arranging a match with Afghanistan. And in March 2006 an MCC team touring India invites the Afghan team over for a game. The MCC and the British Embassy in Kabul sponsor the team's journey – paying for the flights to Delhi, and the train to Mumbai.

On arrival Mike Gatting (the former England captain and captain of the MCC team) graciously offers to give the Afghans some tips in the nets after the game. But when Afghanistan post 356 for seven in 40 overs and skittle MCC out for 185, no tips are forthcoming from Gatting, who is himself bowled for a duck by Hasti Gul.

It is a significant victory. In the match, Nabi top scores with 116 and Hamid performs well with the ball. Both players impress Marlar so much he invites them to come to Lord's for a month that summer to take part in the MCC Young Cricketer programme, from which they will benefit from some world-class coaching.

During the programme, John Stephenson, Head of Cricket and Estates at the MCC, is impressed by their natural talent but frustrated by their lack of discipline. The machismo of the players gets in the way of any guile or tactical play – Nabi tries to hit everything for six and Hamid expects to get a wicket with every ball.

Their stay in London is an eye-opener for the two young Afghans: when Hamid arrives in the city he doesn't even have a pair of proper bowling spikes – he is used to playing in trainers. But Stephenson has a cupboard full of cricket kit and he invites the pair to take whatever they want. It is an act of generosity and the Afghan boys make sure they take full advantage. For days after that, when Stephenson comes back to his office, he finds the two boys rifling through his gear. They clearly find it impossible to believe someone could have so much unwanted, good-quality cricket kit. The two Afghans make an impression on everyone they meet. Paul Carroll, who was twelfth man for MCC in Mumbai (and so was spared his blushes), stays in touch with Hamid and is so impressed by his will to succeed that he asks him to stay on and helps find him a team in England to play for during the summer.

The young bowler turns out for Norden in the Central Lancashire League where he immediately impresses and gains the local nickname of 'the Afghan Express'. In his first game, he takes a wicket with his first ball and follows this up with a stunning eight-wicket haul against the reigning league champions. Hamid is invited back to play the following year.

Another result of victory against the MCC is that the full Afghan team is invited to tour England. The tour is organised by Peter Frawley, a cricket promoter who, phil-anthropically, donates his services and secures funding for the trip. The team plays seven games, mainly against county second teams, and wins all but one. Frawley believes the tour is a turning point for the team as the players finally start to believe they deserve a place in the real cricket world.

The team makes steady progress throughout 2006 and 2007, and by 2008 it is firmly established on the Asian circuit. It has risen from 90th in the world – the position they occupied in 2001 and the lowest possible rank at the time – to the mid-30s. A remaining frustration, however, is the declining security situation in Afghanistan, which means that no one is particularly keen to come to the country, much less to stay there for any length of time. Future success lies elsewhere.

The team's current success has had its effects on Taj, who is now convinced that it is on its way to the World Cup. He talks as if his team is already there, and makes frequent comparisons between his players and the reigning world champions Australia. He hadn't dreamt of being a coach when he was growing up, but he has taken to the role quickly. As a boy he always wanted to be a player, like Imran Khan, the famous Pakistani captain turned politician. It hadn't worked out that way and now he was proud to be coach.

Although Taj had played for one of the academy clubs during the second Afghan trial he had never actually tried out for the national team. With Karim and Hasti eager to play, he thought his skills would be better served on the non-playing side. He thought it might look suspicious and damage their chances if there were three brothers in the squad so, as the eldest, he stepped aside.

Since the ACC has taken an interest in the development of Afghan cricket, they had sent several coaches to advise Taj but none had lasted very long. Taj is hard to persuade and even more difficult to control. But Taj does benefit from a number of ACC-sponsored coaching courses in the period between 2006 and 2008, which set him up, by some distance, as the most qualified coach in Afghanistan. His energy, enthusiasm and absolutely unshakeable belief in himself and the ability of his team also make him an unmanageable force of nature.

Although Taj might not have the experience of playing international cricket, what he does have is determination and he has it by the bucket load. When he speaks he smiles and he laughs often but his eyes always remain focused, they are always busy and thoughtful, fully determined. He knows where he wants his team to be and he has mighty ambitions. He truly believes that his team has the potential to be one of the best in the world.

Taj is full of bravado. He is, or so he says, a master psychologist capable of inspiring his players to greatness. He claims to know, better than anyone, how to inspire his team. Taj has something, and it isn't just braggadocio. He has established a team, got them playing internationals and, for the most part, is managing to keep a squad that isn't getting paid, happy.

Although he speaks about qualifying for the World Cup as if it is a formality, it is anything but. Though their third-place finish in Malaysia has seen Afghanistan admitted to the World Cup qualifiers, an exhaustive series of 50-over matches, they still have a very long way to go. Only four non-Test Nations will make it to the 2011 tournament and Afghanistan are looking up from Division Five – the bottom of the pile.

It is announced that the Division Five tournament will be held in the Channel Islands. The other teams in their group are Botswana, Singapore, Japan, the Bahamas and the hosts Jersey. When the draw is made it is confirmed Afghanistan will play Japan in their first game. The night of the draw, Nowroz has a dream. He dreams Afghanistan will lose, but this, he declares, is a positive sign because he believes that whatever you dream the opposite will happen. Taj is more bombastic than his captain. He predicts they will score 300 or 400 against Japan. Their opponents, he says are weak physically and tactically. The Afghans are stronger both in person and on the pitch.

Taj also has opinions about their other opponents. Botswana is a country he has never heard of, although he correctly guesses it is in Africa and, therefore, they will be strong like the Kenyans. Singapore he dismisses as a one man-team – Kumarage, their captain, is the only good player. The hosts Jersey have, according to Taj, a strong economy and are very rich like the English. Although he predicts the general population of Jersey will be fat with red hair, he thinks the cricket team will be professional and strong. After looking the Bahamas up online, he is amused to see how small the country is. Taj is unconcerned by them – they sound like a club team, which he thinks will be their standard.

If Taj is brimming with confidence, Nowroz is unafraid to voice his concerns about what the conditions both on and off the field might be like in Jersey. Although the Afghan team toured England and Wales in 2006, British conditions are largely unknown to them. The players are used to playing on dry, hard-baked wickets in Peshawar, not grassy, moist wickets like those they'll encounter in Jersey. The ball will bounce differently and it will move or swing more in the air because of the atmospheric conditions – both factors that significantly increase the odds against them.

Nowroz is also concerned about the preparations. The team is hoping to stop off in England on their way to Jersey and play some warm-up games but as the tournament draws nearer it turns out that the players have only been issued visas for the Channel Islands. They will not be allowed out of the airport in London and will be flying straight to Jersey and will face Japan without a warm-up game.

Their worries aren't confined to the field either. There is also the issue of food. In the same way an English cricket team touring in India might worry about getting 'Delhi belly', the Afghan team, who are all Muslims, are worried the food might not be halal, and prepared in accordance with Islamic law. Nowroz is particularly concerned about inadvertently eating pork, seen by Muslims as dirty. The very thought disgusts him. If the worst comes to the worst, he says, he will drink tea and eat fruit and biscuits.

The team's preparations for the tour, even putting aside the fact it won't be playing any warm-up games in England, do not go smoothly. Although the ICC is paying for the flights, the hotel and breakfast in Jersey, the ACF still needs to raise some money for kit, equipment, per diems for players and additional seats on the flights (the team is also taking two dignitaries, including Massoud).

The ACF is seeking sponsorship of US$14,000 to cover the additional costs. It isn't a huge amount but they are having trouble drumming up interest. The kit has already been ordered, the additional flights booked, and if they don't come up with the money to pay the federation will be in trouble.

While the finances don't seem to worry Taj, Mujib, the federation's accountant, wears a permanent look of alarm on his face. He is small and skinny with a wispy beard and although he smiles often it seems to be a smile of fear rather than genuine joy. He has the look of a man who knows at any moment his world could collapse around him and he will be left to pick up the pieces.

A month before the tour, Taj and Mujib take a trip to the Standard Chartered Bank in Kabul. This is the only international bank with permission to operate in Afghanistan. The bank is barricaded by concertinas of barbed wire; armed guards peer out of watchtowers and it is surrounded by large concrete blast walls. To enter the bank you first have to be allowed past the armed guards on the street, then you approach a steel door; here a guard checks you out through an eyehole. If he lets you in, you are frisked and go through a metal detector. Once you have passed this inspection you are allowed through the final steel door and into the bank. The armed guards, all carrying AK47s, loiter around inside and the glass is all reinforced and covered in blast film to stop it shattering in case of an explosion. It is perhaps the safest bank in the world.

When Mujib emerges from his meeting with the bank manager he shifts nervously from one leg to the other and then laughs. The balance, he says is zero. It is completely empty, the ACF has nothing. To lighten the mood, or perhaps because if they don't laugh they will cry, the two burst into uncontrollable laughter and perform a high five.

It is hard to know exactly how much money had made it into the ACF coffers and what it, if anything, had been spent on, but by 2008 Mujib confirms that the pot is empty. According to their accounts in 2003-04 the ICC set aside US$46,294 for Afghan cricket: in 2004-05 this rose to US$115,451, in 2005-06 to US$165,605, in 2006-07 to US$121,961 and a further US$107,453 was set aside in 2007 as the tax year changed. In 2008 Afghanistan cricket was set to receive US$253,213. This, however, was funding that the ICC gave to the Asian Cricket Council for Afghan cricket, and little money actually found its way into the ACF accounts. The Afghans claim that the only lump sum they received from the ACC was around US$30,000, and this was spent on the academy. In 2005, for example, the Asian Cricket Council statements show that the cricket board received an advance of only US$895. Other money would have been used to help the team attend tournaments, to train coaches and umpires, but the fact is that the expected funds had never made it into the coffers of the ACF.

Luckily for the team and Mujib's sanity, funding is soon secured through a sponsorship deal with a mobile phone company. Bashir, a relative of Jagdalek who had gone to the first meeting at the Olympic Committee, set up the deal. He will also be going on the Jersey tour as assistant manager.

However, the sponsorship money is not enough to give the players a per diem and they will have to find money to pay for dinner and, on non-match days, lunch. This is another concern for Nowroz. He realises that, as some of his players are poor, they will struggle to find the money to eat.

During the weeks leading up to Jersey the team holds two training camps; one in Peshawar, where most of the team live and where they can make use of top quality cricket facilities, and one in Kabul. Outside the Olympic Stadium in Kabul is the Afghan National Cricket Academy. It is across the road from the patch of land where the trials were held. The name is far grander than the facilities merit. Since it had been built it had quickly, like most things in Kabul's harsh climate, deteriorated.

Although the academy pales in comparison to the facilities in Peshawar, the team trains in Afghanistan out of a sense of national pride. They want to show their countrymen, as they did during the trials, that although they have spent much of their lives as refugees in Pakistan they are still Afghans.

As the trip grows closer the training picks up in intensity. They practise bowling and catching, do fielding drills and the batsmen try to find form by facing a newly donated bowling machine. By far the most popular activity is dive catching. Taj has laid a dirty old mattress on the floor, he then throws balls to players who dive manically to try and catch them. The idea is to catch the ball in the air and land safely on the mattress. It is only a single mattress and at times the players miss, landing on the hard dirt. One player, who is carrying a bit of extra weight and seems to miss the mattress more than most, is Ahmad Shah. On first meeting Ahmad Shah he seems serious. He doesn't smile very often and has the aloof manner of a superstar. On further exploration it is clear he is shy and nervous, but once he warms up he proves to be a kind man with an easy, happy-go-lucky manner. He is generous and considers himself a bit of a fashionista. He is, apart from a moustache he has styled on his favourite Indian actor, clean-shaven. He wears jeans, short sleeve shirts and, while many of the team wear sandals, he sports a pair of leather slip-on shoes. Despite his shy disposition Ahmad Shah has an eye for the fairer sex. Explaining the extra weight he is carrying, Shah says it helps him hit the ball farther.

The extra weight might be explained by the fact the team has no fitness coach. Not only that, but unlike many teams, neither do they have a specialist bowling coach, nor a specialist batting coach. Just Taj.

Despite this some of the players have incredible style and panache. Nabi, with both bat and ball, and Hamid, with the ball, really look the part. The player with the most style though is Noor Ali, a top-order batsman. He plays as if the bat is an extension of his arm. He oozes grace and poise at the crease. He is explosive and when he gets hold of a ball it shoots into orbit like a rocket. Away from the cricket pitch Noor Ali is quiet, reserved and unassuming.

Most sportsmen, including cricketers, have a carefully controlled diet. Generally, the Afghan players do not. They eat lamb kebabs, rice, chunks of greasy meat and naan bread. There are very few vegetables or fruit on the menu. They guzzle soft drinks and cups of green tea, with two or three sugars, like most athletes drink isotonic sports drinks. Some of the players smoke and Taj and his two brothers Karim and Hasti Gul chew tobacco as well. Some of the players also smoke hashish.

This is not to say that none of the team looks after themselves. Raees, the former captain, appears to eat nothing but fruit. And Gulbadeen 'the Body' Naib, a youngster discovered playing cricket in the Kacha Gari refugee camp where he still lives and who will be making his debut in Jersey, spends all his free time in the gym and drinks protein shakes. Gulbadeen has biceps as big as a man's thighs and strips off his shirt at every opportunity to perform his favourite trick – moving his huge pecs independently. When he does this repeatedly they seem to bounce. Not content with one feat of physical prowess, he also curls his arms to flex his biceps as he moves his pecs. Before coming to cricket he entered and won a number of bodybuilding competitions in Peshawar. He carries around with him a number of competition photos in which he is naked apart from a pair of skimpy swimming trunks, and his body is a very orange colour from the fake tan. It is bizarre in a culture as conservative as Afghanistan's that men take part in something as Western as bodybuilding but the activity is very popular.

Rather than being shunned by his teammates for Western excesses, Gulbadeen is worshipped for his body.

Gulbadeen's inclusion in the squad for the tournament had highlighted a new problem for Taj. It had not been easy to persuade the Olympic Committee to grant him a passport. After the tour of England in 2006 one player and one official used their multiple entry visas to return to England and claim asylum. The player was Khaliq Dad, Allah Dad's brother. This has made the committee nervous about issuing passports. It might also explain why they were only given visas to Jersey.

A number of other Afghan athletes have disappeared on foreign tours. Taj is not overly worried though. He was humiliated when Khaliq Dad disappeared but he wasn't surprised. It also gave him something else to hold over Allah Dad. On an official level the incident was swept under the carpet. Khaliq Dad didn't disappear on the tour, he used his multiple entry visa to return to England legally, paying for the flight himself, and then claimed asylum. If he had done it on the tour the implications for Taj and the federation would have been greater. He knows his current players so much better and trusts them. He has personally promised the Olympic Committee that if any of the players go missing he will be held responsible. It's a huge risk for Taj: he could face a fine or worse he could have his passport taken away and not be able to travel abroad anymore. For those players he doesn't know so well he has asked a senior player to act as their guardian and ensure they don't go missing. For Gulbadeen that player is the former captain and Taj's great friend – Raees Ahmadzai.

As the tournament approaches, Afghan journalists besiege the players with requests for interviews and a press conference is organised. It is clear that most of the journalists know very little about cricket. Some ask to have the rules explained; others can't name a single Afghan player. The line of questioning is basic. One correspondent asks the difference between batting and bowling; another how many players are on a team? Someone says cricket is a Pakistani game and wonders what the team say to that?

The few reporters that know a bit about cricket like to show off their knowledge. Their questions are more like statements and are aggressive. They say it is clear the team is better at bowling than batting and ask if Taj has considered that?

For their part the players are gracious and take the time to explain the rules. Raees, the former captain, and Nowroz, the current captain, along with Taj do most of the talking.

Raees and Nowroz have remained friends even though Nowroz has replaced Raees as captain. The two have an interesting dynamic. Raees will always introduce himself as the former captain, and Nowroz privately complains to Taj that Raees undermines him by talking tactics too much during training and matches. Publicly though the two show a united front. As the tour approaches it seems that Nowroz and Raees develop an understanding and learn to work together. Raees has a quick cricket brain and Nowroz realises he can learn from the ex-captain. Nowroz has an air that demands respect. Raees may make suggestions but Nowroz's word is final.

During the Kabul training camp the team stay at the Saari Chowck Worgon Wall Hotel, which is within spitting distance of the academy. However, that is about all it has going for it. It is a benighted place. The electricity, when it comes, is so weak that the single bare bulb in each room flickers pathetically, unable to maintain a constant stream of light. The lime green walls reflect an eerie glow over everything. There are no beds and the players sleep on single mattresses on the floor – four or five to a room. Around them their cricket kit is scattered: bats, balls, shirts and pads. The rooms smell of musk, cigarettes and body odour. Many of the windows are cracked and they are all covered in polythene to try and keep the heat in and the rain out. There is no central heating or air conditioning. The only toilet is a hole in the floor on the ground floor of the rickety five-storey building.

The nearest washing facilities are in the hammam, the public baths across the busy and noisy Jaday-e-Miywond Road. In the dining room raw meat sits uncovered as flies buzz around it. Koranic verses hang in gaudy picture frames on the wall. Bearded men in traditional Afghan robes sit cross-legged on the floor while an old dusty fan whirls weakly from the ceiling. There are only two dishes on the menu: lamb kebab and lamb stew, served with either bread or rice. The green tea, with spoonfuls of white sugar, is handed out to everyone who enters the room.

The night before they leave for Jersey the players laugh and watch videos on their mobile phones. Despite being poor all the players have mobiles onto which they can download videos from the Internet. None of them has any credit, however, and if they want to talk to someone they call and hang up before they answer. They keep doing this until the person calls them back.

They crowd around the phones and giggle at Mr Bean-type Afghan comedy clips. Other favourites include religious sermons and videos of Taliban insurgents shooting down helicopters. Although none of the players actively supports the Taliban, many are critical of the American troops and their treatment of the Afghans. Despite the fact that Britain also has troops in Afghanistan the players all appear to love the country. Taj explains it is because they play cricket.

On the final night most of the players crowd into one room and consume a great deal of tea. Hasti Gul, 'the Joker' with the lisp, is dancing the Attan, a traditional Afghan dance. He sways and twirls, a broad smile plays across his face. It is clear he can't wait to get playing. Hasti has never been the favourite brother and he wants to use this tournament to prove to Taj he is as good as Karim. He also wants to prove to the team he is in the squad on merit, not because his brother is coach.

Despite the laughter the players are determined. Taj, in his wonderfully colourful way, sums it up when he says he loves Afghanistan and he never wants her to be in a low position: one where others only think of the country related to terror, drugs and violence. He wants to improve the reputation of the country and he wants to start by winning this tournament.

Nowroz, the captain, echoes this sentiment. He dreams of a better Afghanistan and he sees that starting on the cricket pitch. It is a cliché but to them it really is more than sport. Afghanistan has something to prove. They are playing for their very identity and to change the way the world perceives them. What better way to change people's perceptions than through cricket?

Cricket is a genteel sport of discipline, tactics and diplomacy: in other words it is a game that encapsulates all that Afghanistan doesn't in the eyes of the wider world. The team feels if it can win at cricket they can go a long way to changing people's thoughts about Afghanistan. Although their experiences outside of the country have largely been limited to Asia and the 2006 cricket tour of England, the members of the team are all aware of how their country is perceived. What's more, as much as they love Afghanistan, they know it has problems. They want to try and improve the lot of their country and they want to do it in the only way they know how, by playing cricket and winning.

That's not to say the Afghans won't be adding their own touches to the game. Taj says cricket is war by different means, and they certainly play the game as if it is a conflict.

Taj spends his last day in Kabul shopping for the tour of Jersey. He wants a suit, but nothing too silky, and he wants black leather pointy shoes. He wants to look his best in Jersey and make an impression. He finds time to berate a young shopkeeper who says he prefers football to cricket. Taj finishes the argument by telling him the Afghan cricket team is only five years behind the international community whereas the football team is 50 years adrift.

The players are all given suits made by a tailor in Jalalabad. On each of the sleeves a different designer label has been sown, some read Boss, some read Armani and some read Calvin Klein. The tags are not removed but left proudly displayed on the sleeve. Karim announces he is going to Europe, dressed European-style. As well as the suits the players also get new training gear and an official playing kit. The kit they will wear on match days is made up of royal blue trousers and royal blue tops with red sleeves. On the back of the shirts each player has their name and a number. They are also given tracksuits, which are coloured like the playing kit, except on the back they have 'Afghanistan' in white lettering. Their training tops have 'Proud to be Afghan' across the back. The players love the new kit – they realise they are proud to represent their country and want the world to know where they come from. They know that Afghanistan has a poor reputation, centred on violence, war and drugs, but they are not ashamed and want to play their part in changing the minds of people who see them play.

For the Afghan team Jersey is the start of their World Cup adventure, but it also offers the chance for more immediate rewards. They want to show the world that Afghans are civilised, can play by the rules, can integrate and can compete. What better way to do this than by playing in Europe and by winning? They also know that if they win the competition they will send a message to those who doubt them in Kabul. Although they have support from Sherzada Massoud and the Olympic Committee, many within the country still view cricket as a funny foreign sport, particularly in the Tajik dominated government. Taj is aware that a failure in the tournament will be pounced on by the press and might weaken his chances of continuing to develop the sport. Much is riding on victory in Jersey.

Chapter 5

World Cup Dream

JERSEY, MAY 2008 – PART I

The players wear their new suits from Kabul to Dubai, from Dubai to London and from London to Jersey. The stop-off in Dubai is full of incident. The departure lounge is a maze of glitz, glamour and over-the-top capitalism. In the duty-free there is a Ferrari that you can win in a raffle, there are shops selling Rolexes, Tag Heuers and Jaeger Le Coultres and, in contrast to Kabul Airport where all you can snack on are stale crisps and flat coke, here one can dine on caviar, sushi and lobster, while drinking champagne. There are also shops that sell gold, diamonds and designer clothes. Kabul might only be a two and half hour flight from Dubai but it is, in the glamour stakes, a galaxy away.

Though most of the players have been here before they still are mesmerised. Their first stop, however, is not to one of the swanky restaurants, which are out of their budget, but to the food court where they head straight to McDonald's.

In their matching suits, with movie-star looks – hair gelled back, sunglasses on, shirt collars upturned or big tie knots – they look every part the glamorous cricketing stars. They are soon surrounded by a group of Arab girls who ask them for photos and autographs. The girls don't know who they are but they squeal to each other that they must be famous because of the way they are dressed.

One girl, in her early twenties, cries with delight as she wraps her arm around a player for a photo. Another asks where they are from. A third asks what they do. On discovering that they are Afghan cricketers, the girls are even more impressed. After the initial flurry of conversation the group reach an impasse. Both are from very conservative societies and are normally unable to mix freely with the opposite sex but in the neutral territory of Dubai Airport they have been given the opportunity to do so. For Sami, who dreams of being a model and has been the centre of the attention, it doesn't end well. Not wanting to see them leave he racks his brains for a parting quip; as the girls walk away he calls after the largest one and tells her to stop being so fat. The boys burst into laughter but the girls, understandably, look horrified. Sami freezes and realises that his joke has fallen flat; he hadn't intended to be mean or insulting. But regardless, the girls immediately delete all photos of the team from their digital cameras. The players' first brush with celebrity ends badly.

Taj has no such problem. His charm is endless. In the smoking room he puffs away feverishly on a cigarette and approaches a skinny, grey-haired man in blue jeans and a button-down shirt. Soon he has found out that the man is American and when Taj reveals that he is from Afghanistan, the man smiles. But when Taj says he is heading for the Cricket World Cup and the first stop is Jersey the American looks baffled, he has no idea about cricket or even where Jersey is. The American's confusion amuses Taj and he laughs as he leaves the smoking room, almost losing his footing as he steps onto the escalator. Escalators are not entirely new to Taj, there is one in a city mall shopping centre in Kabul, though he rarely visits it. He has used them on his travels but they remain a bit of a novelty and he prefers to take the stairs.

He then runs into a Japanese tour group. When he asks if they speak English, one responds, 'Little, little,' which sends Taj into a hysterical laughing fit. He then takes a cowboy hat off one of them and tries it on, posing this way and that. They titter amongst each other. Taj notices that one of them, a man in his 60s, is wearing spectacles. Taj calls him 'four eyes', then, seeing that he has a pair of fold-down sunglasses attached corrects it to 'six eyes'. He wins them over with this comment and the group all laugh and queue up to shake his hand.

Taj leaves the Japanese tourists and spies his next target, an attractive, blonde mother and daughter. He asks them where they are from. They are German. Not a cricketing nation; he moves on.

His next stop is a middle-aged man in spectacles. He is, Taj soon discovers, from Belgium, not a cricketing nation either. They play football Taj announces shaking his head in dismay. The Belgian looks bemused. It is obvious Taj thinks less of non-cricketers. He sees them as inferior, less trustworthy and not as decent. For him cricket is a marker by which to judge people; those that like the sport are trustworthy, decent individuals, they are gentleman who know the importance of team spirit and have a never-say-die attitude. They can follow rules, understand complex tactical situations and are also brave. Taj is fond of reminding those who doubt the bravery of how hard a leather ball is, sometimes if he has one to hand he might toss it at them to emphasise his point. Those that don't like cricket are bounders and cads; they are untrustworthy, unreliable, cowardly and above all stupid. The rules of cricket are complicated and the only reason people wouldn't like it, he thinks, is if they are too stupid to understand them.

In all the journey takes over 24 hours, and the players are looking more than a little dishevelled, but as the plane comes into land in Jersey they straighten their ties, tuck in their shirts and put their creased jackets on. They are playing in their first World Cup qualifier and they want to make a good impression.

Karim makes sure he is one of the first off the plane, saying how proud he is to be an Afghan and that it's his mission in Jersey to show a different side of Afghanistan. But, being Karim, he is not entirely altruistic: in the same breath he says he wants to win player of the tournament and score the most runs. This statement reflects how all the members of the Afghan team feel about playing international cricket – it is at once essential for the reputation of the country and a personal glory mission.

It is a beautiful clear spring day and upon arrival the difference between Kabul and St Helier is immediately clear. Kabul Airport is a mess: bombed-out planes lie to one side of the runway, their bodies broken and bullet ridden, reminders of years of civil war and American bombing raids. Brand new fighter jets belonging to NATO sit on the opposite side, symbolising the ongoing conflict in the country. The airport is fortified with guard towers and heavily armed soldiers. The terminal is a cavernous, empty building with one luggage carousel that never works. It too bears the marks of war – chipped marble, bullet holes and windows without glass or panes. It is a sorry sight. The airport at Jersey is also small – like Kabul it only has one runway – but it is modern, neat and clean. The only planes are small propeller-powered island hoppers or smart-looking British Airways jets. There are no fighter planes and no military garrisons.

Jersey and Afghanistan could hardly be more different. Everything Afghanistan isn't, Jersey is. Jersey is completely surrounded by water; Afghanistan is completely land-locked. Jersey is wealth (the GDP per capita is US$57,000) to Afghanistan's poverty ($800). Unemployment on the island is around 2.4 per cent; in Afghanistan it is 35 per cent. The average life expectancy for an Afghan is under 45 years, whereas someone from Jersey could expect to live until they are almost 80. In Jersey fewer than five babies per thousand die before their first birthday; in Afghanistan it is 153, one of the worst rates in the world. The average age of the Afghan population is around 17, in Jersey it is almost 43; Afghanistan is a very young country: leaders, experience and skills are in short supply.

The people of Jersey are well educated. *The Jersey Evening Post*, the only newspaper published on the island, estimates that 93 per cent of the population will read their newspaper each week. In Afghanistan only about 35 per cent of the population can read.

About the only thing Afghanistan has going for it is its size and population. Jersey, which is only 116 square kilometres, has a population of almost 92,000, Afghanistan, population 28 million, covers an area of 652,000 square kilometres. But size is deceptive in cricket terms. Jersey might be small but it has six cricket pitches, Afghanistan has none.

As the bus rumbles from the airport towards the hotel, Ahmad Shah, another of the elder statesmen of the team, looks out the window and says the view is one of the most beautiful things he has ever seen. To British eyes, Jersey has caught up with trends slower than the British mainland, and can be reminiscent of British small-town life in the 1980s. But as the young Afghan players gaze out of the windows at the small houses, gardens, streets and green fields, a sense of peace and security settles over them.

This sense of peace makes Ahmad Shah melancholic and homesick. Although he spends most of his time in Rawalpindi in Pakistan, he still has a family home in

Paktika province, Afghanistan. He is sad, as he hasn't been able to visit his home for months. After a recent tour abroad he appeared on television. He has heard rumours that the Taliban didn't approve and, as they control large areas around his home, he is anxious for his family and scared to visit. When he does go he has to travel early in the morning or late at night and in disguise. This brings its own worries, as the area is not safe. As well as the Taliban, there are criminal gangs and kidnappers who work purely for financial gain. The American army also has several bases in his province and Ahmad Shah, more than most on the team, is suspicious of them and their motives.

The team's hotel is a ten-minute walk from the seafront. It is an ageing three-star establishment, but its atmosphere strengthens the players' feelings of peace, security, and comparative luxury – certainly relative to the Saari Chowck Worgon Wall Hotel in Kabul. On the ground floor are the lobby, a bar, a dining room and a room for activities such as dancing and bingo. The only other guests apart from the team are old-age pensioners and, on one of the first nights, a wedding party.

It is the first of many surprising events for the Afghan players. The bride is in her late thirties and is wearing a traditional white dress; the groom is dressed in a kilt. Taj finds the man in the kilt particularly strange and says so, a little too loudly. To try and make amends for the offence he causes, he charges into the bar to offer his hearty congratulations to the happy couple. He also wants to tell them about the Afghan cricket team. The bride is smitten with Taj, perhaps made bold by the occasion, and the drink. She contemplates kissing his cheek, but mid-lunge thinks better of it, settling on a handshake. The couple introduce their child, a boy of about eight. Taj's imagination is sent into overtime; they have only just got married, how is it possible they already have a child?

In Afghanistan to have a child outside of marriage is considered sinful: no man would willingly marry a woman who has borne a child outside of wedlock, a birth outside the marriage leaves the woman damaged. In many areas, sex outside of marriage is punishable by death. It is just one facet of Western life that bewilders and shocks the team. After his initial blunder, Taj keeps cool. He has the ability to take most things in his stride.

Taj has another bizarre experience the night before Afghanistan play their first match against Japan. Walking past the activities room he hears loud, live music. The song, although he doesn't recognise it, is 'Is This The Way to Amarillo'. Taj opens the door and guffaws. The song is being played live by a perma-tanned elderly couple as about 12 other pensioners dance in line, swaying and bucking slowly to the music. Taj can barely believe the sight: it is, he thinks, the first time he has seen old people dance. In Afghanistan such behaviour would be seen as uncouth: the elderly are revered and remain very much a part of the family. Not only would they never dance but also they would never go on holiday on their own. They would remain in the family home and be supported by their children.

It is not only alien cultural practices that are disturbing the team ahead of their first qualifier. The morning after the disco, food becomes an issue, as they thought it might. Although breakfast is provided, it is not to their tastes. Sherzada Massoud, the president who has no real need to be on the tour, nevertheless complains to anyone who will listen. The only thing he is eating is the fruit. The two greasy fried eggs that Taj has helped himself to do not meet with Massoud's approval. Taj doesn't share the president's militant stance on cooked food, but he is still not impressed. He says it isn't tasty and he reflects on all the Afghan foods he is missing. He talks about the pilau rice, the meat kebabs and the lamb; the memory is so vivid that as he talks he starts to lick his lips. The eggs just make him frown.

Breakfast is the only inclusive meal the players get so they are forced to eat it. Later, when Karim goes to an Indian takeaway and buys half a chicken and some naan bread, he is shocked to find it costs as much as a whole lamb in Kabul. Karim is homesick. On the way back from the restaurant he makes a list of everything he misses: his children, his mother, his brothers and sisters and the food. Tellingly he omits his wife from the list. It is not that he isn't missing her, in private he will admit that he is, it's just in public it would be inappropriate to talk of her in front of anyone but family and very close friends.

The lack of funds and the high living costs in Jersey lead the players to develop some ingenious ways of finding food. First they try to get hold of some more money. Noor

Ali, a quiet man who idolises Ricky Ponting, and Sami, the player who dreams of being a male model, both have brothers who live in London. Sami's brother works at Heathrow Airport as a baggage handler while Noor Ali's is a bus driver in Walthamstow. The two cricketers persuade their brothers to wire them a few hundred pounds. The money is the team's lunch and dinner fund for the week. They are provided with lunch on the days they play matches but otherwise they have to fend for themselves.

The money they receive is still not enough and so some further improvisation is required. Nabi happens upon the St Helier branch of McDonald's. It's a welcome sight for the players who were impressed with their meals at Dubai Airport. Not only is it the cheapest food available but the players all agree it is also the tastiest food they have come across. What's more the Filet-o-Fish and chips are halal. Nabi, with his sportsmen's physique and Afghan robes, cuts quite a figure in the restaurant. He discovers that by smiling at the staff they will give him 'two-for-one' vouchers. Before long he has collected a large pile. He becomes so confident that he starts just walking up to the counter – even if he isn't ordering anything – and smiling with his hand held out for more vouchers. The players can't believe their luck. Soon the whole Afghan squad is eating lunch and dinner in McDonald's for half price.

The game against Japan approaches very quickly. McDonald's feasts aren't ideal for the general fitness of the team and there is only one practice session before the game itself. They have little time to prepare for the huge change in playing conditions and the beginning of such an important tournament. Nevertheless, on the way to the practice field the day before the game, they are arrogant, bullish and more than a little confident.

Karim, the self-appointed star, is excited. He wants to start with a bang and predicts he'll score a century. And Taj, in contrast to the widely held idea that cricket is a genteel sport, believes that cricket is not a game for wimps, it is a physical challenge between two teams more than a tactical one. The physically stronger should normally win. Imagine then, Taj's amusement when he sees the Japanese training with soft balls. He concludes that there will be little opposition from this team. As if to prove their physical superiority, Karim, on cue, takes a hard leather ball in the face and barely flinches. Despite Karim's protests, Taj makes him sit out the rest of the session. He uses the time to spray paint his white wicket-keeping pads blue, so they match Afghanistan's blue and red uniforms.

The teams share a bus to and from the training session (on match day they will have separate buses in case emotions are running high). Although Taj finds it amusing that the Japanese practise with soft balls, it really irks him that they don't show respect to their Australian coach. The Afghan players board the bus back to the hotel at the appointed time and have to wait for ten minutes for the Japanese team. As each minute passes Taj becomes more and more agitated. When the team finally boards the coach is the last one on and there are no seats left. None of the players offers him theirs.

Taj can't believe it. He makes one of his own players offer up his seat but the coach refuses to take it. To Taj this is against everything that cricket stands for. Cricket is meant to be a game of discipline and respect, of order and decorum. He can't believe the Japanese have shown their coach so little respect.

When Taj gets back to the hotel he is in a bad mood. He thought all nations that played cricket would derive the same lessons from the game that he has. 'A player should always respect his coach'; that, he believes, is one of the tenets of the game. Without that respect the team would fall apart. He thinks less of the Japanese team as a result of this but it makes him more confident about the coming match: a team that doesn't respect its coach can't be good on the pitch.

Perhaps it's the tension, but his bad mood develops into a general feeling that people in Jersey are looking down on the Afghans. He says people think he and his team have come from the jungle and that they are wild. Taj doesn't go as far as to say Jersey is racist – he knows what it's like to be looked down upon because he grew up as a refugee in Pakistan and was looked down upon by many non-Pashtu Pakistanis. Jersey is nowhere near as bad as that – but he does think it is isolated and not used to visitors such as the Afghans. Being an island it is naturally more of a closed society than most, but the perception they are looked down upon simply spurs him on. The team feels the same. More than ever they want to show they are good messengers for Afghanistan and they want to do this by winning the tournament. On the pitch the Afghans promise to fight, and although their attitude to cricket might raise eyebrows among the old guard, they feel that winning will show that Afghans haven't been beaten by war and that, for them, is the most important message.

The big day finally arrives. It is overcast and the air is full of moisture, which will make things tough for the batsmen. The alien conditions are compounded by the presence of grass on the wicket, which will make the ball zip through lower. Despite this, when Nowroz wins the toss, he elects to bat. He is sure if they can post anywhere near a decent total his bowlers will destroy the Japanese – particularly as the forecast suggests it will rain later. He also thinks now the wait is over it's best to get his batsmen out there, the conditions might be tough but the sooner they start playing the better. Besides that Japan is considered one of the weakest teams in the group so who better to start against?

Nowroz jogs out onto the pitch with Karim, his fellow opener. Karim strides out, looking confident, swinging his arms in windmills to loosen up and shuffling from side to side, but Karim always looks confident. Nowroz is trying to decipher what is going on in his head. He doesn't doubt that Karim has talent but he is concerned about his temperament. He can be cavalier and careless, often prone to a rush of blood to the head, and today Nowroz needs him to focus and score runs. He has scored well in Asian tournaments and although he is Taj's brother he opens the batting on merit, not bias.

At the crease the two look very different: Nowroz, straight backed and tall, looks regal and confident, but Karim, short and squat, looks ready for war. Nowroz is the officer, he thinks things through and plans ahead, but Karim, who plays with heart, will sweat blood to score runs and will get dirty in the trenches. He once continued to play when a ball struck his head and opened a cut. When he came off blood was gushing down his face, he had thought it was sweat. Karim is the fighter, he is pugnacious, arrogant, supremely gifted and often mercurial, but he is also driven.

Before the start of the innings Karim meets Nowroz in the middle of the pitch, bumps his fist, fixes him with an icy stare and utters one word. 'Shabash.' Come on. This reassures Nowroz, he's never seen Karim so determined.

When the Japanese start bowling, it's clear the Afghans were right to think they wouldn't be very strong – that seemed obvious during training the day before – but then they only had an Astroturf pitch to practice on, this is going to be very different. Despite their comparative lack of talent every ball is swinging like crazy.

Although Nowroz is finding it tough going at the crease, he wonders how the Japanese will feel facing one of Hamid's thunderbolts. He has a couple of spinners but he probably won't use them much today. The Japanese are shorter than his team and, he thinks, not used to pace – he'll try and terrify them with speed and movement. But for now Nowroz needs to put these thoughts out of his head and focus on his batting. He is the captain and has to lead from the front. Perhaps they have been a bit cocky coming into the game, but if he scores some runs then that will settle everyone.

Gradually Nowroz and Karim start to find their rhythm. Nowroz smashes 22 runs off 20 balls in under half-an-hour, including three fours and a six straight back over the bowler. Karim thumps ten fours in his innings, but only picks up another seven runs in singles and is out for 47 – not quite the century he was hoping for but not a bad start in a 50-over match. His knock comes in at just over an hour and in only 46 balls. However, Karim is not happy, not only did he not get a century but he had missed his half-century by three runs. The players often chastise Karim for taking crazy risks and although he can't seem to stop himself doing it, he is his harshest critic. When he is out he slumps down in a chair, replaying his shot selection over and over again.

Shortly afterwards Nowroz is clean bowled by Patrick Giles-Jones – a hulking great Australian who towers over his Japanese teammates. He curses as he slinks back to the pavilion. Despite his disappointment he knows it's not a bad start; Karim and Nowroz had posted 69 runs between them. The next three batsmen, Asghar, Nabi and Ahmad Shah, continue the steady run accumulation. With five wickets down they are on 141 runs, not a great total, but on this wicket and in their first game it'll do. Taj believes, at this point, that the team can easily get over 200 and that is very defendable. But suddenly the wickets start to tumble. Sami is out, clean bowled for a duck, and Raees follows shortly after, lbw for one. Gulbadeen, who had started the day by being given his first cap, comes in to bat at No. 8.

Taj had presented the cap on the pitch before the game. The players gathered in a semi-circle for the event. He had given a speech in which he reminded the players of the difficulties they had all come through to join the national team, the same hardships that Gulbadeen had encountered. He urged them to support and encourage him. Though tactically naive and over-emotional Taj is a skilled and eloquent orator. After Taj's speech, Gulbadeen walked towards Nowroz, took the hat, shook his hand and then kissed the badge.

Now, standing at the crease, Gulbadeen definitely looks like he belongs there. Everything the Japanese throw at him he manages to deal with – at once building on the total. He hits a massive six over long off and drives two fours through the covers. Gulbadeen stays rooted at one end while other players lose their wickets at the other. He bats sensibly, punishing bad balls and leaving the tricky ones. Unfortunately, when Hasti Gul is out for one and Dawlat for a duck, the innings is over. Against mediocre bowling, Afghanistan have posted a disappointing score of 179. Despite Gulbadeen's doggedness, the team's cavalier attitude means their innings has ended early. Taj is not overly impressed. While they were not far short of his intended target of 200, his main concern is that the team was all out with 14 overs still to play. Not batting out the overs is a sin in one-day cricket. If they had shown a bit more patience with the bat they could have faced a further 84 balls. This is their first ever global tournament and the players have been guilty of trying too hard to score big and impress everyone.

Lunch – which consists of salads, chicken, quiche, potato salad, coleslaw and bread – is served and prepared by a group of retired women. The women had gone to great lengths to make sure the Afghans would enjoy their food. They had difficulty finding halal food in Jersey, but, they stress, they had found it.

Taj and the players are initially sceptical of the food. He wonders aloud if there is donkey meat in the quiche. Luckily, he speaks in Pashtu so no one can understand him. In Afghanistan men will often say exactly what they think without considering the offence it might cause, like Sami's comment to the girl in Dubai Airport. It's not that they mean to be rude, ungrateful or arrogant, Afghans are just not used to the finer points of polite society. It is a male-dominated society full of machismo and men simply say what is on their minds.

Despite their concerns about what is in the food, the players pile up their plates and eat. It's a free meal and everything else in Jersey is extremely expensive. Unlike the Japanese, who sit on the chairs provided, the Afghans take off their shoes and sit on the floor cross-legged, some in the clubhouse, others out on the grass around the pitch. There aren't many spectators, maybe 20 or so, but with the umpires, scorers, catering women and the opposition, there are about 40 people in total and all eyes are focused on the Afghans. One or two of the players use the knives and forks provided but most eat with their hands. The women find it strange that they don't use the chairs or cutlery. But at least, they joke, they won't have so much to wash up.

After lunch the players head to the changing room; they wash and then pray and then they are ready to play cricket again. Dawlat, a heavy-set and ungainly fast bowler, who swings the ball with some ease, opens the bowling for Afghanistan. Dawlat is a romantic and has not yet found a wife; he dreams of finding true love. The team call him 'the Doctor' as he worked as a nurse in a hospital and is the most educated member of the team.

He doesn't have to wait long for a wicket. Three balls into his first over, one of the Japanese openers edges the ball and is caught behind by Karim. The second wicket comes with 15 runs on the board. The Afghans are bowling fast and the Japanese can't cope with the pace and swing. Hasti Gul, who'd got out for one run, takes three wickets and Karim four catches. The Japanese are all out for 87 but manage to stay in until the 40th over, longer than the Afghans. Their top-scoring batsman only gets 19, which is less than the 29 extras (including 19 wides) the Afghans give away. This is another cardinal sin in one-day cricket. When Afghanistan bowl accurately they are almost unplayable, but in one-day cricket it is imperative to give away as little as possible, make the batsmen play every ball and keep the fielding tight. Afghanistan have a lot to learn – not just about playing internationals but also about disciplined performances with bat and ball. As he predicted, the Man of the Match award goes to Karim for his quick-fire innings and four catches.

Celebrations are muted but the players are pleased with the win. After the game, Nowroz, the captain, takes Gulbadeen, the rookie, outside for a talk. He asks him how he's feeling and Gulbadeen replies that he feels proud, happy and honoured to be playing for his country. It was, he said, the sweetest moment of his life. Gulbadeen normally smiles but after the match his smile is wider than usual. You only get one debut, he says.

The win is satisfying given the circumstances. The conditions were difficult and took some getting used to, and the players feel they have done well. The Japanese had toured England prior to the tournament and had got used to the conditions, the Afghans had not had a chance to acclimatise. Taj is just happy to have a win under his belt; he'd promised the nation so much and now he has to deliver. He is aware that the games will get harder and he can't afford his team to slip up. He brushes his fears aside though, the team has won and will keep winning. Taj has worked out that if the team is to get to the World Cup it will have to win 30 games. One down, 29 to go!

Chapter 6

Praying for Rain

JERSEY, MAY 2008 – PART 2

The press in Afghanistan report extensively on the victory over Japan. Pajhwok News Agency reported it as a 'thrashing'. It was good to finally have some positive news. In the week before the game, there were distractions from home as violence had once again flared. Two suicide bombs had exploded, three NATO troops had been killed and scores of Afghans had been murdered in violent clashes. Even if this was not an extreme week by Afghanistan standards – suicide bombs and high death rates are becoming all too familiar – it is an unwelcome reminder for the players of real life at home.

In 2004 around 500 civilians were estimated to have died as a direct result of fighting. By 2006 Human Rights Watch, a well-respected New York-based non-governmental organisation (NGO), estimated that the figure was over 900 and by 2007 it stood over 1,600. In 2008 it was set to rise further. Naturally each incident raised worries that a family member or friend may have been caught up in the violence. Not many of their opponents have to deal with this kind of news on a daily basis. When the players talked to their friends and families back in Afghanistan and Pakistan they hoped the good news from the cricket field would lift spirits. Victories, like those against Japan and now hopefully the Bahamas, do have a positive effect, however limited. It is another motivation factor for the team.

There is no time for the players to rest as the game against the Bahamas takes place the following day. Perhaps surprisingly given its location, the Bahamas is not an established cricketing nation. They only registered with the ICC in 1987 and had to wait until 2002 to play in their first tournament, the ICC Americas Cup, in which they finished fifth out of six teams. In 2006 they played in the tournament again, this time finishing last.

Taj's assessment of them as sounding like a village team is borne out in the game itself, in which, despite or perhaps fired up by the reports of ongoing violence at home, Afghanistan are again the victors. They bowl the Bahamas out for only 46 runs in under half their overs. Once again, the star of the show is the rookie Gulbadeen. His bowling is perfect, the line and length superb, and he takes the last five wickets in just over 20 minutes. With his last three balls he takes a hat-trick. No matter what the standard of cricket, this is an impressive achievement. He celebrates the final wicket by wheeling away, arms spread wide like an eagle and running around the pitch like a footballer who has just scored the winning goal. The celebration, accompanied by a high-pitched scream and cheering teammates, is by cricket standards over the top and inappropriate and some eyebrows are raised in the small crowd and among the officials.

They might have been more forgiving if they had known the youngster's life story. His father disappeared when he was a boy. His mother was sick with hepatitis, his younger sister had a club foot and, as the eldest son, he was left in charge of providing for his family. The family soon lost their home and had to move into a room in an uncle's house. The family continue to live on handouts and the generosity of relatives.

Afghanistan chase down the score in six overs but in their excitement manage to lose five wickets. Karim goes for 11, Nabi for seven and Raees for two. Once again their almost suicidally aggressive batting comes close to undoing their good work with the ball.

Gulbadeen wins Man of the Match and draws glowing praise from one of the umpires. One says he has never seen such good bowling from someone so young. Gulbadeen beams with pride and celebrates by flexing his pecs.

Afghanistan face Botswana next – a team with as short a cricket history as their own. Whereas the Afghanistan team was started by refugees who learnt the game in Pakistan, Botswana's team is made up of south Asian and South African expats living in the country. They joined the ICC in 2001, the same year as the Afghans. In their first tournament, the Africa Cup in 2002, Botswana beat Namibia, Tanzania, Zambia, Zimbabwe and Kenya to reach the final, where they lost against South Africa. Botswana's achievement is remarkable for an emerging nation and they have a record that should dampen the Afghans' overbearing self-confidence.

Nowroz wins the toss and puts Botswana in to bat – a tactical change but, given the strength of the bowling, a good one. The Afghans must be more disciplined in their batting and knowing how many runs they have to make to win must concentrate their minds.

The decision is justified when they bowl Botswana out for 128 in the 35th over. Pace bowler Hamid Hassan, starts to show his true ability. He takes three for 19 in seven overs. Even more impressively, Mohammad Nabi takes four for 20 in less than six overs.

Despite having the upper hand, the Afghans get a fright at the start of their innings when Nowroz is out on his second ball for one. Unlike in previous games though, this does not trigger a collapse. Karim and Noor Ali, an elegant batsman and the only one on the team who hadn't learnt his cricket in Pakistan, ensure it is an easy win. Karim top scores with 62, playing a calmer innings than his big-hitting rampage against Japan. He only scores six fours and no sixes before he's caught out. Noor Ali smashes an unbeaten 48 off 40 balls. Nabi falls for five and it is left to Asghar Stanikzai to come in and score the three runs needed to ensure victory. Afghanistan reach 129 for three in 19.5 overs. Karim is once again named Man of the Match. It's an extremely impressive win against a strong team.

While Afghanistan are sweeping aside Botswana, rain has disrupted the other games in the group. Jersey's match against the Bahamas is shortened to 32 overs and Japan's match against Singapore is cancelled. With Jersey beating the Bahamas, Afghanistan and the Channel Islanders are now in pole position. If Afghanistan beat Singapore in their next match they will qualify for the semi-finals.

Singapore, a former British colony, has a long history of cricket. The first recorded game in the country was in 1837 and the nation joined the ICC in 1974 – they've already appeared in the ICC Trophy six times. Although they have never qualified for the World Cup, the structure of the game in Singapore is well organised and their players are of proven quality.

Despite their pedigree, Singapore lost heavily against the hosts Jersey in the first game of the tournament and, in their second game, had scored an unconvincing victory over Botswana, chasing down the total of 183 in 48 overs but never really dominating the match. Their third game against Japan was abandoned due to rain, so they come into the match against Afghanistan with one victory and one loss, but with a match in hand. If Singapore want to progress they will have to win against Afghanistan – fast becoming known as the cocky upstarts of the competition.

Taj does not seem overly concerned by Singapore; he has seen them play before and belittles their potential. As with a lot of sides that Afghanistan encounter, they feel it is naturalised rather than locally produced players that are the ones to watch. Chaminda Ruwan Kumarage, the captain, is the only threat according to Taj. He was born in Sri Lanka and played grade A cricket there, but he qualifies for Singapore as he has lived in the republic for over four years.

Afghanistan win the toss and put Singapore in to bat. Rain limits the match to 30 overs – the grass is green and heavy and the outfield is very slow. On a very sticky wicket, Singapore battle their way to 145. Ruwan top scores with 32 off 45 balls. It proves to be a good score, considering the conditions and the reduced number of overs.

As they go into bat though, Afghanistan's confidence is high and they start well. Taj instructs them, despite the reduced overs, to play patiently. Needless to say, opener Karim bats in the only way he knows how, swinging for the fences, hitting hard and big. He scores 22 runs, including five fours, off the first 21 balls. Taj yells at him from the boundary to stop being so reckless. Nowroz heeds his coach's advice and is more patient, facing 29 balls for only five runs. The wicket is awkward; the balls are again staying low and swinging. To start with Nowroz and Karim seem to be reading the conditions well, but after 40 minutes optimism diminishes. Nowroz is clean bowled and Karim caught. Noor Ali and Asghar, who follow them to the crease, are both out for ducks and suddenly Afghanistan are 27 for four. Their chances of getting to the semi-finals are rapidly disappearing.

It is incredible in cricket how quickly the momentum and mood of a match can change. With Karim and Nowroz at the crease Taj laughed and joked with his players. Victory, he thought, was a mere formality. Now the team is four wickets down a dark depression has descended over him.

He paces the sidelines, smoking one cigarette after another. He doesn't seem to know what to say to the players so gets them to rearrange the chairs they sit on as they wait to bat. He looks lost. The team needs him to be calm and to reassure them but as the wickets fall he becomes visibly more anxious. Taj is paralyzed by the fear they might lose. In a panic he gives those going into bat conflicting advice.

Nabi comes in at six and plays himself in, sparking thoughts of a mini-revival. But when he is caught in the deep for 24 all hopes of victory are dashed. The fall of his wicket triggers a total collapse: Hasti Gul and Dawlat are out for ducks, and Ahmad Shah and Raees Ahmadzai do little better, scoring three apiece.

Christopher Janik is the architect of Afghanistan's downfall. A slight right-arm, medium pacer, he picks up astonishing figures of five wickets for nine runs, bowling a good line and length. Afghanistan's final six wickets fall for only ten runs. The team are all out for 76. A disastrous display.

Although Hasti Gul is bitterly disappointed with his performance, he shrugs and says it's cricket and sometimes in cricket you lose. He knows though that Afghanistan should have done better. But in the changing room tempers flare. Karim accuses Taj of stopping him playing his natural game. He says Taj took away his freedom to play the shots he wanted by asking them to be patient.

Although Taj was right – the team did need to play with more patience – they were unused to such restraint and it confused them. They tried to play in a way that was foreign to them and they came unstuck.

Noor Ali, who was given out lbw, complains to Nowroz that the umpire had got it wrong and that he shouldn't have been given out. Nowroz snaps back at him. It's the first occasion anyone has seen the captain lose his temper during the tournament. Nowroz doesn't even look at Noor Ali as he speaks. He buries his head in his hands and tells him not to bullshit him. It was lbw – now is not the time for excuses – they must plan for their next game. For the first time Nowroz is showing the strain of captaining this bunch of mavericks.

Taj, plagued by doubts and insecurities, wonders if he has let his team down. In the changing room he tries to gee them up. He tells them they are not out, that they shouldn't feel the pressure and that they can still make it through to the semi-finals. Despite his positive words his body language tells a different story. During the match he had huffed and puffed, scratching his head and looking completely out of ideas. Now he seems close to tears. This first defeat in the competition has shaken him and he lashes out at anything he can find to blame – the damp, cold Jersey weather, the wet, sticky wickets and the slow outfields have all conspired against his team.

Afghanistan only have one game left – against the hosts Jersey, who are unbeaten, and Singapore have the Bahamas and Japan to play. Two victories by Singapore, which seem assured considering their performance against Afghanistan, would mean Afghanistan have to beat Jersey to go through. Even if Afghanistan beat Jersey it is not certain they will qualify. Afghanistan and Singapore would then be equal on points and qualification would be decided by superior run-rate.

For the first time on the tour the players begin to question Taj's leadership and tactics. In public though, at least for the moment, they are still defending him. Paul Carroll, the MCC member who brought Hamid over to play in England, has flown to Jersey to watch him play. During the game he is disappointed by some of Taj's decisions and thinks the team needs someone with more experience at the helm. They need someone who has played first-class cricket and knows when to go for it and when to stay calm and defend. They need someone who can plan an innings and get the players to carry out his plans. After the match he outlines his thoughts to Hamid, but Hamid refuses to hear anything against his coach. Taj discovered him and brought him through the youth ranks. In his heart Hamid knows Paul is right but he can't, at least not yet, bring himself to voice his concerns. The Afghan team needs to stick together. They need to get behind Taj and make sure they win their next match.

After the game, Taj calls his mother. Unlike his father, she has always supported his cricket playing. He is surprised to find her sounding upbeat and even more surprised when she congratulates him on his victory. He starts to correct her then realises what has happened: his sisters and brothers have lied to their mother about the result. Whenever the team loses she becomes stressed and emotional, and in her old age they are worried a defeat might give her a heart attack. Taj twigs and plays along with the charade. It is hard, as he wants to ask her advice. When he is down and in need of support she always has wise words to offer but today he needs to be there for her. He pretends they won.

After the Singapore game, Taj complains that the British weather is the enemy of Afghanistan, and that had it been sunny and had the pitch been hard they would have won easily. But later that evening it becomes apparent that rain now could be their saviour, in the sort of complicated fashion that only cricket can come up with. If it rains and the next day's matches are cancelled, then the points would be shared and Singapore would be denied the chance of overhauling Afghanistan in the table. The Afghan players go to sleep that night praying for rain – it's their best chance of getting through to the semi-finals.

As if in answer to their prayers, Friday starts with rain, torrential rain. In the morning it seems likely that there will be no play that day and Afghanistan will avoid their match against Jersey. However, something strange happens. The ICC holds a technical meeting to confirm proceedings following the downpour and word comes out that Afghanistan have given permission for Singapore to play a reduced overs match against Japan in the afternoon. On top of that they have 'agreed' that all teams will then play the final fixtures the following day (which had been scheduled as a rest day). The final matches would then be Afghanistan versus Jersey and Singapore versus Bahamas. This provokes fury in the team. With only two points between the teams, presuming Singapore beat Japan, it means that if Afghanistan loses to Jersey they will almost certainly go out. And even if they win, Singapore have been given an easy chance to get the necessary run-rate to progress instead of them. Who, demand the team, could have agreed to this?

Taj is flabbergasted and enraged. He smells a conspiracy. Nobody, he says, wants Afghanistan to win. The whole of the ICC are against them. Bashir, who despite taking on the role of tour manager, is in effect only given the title of assistant, is incandescent. He wonders why nobody asked him about this?

The truth is that the ICC has been given the name and contact details of tour manager Rais Jaji, a friend of Massoud's and the man who fought with Hasti during Afghanistan's first tournament in Malaysia. He has done little on the tour so far, he is lazy, uninterested and appears to regard the tour as something of a jolly. However, for some reason, most likely that he is on the ICC list as the official manager, he was invited to the technical meeting. When the motion was rather hopefully put forward that Singapore be allowed to play all their remaining fixtures, all present agreed, including Rais Jaji. By agreeing to this the manager has almost certainly put his own team out of the competition. While Rais has many faults, he isn't stupid, he just doesn't speak English. He didn't understand the question or its implications. Now it looks likely that Afghanistan will go out of the tournament on a misunderstanding.

Bashir frantically runs around the lobby of the hotel, sweating profusely and looking even more troubled than usual. He asks anyone and everyone who looks official how this decision can be changed. By this stage his suit is crumpled, every five minutes he takes a break from negotiating and heads outside for a cigarette, he looks exhausted. He simply can't believe Afghanistan are going out for something as stupid as a technicality. Rais Jaji has annoyed Bashir from the start; he receives all the benefits and the prestige of being tour manager, yet Bashir has to do all the work. It was Bashir, not Rais, who had spent hours getting visas, arranging sponsorship, setting up the training camps, liaising with the ICC, ordering the kit, trying to find the players money for food and booking flights and now, because of Rais, they're going home early. Going home, unless Bashir can come up with a miracle.

Finally Bashir is rewarded for his persistence. When he eventually finds the technical director he is told that if he writes a letter saying there has been a misunderstanding and that Afghanistan would like to go back to the original tournament format then that could be done. Bashir is beside himself with joy. He writes the letter outlining the mistake and asking the ICC to stick to the tournament rules. Singapore, he says, should replay the match with Japan the day before the semi-finals and today's, Friday's matches should, as was decided that morning, be cancelled due to the weather. As quickly as it had started the crisis is over, once the ICC receives the letter it is a mere formality to return to the original plan. Barring a miracle and a momentous victory by Singapore, Afghanistan would now take their place in the semi-finals.

Fate has smiled upon them. Singapore do beat Japan, but only by 52 runs. Although Singapore score 201 and Japan only 67, the Japanese innings had been interrupted by rain and they only batted for 27 overs. The Duckworth-Lewis calculation reduces Singapore's total to 118 off 27 overs. Not enough to overturn the run deficit. Afghanistan are now through to the semi-finals.

Luck had played its part. The weather, the cancellation of their match against the strongest team and an accommodating ICC committee have all helped them get through. However, if they are to make it to the World Cup they will need to improve drastically because they probably won't get so lucky again.

The Afghans draw some criticism for their tactics. Other teams, journalists and even tournament officials feel they have cheated their way to the semi-finals. They think, in the spirit of fair play, that Afghanistan should have stuck with what was agreed at the technical meeting. But Taj gives the argument short shrift. His team wanted to win and they did all they possibly could, within the rules, to ensure that. It's hard to imagine England, South Africa or Australia sticking to a decision that would almost certainly eliminate them from a competition.

This does not help Afghanistan's reputation or their

image. Afghanistan have not proved to be a popular team, one journalist derides their batting style as kamikaze and other aspects of their game come under the spotlight. The way they appeal at every conceivable opportunity is seen as unsporting, but Taj insists this is his team's right. The umpire is the expert, he says, and it must be left up to him to make decisions. Afghanistan are new to international cricket and although their appealing is over the top and does need to be toned down, they are finding their feet at this level. They are excited to be playing, excited to be representing their country and that spills over onto the pitch. In an age where professional sportsmen seem to not care if they win or lose as long as they are paid handsomely for their endeavours, the Afghan approach is refreshing.

There is also a feeling among the other teams at the tournament that Afghanistan are too big for their boots. Taj's bombastic approach to media management doesn't help their cause. He says, through the media, that other teams are scared of his team, that they are weak and that his team will score hundreds of runs in each innings they play.

The Afghans' chatter on the pitch also fails to endear them to many of the other teams. In between overs the players make constant reference to the 2011 World Cup. This is where they want to be and they hype each other up by reminding each other of it very loudly. To most teams in Division Five, three tournament wins away from a World Cup appearance, the thought of making it to the finals seems ridiculous. It would be like a non-league football team shouting 'Premier League here we come' after every goal they score. To the Afghans there is nothing ridiculous about their convictions. They know where they want to be and it isn't in Division Five. They have hope, a plan and a ridiculous amount of self-belief. They are sure they will make it to the World Cup.

Another complaint is that as the team learnt the game in Pakistan, and some of the players were born there, that they aren't really Afghan. People think they are Pakistani. This is a ridiculous accusation expressed by some opposing players, journalists, supporters watching the games and other coaches. Taj is incredulous that after all the troubles Afghanistan have been through that people would bring this up as proof that they aren't really Afghan. The refugee camps are pitiful places with no facilities; few had running water or electricity. It is impossible to think of any advantage in living there. Yes, it was where they had come into contact with cricket for the first time but they played on rutted dirt tracks, used bricks as wickets and often made their own bats out of wood and their own balls out of plastic bags and rubber bands.

What makes the accusations all the more galling is that the majority of star players in the other teams really have been drafted in from other countries. Japan have some Australians, Norway are made up almost exclusively of Pakistani immigrants, Germany have a Brit, a South African and some south Asians and the Americans don't have a single US-born player in the team but draw heavily from the Caribbean. Even Jersey's star player, the captain, is a foreigner, an Australian by the name of Matt Hague.

The Afghan players are all Afghans and the only other team in the competition that can claim to be wholly represented by people from their country is Nepal.

Cricket has some bizarre rules. And one of the most odd is that to play for a country you only needed to have lived in the country for 183 days of the four previous years, and a number of nations take advantage of this loophole. While many of the Afghanistan team had grown up exclusively in Pakistan there is a very good reason for this, their country has been a battlefield for the past 30 years. They all have Afghan parents, Afghan heritage and, if it wasn't for war, would have grown up in Afghanistan.

On their day off after making it to the semi-finals Sherzada Massoud, Taj, Karim, Gulbadeen and Nowroz head to the beach as a diversion. Massoud, who normally dresses in smart Afghan clothes, is wearing a pair of tracksuit bottoms and an Inter Milan football shirt. He is clearly unimpressed by the beach, the sea and the surroundings and says that in Afghanistan they have rivers with better views than this beach.

However, not everything in Jersey disappoints Massoud. He is quite taken with the traffic lights. He tells the team that when the man turns green they can walk but until that point they have to remain on the curb, even if no car is coming. This, he tells them, is called 'rules and regulations'.

On the beach Nowroz and Karim see a brown animal and can't figure out whether it is a bear or not. It turns out to be an obese Labrador and they laugh as the dog strains on his leash almost pulling its owner over. They ask what the dog's name is, Chip is the reply. As the owner heads out of earshot, Nowroz howls with laughter. In Afghanistan people don't keep dogs as pets, the only dogs you see are either pathetically skinny and mangy strays or massive fighting dogs. Dogs are generally seen as dirty and no one would let them in their house, let alone stroke them for pleasure. Afghan fighting dogs, which have their ears cut off so they don't get ripped off in a fight, have names such as Rambo, Tiger, War or Bee. Nowroz can't believe someone would give a dog such an ugly name. Even a simple walk on the beach reminds the team how far away from home they are. Everything here is so different. People keeping dogs as pets – how ridiculous!

Afghanistan's journey to the semi-finals has made big news back home and the BBC send Emal Pasarly, a seasoned Afghan journalist from the Pashtu section of the World Service, to cover events. Emal has covered cricket since 1997 but commentating on Afghanistan playing in a World Cup qualifier will be the highlight of his career. In Pakistan, cricket vocabulary is infused with English turns of phrase mixed with Urdu, even the Pashtu speakers use English words such as 'wicket' and 'six'. Now Emal is set to broadcast cricket in Afghanistan he faces quite enormous challenges: there is no history of cricket in the country and many of the audience have no idea about any of the fundamentals of the game – let alone understanding what a six or a wicket is. They don't even know what a cricket pitch looks like. As a result

Emal feels he has to devise a whole new Pashtu vocabulary to describe the game.

He grew up as a refugee in Peshawar and had learnt English by watching cricket. He used to watch games on TV and listen to the radio and repeat what he heard, even though, at first, he didn't understand what he was saying. He would say 'howzat' all the time and for all situations, without knowing what it meant. Over time though, his English improved and in 1992 he decided to go to university in England. Emal was always clever and was lucky enough to get one of the scholarships offered to Afghan refugees by international aid agencies. He chose Canterbury as his destination. Not because of the courses on offer or the reputation of the University of Kent but because the city was the home of Kent County Cricket Club. Emal spent his days in the British Council offices in Peshawar reading week-old newspapers and had fallen in love with the county and the club. When he arrived in England he would travel to the ground every day just to look at it. In his first year he never got to see a game, he arrived during the off-season and then his work took over.

In order to devise his new cricket vocabulary Emal decides to use words from the Pashtu dictionary and modify them. He relies heavily on an Afghan game called toop danda (which literally translates as 'bat and ball' and is similar to baseball). The bowler becomes the 'toop achonky' or ball dropper/thrower. The batsman is called the 'manda joronky', or run maker, and the wicketkeeper is simply called 'satonkey', the same word used for a football goalkeeper.

Fours he has christened 'salor' and sixes 'splag'. Over time and with audience participation these become 'salo-reza' and 'splageza' – the '-eza', listeners feel, making the words sound more exciting. Emal's enthusiasm for the game and the fact that the Afghan cricket team is playing its most important game ever prompted him to ask his bosses at the BBC World Service to allow live commentary on the match. Despite their initial scepticism, Emal is persuasive and they finally agreed. He envisages an audience for cricket in Afghanistan that simply would not have existed without this match. It's a major national event. He sets up an Internet message board and as the countdown to the match gets underway he starts to receive hundreds, if not thousands of e-mails, about the team. This is the most important match in Afghanistan's history and this is the first time he has ever commented on a live Afghanistan game. His excitement matches that of the team and the growing number of fans back home. He starts to get reports of thousands of people gathering in the Internet cafes in Kabul. If Afghanistan win the next game, they are through to the final and the next round of World Cup qualification.

Chapter 7

Hero of Afghanistan

JERSEY, MAY 2008 – PART 3

The build-up to the semi-final against Nepal is tense. Both teams are desperate to win. Victory is essential to keep the World Cup dream alive, as the two losing semi-finalists will remain in Division Five. Added to this, the two have history. Afghanistan beat Nepal in the third-place play-off match in the 2006 ACC Trophy and Nepal are out for revenge.

Cricket was first played in Nepal in the 1920s. In the 1940s a federation was formed to promote the game among an aristocracy who had learnt to play it while being schooled in England and India. After Nepal joined the ICC in 1988 the game started spreading and gained a following among all social classes. They are taking the tournament seriously. For Jersey they have appointed a top quality coach in Roy Dias, a Sri Lankan, and the first of his countrymen to hit a thousand Test runs. He has a lot more experience than Taj, both as a player and as a coach, but even he is feeling the pressure.

On the bus to the game the players are quiet and nervous. They know Nepal are a good team with some exceptionally talented players. In particular they are worried about the main strike bowler, Meheboob Alam. In an early match against Mozambique he had taken a ten-wicket haul to win the match single-handed.

Things get better once they arrive at the ground. For once the rain has stopped and the day is clear. The wicket is drier than it has been and occasionally the sun even breaks out of the clouds, warming the sparse crowd that has gathered to see this vital qualifier. Massoud has dressed up for the occasion. Gone is the Inter Milan football shirt, he's wearing a smart, neatly pressed, beige shalwar kameez underneath a suit jacket. He looks regal and distinguished.

Afghanistan win the toss and elect to bat. They feel, with the unpredictability of the Jersey climate, that it might rain later, and they much prefer to bat on a dry wicket. Despite the wicket being dry the outfield is very heavy, as it has been all tournament. This will make runs harder to come by so the Afghans expect a low-scoring contest.

They start safely and in the first 40 minutes they make slow but steady progress. Karim posts 18 and, backed up by Ahmad Shah, Afghanistan reach 26 for no wicket. When Karim is bowled though, the batting starts to wobble. Noor Ali, who comes in next, is out for a golden duck and Ahmad Shah heads back to the pavilion shortly afterwards as Afghanistan slump from 26 for one to 29 for three. Nowroz, who comes in at No. 4, gets an edge and is caught in the slips for seven. Thankfully the rest of the middle-order avert disaster: the next four batsman, Asghar, Nabi, Raees and Sami, steady the ship, adding 99 runs between them. Nabi top scores with 48. Finally, Afghanistan's tail collapses and they go from 119 for five, to 142 all out.

Taj is worried that they don't have enough runs on the board, but Nepal's batting line-up proves even more fragile. The bowlers tear through the innings – benefitting from the drier conditions by really making the ball zip through. Dawlat leads the haul with three for 18, ably supported by Hamid with two for 12, Hasti two for 13 and Nabi two for 15. Nepal are all out for 105. Afghanistan have bowled themselves into the final by a margin of 37 runs.

After the final wicket falls, Taj oscillates between tears, smiles and hysterical laughter – back-slapping his colleagues and anyone else who comes near him. More than anything he is visibly relieved and declares it to be the proudest moment of his life.

Afghanistan have qualified for Division Four. By getting through to the final they have cleared the first obstacle on the way to the World Cup. But Taj knows that after all the claims and boasts he has made, they also need to win the final against Jersey.

The day of the final is fine and sunny and a crowd of around a thousand, the largest of the tournament, turns out – largely because the host nation has made it through. Jersey come into the match unbeaten. Peter Kirsten, their tough, no-nonsense coach who played for South Africa, has instilled a level of professionalism in them that few, if any, of the other teams at this level can match. And no one would claim that Afghanistan are even close to that standard. This professionalism, coupled with strong team spirit, some experienced players and home advantage compensate for the fact that they are not the most naturally talented team. They are extremely tough opponents.

Jersey's Australian captain, Matthew Hague, played grade cricket in Melbourne and Ryan Driver, their towering medium-pace bowler, played county cricket for Worcestershire and Lancashire. The Jersey players are all employed in jobs that the Afghan players can only dream of – as financial advisors and civil servants as well as accountants and teachers. For them cricket is a part-time passion – for Taj and his team it is the focus of their lives.

Before the game, undoubtedly the biggest in the nation's history, Nowroz gathers all the players on the grass around him and delivers a rousing captain's speech. He tells them that the most important thing to remember is discipline. Even if they lose they must do so in a dignified way, so that they will be remembered as a credit to the country they love. The one thing he really emphasises, he thinks successfully, is not to get angry and lose control. Nowroz reminds the players of their days playing in the dusty refugee camps of Pakistan and how far they have come. He finishes by asking them to visualise the joy of holding the trophy in their arms as they touch down in Kabul Airport.

The speech seems to work – when they go onto field they play the game of their lives. The match starts like a dream for Afghanistan. With a mesmerising display of fielding and bowling, they skittle Jersey out for 80 runs in 39 overs. Jersey are powerless to resist the pace and ferocity of the bowling attack. Hamid is the pick of the bowlers with four wickets. He destroys Jersey's middle order giving up just 27 runs in 9.5 overs. Hasti also returns impressive figures, taking three for 17 in ten overs. Afghanistan's bowlers have again swung the tie in their favour.

When Karim and Ahmad Shah open the batting, scoring ten runs off the first over, victory looks all but assured. They only need 70 runs from 49 overs and with all their wickets in hand they don't need to rush. But predictably Karim has other ideas. He wants to score runs and he also wants to get Man of the Match and win the final for Afghanistan. To do that he has to be on strike.

In the second over Ahmad Shah hits a shot, goes to run and then checks himself, realising he doesn't have enough time to make it. Karim though doesn't seem to care and keeps running towards the striker's end. He hurtles down the crease screaming at Ahmad Shah to swap places. Ahmad Shah remains rooted to the spot, he knows to run is suicide. The throw comes in from the fielder and the bowler breaks the wickets.

For a moment there is total silence across the field. The crowd and the players are transfixed and Taj stands mouth open, completely still and aghast. This is the calm before the storm. When the umpire raises his finger to send Karim back to the pavilion, the insults begin to fly.

Karim curses Ahmad Shah and screams at Taj, asking him why he put him to bat with a bisexual? As he reaches the boundary he flings his bat through the air and it clatters to the ground. The crowd takes a collective gasp as Karim stomps through to the changing room, ripping off his pads and gloves and throwing them about as he does so.

The looks on the faces of the spectators say it all: this just isn't cricket. The only saving grace is that most of them don't understand Karim's foul-mouthed Pashtu tirade. They are shocked enough that he threw his bat away as he stormed off the pitch. His colourful language would have sent them over the edge.

Taj is particularly upset: not only does the run-out put the match in jeopardy, but he is also upset for his favourite brother. Taj thinks that Ahmad Shah should have taken the fall for Karim. His fury at the not-out batsman leads him to pronounce that if Afghanistan lose, Ahmad Shah will never play for the team again.

On his day Karim is very good. In Peshawar he would routinely hit hundreds with knocks of style and panache. He is the least fearless and most uninhibited of the Afghan players at the crease. He loves to pull the ball – stepping easily into wayward or loose deliveries. However, he hasn't really found his best form in Jersey yet – scoring 47, 11, 62, 22 and 18 in the previous games and he had hoped to make a mark in the final. Now he is out for three and the team is wobbling in a game that should be a formality.

Karim's outburst has a negative effect on the other players. Nowroz has been trying to get the team to play with patience, to relax and not to panic. But all that has changed now. It seems Karim had failed to remember his captain's advice and the rest of the team are sent reeling by his astonishing outburst. From being ten runs for no wicket in the first over they rapidly collapse to 42 for 7. It is another disaster in the making. The situation is not helped as Karim loudly announces to whoever will listen that if he was still in, they would have won by now.

When Ahmad Shah is out he is greeted by silence in the pavilion and he sits away from his teammates, ignored for the rest of the innings. Emal Pasarly, the Pashtu BBC correspondent, is not surprised at the unfolding disaster. He says that this behaviour is typical of Afghanistan, because they are hot-headed and impatient. They had been cruising and now they have thrown it all away, with Karim's outburst serving as the catalyst. This, Emal felt, is all too common. In Kabul, he says, the interest in the match is intense. Although there is no TV coverage at home, Emal is relaying a ball-by-ball commentary and thousands have again crowded into the capital's Internet cafes to keep up with the score. Rumour has it the BBC website has already received over a million hits during the match.

Less than an hour ago these Internet cafes had been full of happy, excited fans – potential converts to the cause of cricket in Afghanistan. Now the atmosphere has changed – people are edgy or disappointed. This isn't what they expected from cricket.

On the boundary Mohammad Nabi moans that it isn't Jersey who's getting them out, they are getting themselves out. Karim continues his unhelpful comments but now Nowroz gives him short shrift and tells him to shut up. Inside the dressing room there is bewilderment and unbearable tension. Sherzada Massoud lies on a bench: he can't face watching the match and is shell-shocked by the turn of events. He hasn't moved for the last hour, as the Afghanistan players, their wickets falling, stumble in and out of the room.

Back outside, Taj is a nervous wreck. He strides back and forth bizarrely kitted out in a puffa jacket and tartan cap, which he has somehow acquired during the tournament, chain smoking and visibly shaking with anger as he sees his dreams being crushed by the unpredictability of sport. Sometimes he hates the game. Although his team are through to the next stage of the qualifying competition Taj is very competitive and can't bear the thought of losing the final. He had also promised his mother that he would bring the winners' trophy back, so they just have to win.

Coaches normally go out of their way to manage their supporters' expectations. They talk of never underestimating the opposition, of the difficulties in the unusual playing conditions, of the possibility of injuries, anything to avoid looking complacent or looking like a fool if the team loses. This kind of behaviour just isn't Taj's style – in his dealings with the media he lets the dramatic side of his personality do the talking – it's high theatre with big claims and emotional language. Before he left for Jersey he said he would throw himself in the Atlantic if they didn't win the tournament, he talked of scoring 400 runs against Japan and also bragged that his team was capable of beating England.

He is now reaping what he has sowed. The pressure that he has heaped on his own shoulders and those of his team is beginning to tell. He has told the world how brilliant his team is and now, if they fail to win, he will look like a fool. In the eyes of the Afghan public, defeat for such a brilliant team could only possibly come about because of poor coaching decisions. Their defeat would be seen as his failure.

With seven wickets down, Hasti Gul, the elder of Taj's two brothers, is in next. Although he classes himself as an all-rounder he is not really a batsman. Hasti's scores in the tournament so far have been one, a duck and one. He had come into the game in bad form but his bowling against Jersey was impressive – ten overs, 3 wickets for 17 runs. He decides not to wear a protective helmet but strides on to the pitch in an Afghan baseball cap – allowing the fielders to see the intense look of determination on his face as he takes his guard from the umpire.

Asghar, Afghanistan's last specialist batsman, is at the other end. But not for long. He is soon out, lbw for ten. His innings has taken 65 balls and lasted an hour and a half. He has batted exactly as Taj wanted but has not managed to see the game out for Afghanistan. As he trudges off the pitch he removes his helmet, and the Afghan flag he uses as a bandana is drenched in sweat. Asghar's despair is compounded by the knowledge that he is the last recognised batsman and now the tail is exposed to the Jersey bowlers. The situation now looks very bleak as Afghanistan find themselves eight men down for 62 runs – still needing 19 runs to win. Only Dawlat and Hamid are left to bat.

The decision is made to send in Dawlat, the fast bowler, to join Hasti Gul. With the bat he looks awkward and clumsy, he is tall – a few inches over six feet – and he looks like an adult playing with a child's bat. At the crease he hunches over it and shuffles uncomfortably. Hasti Gul knows that if the Afghans are going to win he will have to score the runs.

On the pitch Hasti looks and acts like a man possessed. His determination and focus transform him into a proper batsman: he judges every ball perfectly and nudges Afghanistan closer and closer to the total. As his confidence grows he unleashes two massive sixes: one over long on and one over deep square leg. When he clips another ball to fine leg, pushing the score to 80 the players flood the pitch thinking they've won. But as the umpires and match referees fight to impose order it dawns on them that they have to score one more run to win. Four balls later the run comes. Hasti has scored a patient unbeaten 29 off 40 balls. His highest score, by some way, and the

Taj Malik Alam in Afghanistan, 2003. (TAJ MALIK ALAM)

Karim, Taj's brother and opening batsman. (LESLIE KNOTT)

The Afghan team before their first tour to England in 2006.
(TAJ MALIK ALAM)

Noor Ali with his idol
Ricky Ponting in South
Africa. (NOOR ALI)

Rahmat Wali, the Afghan
national team player killed
by American forces in Khost
province. (AHMAD WALI)

The Afghan cricket team training before their first World Cup qualifier in Jersey. (LESLIE KNOTT)

The Afghan cricket team. *Back row, left to right*: Hamid Hassan, Raees Ahmadzai, Nowroz Mangal, Taj Malik Alam, Ahmad Shah, Samiullah Shinwari, Dawlat Ahmadzai, Jalat Khan.
Front row, left to right: Asghar Stanikzai, Noor Ali, Rashid Zadran, Karim Sadiq, Gulbadeen Naib, unknown. (Hasti Gul Abid not present.) (LESLIE KNOTT)

Above: The Afghan National Cricket Academy. (IQBAL SIKANDER)

Right: Nowroz, the captain, in Tanzania. (LESLIE KNOTT)

Below: Taj Malik Alam in Dubai at the World Twenty20 qualifier. (TIM ALBONE)

Above: Taj's brothers Hasti (*left*) and Karim. (LESLIE KNOTT)

Left: Noor Ali (helmet) and Karim stride onto the pitch to open the batting. (IAN JACOBS)

Below: The Afghan cricket team on Haj. (RAEES AHMADAZAI)

Sharpour celebrates a wicket against Scotland in Benoni, South Africa. He took 3 for 36. (IAN JACOBS)

Mirwais, who is nicknamed Freddie after Andrew 'Freddie' Flintoff, bowling for Afghanistan. (IAN JACOBS)

Afghan fans celebrate in Dubai. (IAN JACOBS)

Afghan fans flood the pitch after the semi-final victory and qualification for the World Twenty20. They were kept from the pitch after the final victory by a plea from Taj and apparent threats of deportation by the UAE authorities. (IAN JACOBS)

Asghar, the Adrien Brody lookalike, pulls a shot against the UAE. (IAN JACOBS)

Hamid Hassan, the Rocky fan, celebrates a wicket against the USA. (IAN JACOBS)

Captain Nowroz celebrates winning the World Twenty20 qualifier. (IAN JACOBS)

The Afghan team celebrates beating Ireland and qualifying for the World Twenty20 in West Indies. By winning the final they will be in the same group as India and South Africa. (IAN JACOBS)

most important innings anyone has played during the tournament.

Once again the players flood onto the pitch. Hasti and Dawlat grab a stump each. Taj's tear-stained face, showing all the strain of the previous week, is red and his voice hoarse and cracked. Finally, he thinks, the country with nothing, the country marked by tragedy has achieved something. We have played a game foreign to us, in a foreign land, against a foreign team, with more experience, more money and a better infrastructure and we have won. My team from Afghanistan has won its first competition and is on to the next qualification stage in the World Cup.

Players fall to the ground all over the pitch; they drop face first as if they are fainting. They kiss the grass, sob and thank Allah. Five Afghan immigrants now resident in Luton and who have flown in for the final, charge onto the pitch carrying the Afghan flag. Exhaustion and the emotion of it all cause Hasti to drop to his knees. Players help take his gloves off and his hat is soon lost in the melee. Taj charges towards him and embraces him, kissing him on the cheek and calling him his hero and shows him that he has changed the entry in his mobile phone book from 'Hasti Gul' to 'Hero of Afghanistan'.

The players hoist Hasti onto their shoulders and cries of 'Allah Akbar' soon bellow out. Dawlat is also hoisted up and he waves a stump in the air. The players cry that today Allah has shown his hand, how else could this nation riven with war and desperately poor, win? It is all Allah's will.

Geoffrey Boycott, the former England captain, arrives to present the trophy and the Man of the Match award. Before the presentation he comes over to the players to congratulate them. Taj is overjoyed to meet him and tells him he is a cricketing legend. Boycott responds enthusiastically about what an exciting match he has just seen. Although the Afghans are the antithesis of Boycott as a player – they are fast, furious and cavalier – whereas Boycott would occupy the crease for hours and methodically, calmly eke out a score, both are outsiders and seem to have a common bond. Although it was a low-scoring game, he says it was very exciting, he keeps repeating the word 'exciting' as if he can hardly believe such a low scoring game can be so exhilarating.

During the presentation Boycott turns to the Afghans and makes a speech. He says that considering where they have come from, what they have achieved in Jersey is remarkable. There is genuine warmth in Boycott's words and he seems honestly impressed by the Afghans. He has understood the sacrifices, the hardship, the effort and the skill that has gone into winning this tournament. As an ex-cricketer who played at the very highest level, he can see how much the players have invested emotionally and he can tell how much victory means to them.

Hasti Gul, unsurprisingly, wins Man of the Match. As the trophy is presented, Sherzada Massoud takes off his watch and in a grand gesture places it around Hasti's wrist. Cricket might be a team sport but it is clear who the hero is. After victory, Karim is quick to forgive Ahmad

Shah; he doesn't apologise for his tirade but the two are quickly talking again. The ICC issues Karim with an official warning for his behaviour. On the coach back to the hotel Hasti can't stop grinning. When they get back to the hotel the team celebrates with a swim in the hotel pool.

Despite the victory, there are murmurings of discontent among the squad. They are unhappy with the guidance they received from Taj and feel he lacked the calmness and maturity to help them through the pressurised situation. They have won, but they have been lucky. Despite the victory, Taj's future looks more and more uncertain.

Chapter 8

Back in Perspective

KABUL, JULY 2008

No sooner had the fantastic news of the team's victory in Jersey been broadcast in the Internet cafes in Kabul and on the radios throughout Afghanistan that the war took a particularly bloody turn. By July, the middle of the summer and what was becoming known as the 'fighting season', things were getting really bad.

All the progress Afghanistan has made in cricketing terms, culminating in the celebrated victory against Jersey, was in stark contrast to events at home. It seems that every step the team takes towards international recognition and acceptance is matched by a backwards step in the conflict.

The first ten days of July are some of the most violent of the Afghan war. A number of attacks kill hundreds: a suicide car bomb at the Indian Embassy in Kabul kills

41, a US missile strike accidently kills 27 civilians on their way to a wedding party in the east of the country. A US helicopter is shot down by insurgents, ten Taliban die when the roadside bomb they are planting detonates prematurely, the Taliban execute an Afghan MP and eight policemen are killed in Kandahar province after the Taliban storm their police outpost. The horrendous list of violent incident goes on.

Drug production in the country is adding to the instability: the opium poppy harvest for 2007 was registered as 193,000 hectares, the highest of any country in the world. Some estimates suggest that 70 per cent of the world's heroin comes from Afghan poppies.

Afghanistan has a young society, around 44 per cent are under 14, and the violence affects them greatly. The special representative of the UN Secretary-General for Children and Armed Conflict announces that Afghanistan is the worst place to be a child. While Kabul remains relatively safe, except for the odd suicide bomb, the south and east of the country are becoming increasingly lawless.

In another violent action, the Taliban carries out an attack on Kandahar prison, releasing over 800 prisoners, many of whom are Taliban fighters. The prisoners had long protested that the conditions they were held in were inhumane, many had been held for years without charge, and just before the attack over 200 had gone on hunger strike, with over 40 using needle and thread to stitch up their own lips. At least 15 policemen, eight prisoners and the two suicide attackers die in the fighting.

The US, which has the largest number of troops in Afghanistan, had significantly increased their troop numbers in the first five months of 2008. In January they had around 26,000 troops in the country. By June it was over 48,000.

The Afghan players, now back from Jersey, are not immune from the violence spreading across their country. In one incident Raees Ahmadzai was shopping only 200 metres from the Indian embassy when a bomb went off outside it. He was lucky to escape unharmed. All around him were dead, dying and injured people. Shards of glass from windows had been sent flying and blood had pooled in the street.

It is with this sense of unease at home that the team sets off to Malaysia in July to take part in the ACC Trophy Elite – the premier 50-over tournament for non-Test playing nations in Asia. What a difference a victory makes. On the back of that win in Jersey, Afghanistan are one of the favourites to lift the trophy. Other contenders for the title are the UAE, who are in the same group as Taj and his men, along with the outsiders Saudi Arabia, the host nation Malaysia and Bahrain. In the other group rivals from previous tournaments, Hong Kong and Nepal, are expected to come out on top.

In previous ACC Elite tournaments, the two finalists have been invited to take part in the Asian Cup to face the highest-ranking teams in the region: Pakistan, India, Sri Lanka and Bangladesh. The games are televised and the tournament is a real money-spinner. The Afghan players therefore believe that a victory in the ACC Elite will set them on the course to international fame and wealth.

They approach the tournament with confidence and ambition. The group stages go according to plan and they beat Malaysia, Saudi Arabia and Bahrain to qualify for the knockout stage. In the semi-finals they are to face Hong Kong with what they think is a guaranteed place in a televised tournament at stake.

Hong Kong win the toss and elect to bat. Afghanistan's bowlers restrict them to 154 for nine in their 50 overs. When Afghanistan go into bat they are confident, but it doesn't last long. Nowroz, the usually reliable captain, goes with one run on the board, precipitating an innings collapse. Only four players get into double figures with Ahmad Shah top scoring with 36, followed by Karim with 17. Afghanistan are all out for 129 in 44 overs and with defeat any chance of reaching the final and the Asian Cup vanishes.

The players react badly to the loss, and once again Taj is the focus of their resentment. They complain that he has let them down: he is too emotional, his boasting heaps unnecessary pressure on the players and, perhaps most damaging of all, his coaching and training are not professional enough to take the team forward. The team complains of poor tactical decisions and woeful training sessions that lack proper structure. Every aspect of his management comes in for criticism; including his match day superstition – Taj always instructs the coach driver to beat the opposition's bus to the ground because if they arrive second he believes they will lose the match.

The players demand that he be sacked and it is all fuelled by the belief that by losing to Hong Kong the team has missed out on appearing in a major, televised tournament. As it turns out, neither of the finalists is invited to play in the Asian Cup so the motive for the players' bitter complaints about Taj – their perceived loss of fame and fortune – proves to be a hollow one. But the tide of anger that has been unleashed on their coach has been building for a long time.

Taj reacts to the accusations with dismay – he feels betrayed. He has known most of the players all their lives and feels personally bound up with the fate of the team. How much of his own life has he given up for the Afghan cricket dream?

The players' judgement of him is seemingly corroborated by an outside observer. Emal Pasarly, the BBC Pashtu correspondent who commentated on the Jersey tournament to the excited Afghan population, writes an article for the BBC website after their loss in the ACC Elite Trophy. He says the team needs a professional coach who has played high-level cricket and has a strong tactical sense. This article may have been the final straw for Taj.

After the tournament, and in a state of emotional confusion, Taj makes a difficult decision and offers to resign. The players have sown the seeds of doubt about his role within the team, and the fact that his friends are turning against him is disenchanting – he doesn't think that he can regain their trust and confidence. He feels considerable resentment too that he devoted every ounce of his considerable energy to the cause for seven years only for the team to reject him. Taj offers his resignation, hoping for an honorary position on the Afghan Cricket Federation as the least reward for all he has done for the sport. But this does not turn out to be the case.

On his return to Kabul from Malaysia, Taj hears rumblings that his old nemesis, Allah Dad, is about to stage a comeback. After his sacking from the federation in 2004 his relationship with Taj had broken down completely. The two didn't talk; they bad-mouthed each other in public and accused one another of being corrupt. But now, after the team's poor showing in Malaysia and with Taj's resignation in the offing, Allah Dad sees an opportunity. He realises that Taj is vulnerable and decides to press home the advantage. The team's unhappiness with Taj's coaching methods give Allah Dad the perfect opportunity to get back to the helm of Afghan cricket.

With the team's support, Allah Dad calls a general meeting of all 20 cricket-playing provinces. Although Karim and Hasti back their brother (or at least claim to) many of the others, including some of his oldest friends, turn against Taj. Allah Dad proposes an election to vote in a new Cricket Federation. It is him and his gang versus Taj and Sherzada Massoud.

The election result is a comprehensive victory for Allah Dad who wins 19 of the 20 votes. Taj claims that Allah Dad influenced the vote by throwing parties and making cash payments to the provinces; something Allah Dad strongly denies.

Taj is understandably distraught when the election result is announced. Rather than the reward he was expecting, Taj is kicked out of cricket in Afghanistan altogether. He is left with nothing – no money, no credit for what he has achieved and few friends to support him in this desperate hour. He is broken – brought to his knees by the humiliating public rejection and, after seven years, no reward for any of his past efforts.

Whatever the players think about Taj and his coaching technique, without his enthusiasm and passion they wouldn't have got through Jersey. To completely sideline him seems harsh but Allah Dad absolutely refuses to work with him again – he's never forgiven Taj for his own cricketing exile.

Taj's misery is compounded soon afterwards when he catches malaria. But his preoccupations are again put into perspective by another grim reminder of all they are trying to escape from through cricket. Wednesday 27 August 2008 is the day the war directly impacts on the Afghan cricket team. American forces raid the home of a former player, Rahmat Wali, and shoot him dead. In the raid they also arrest his brother, taking him off to Bagram airbase on the outskirts of Kabul. The victim, who was only 28 when he was shot, had played for the Afghan team under the Taliban and had kept his place in the early years after the fall of the regime. Rahmat played international cricket but had been dropped for the World Cup qualifier in

Jersey and the ACC Trophy Elite simply because the team had improved beyond his ability. He was a popular figure though, and the players still considered him very much part of the team.

The shooting takes place in the small village of Kheder Piran. The village is in Khost province in the east of Afghanistan, the same province that Nowroz, the captain, and Noor Ali call home. It shakes the team to their very core. The Wali brothers had been involved in a previous incident. In the early months of 2008, Rahmat and Ahmad had been arrested by the Americans and accused of being Taliban. They were taken to Bagram and detained for 16 or 17 days. Then they were released without charge.

Six months later the Americans came back for them. Just before midnight on 27 August, Ahmad Wali was woken by the sound of gunshots close by. The Americans broke into the house looking for him; they cornered him and tied his hands behind his back. He asked them what they were doing and why. They told him to shut up. It was then Ahmad saw his brother, lying on the floor of his room, his hands tied and his head covered with a sack. He was dead. The Americans, Ahmad claimed, said that if he didn't cooperate he would meet the same fate. They asked him where the weapons were and where the foreign fighters were hiding? Ahmad was again taken to Bagram airbase and again released without charge, but this time he returned to the house without his brother.

Nowroz was closest to Rahmat Wali, they lived in the same province, had played cricket for Afghanistan under the Taliban and would play together for Khost. The captain is convinced his teammate wasn't a Talib, he says there was no way he was involved in the insurgency, he only loved sports. Ahmad Shah said he considers Rahmat one of the most pious people he had met. Asghar also cannot believe the American line that he was Taliban. Noor Ali, who also comes from Khost, takes the death very badly, like Nowroz he was close to the player. The effect on the whole team is profound. They are astonished that one of their own, a cricketer, who by playing for Afghanistan did so much for his country, could be accused of supporting the Taliban and then be killed because of it?.

When Taj first hears of the news that an international cricketer has been killed in Khost, he thinks it is Nowroz. When he finds out the truth he is no less upset, Rahmat, he says, was a great man. The players' anger reaches the ears of the authorities. The ISAF claim that during the incident the international troops fired in self-defence. Rahmat was holding a gun, they say. The official line is that he was killed because they believed he was an 'IED facilitator' – in other words someone who enables people to build improvised explosive devices or roadside bombs. His brother Ahmad vehemently denies that Rahmat had a gun, and claims the family has been targeted because someone with a grudge against them has fed false information to the Americans – an all too common occurrence. Protesting his brother's innocence he asks why the Americans had released them without charge the first time they were arrested. And why, after searching their house and arresting him for a second time, he had been released again. Surely they had to show some convincing evidence for their action. But none was forthcoming.

Details of the troops involved in the raid prove impossible to verify. Ahmad Wali claims they were wearing grey uniforms not the normal camouflage. Although the ISAF confirm that the raid took place, they refuse to disclose the nationality or unit of the soldiers involved. The secretive nature of the mission indicates that the troops who carried it out were probably Special Forces operating outside of ISAF's command. ISAF say no investigation will be made, as it isn't 'warranted'. The Wali family received no compensation, despite the fact no charges are ever laid.

For the Afghan team fighting to represent their new government and country it is hard to accept that one of their own has been killed at the hands of those who are meant to free them. That no one is brought to justice and no investigation is launched makes it even harder to bear. It is under this very dark cloud that the team travels, without Taj, to Tanzania to take part in Division Four, their next World Cup qualifier.

Chapter 9

A New Approach

DAR-ES-SALAAM, OCTOBER 2008

The tumultuous events of the summer have resulted in the appointment of a new coach to the Afghanistan cricket team: Kabir Khan. The ACC has been heavily involved in this appointment and is paying half his salary: further proof of its commitment to Afghanistan as a developing cricketing nation.

Kabir's credentials are impressive – perhaps no more so than others coaching at the same level – but there are many points on his CV that make him a perfect fit for the team. Although he is only 34, Kabir brings with him a wealth of playing and coaching experience. He's played first-class cricket in Pakistan, appearing for the national team in Tests and one-day internationals. He has played and coached in Scotland and coached the UAE national team. Although he comes from Peshawar, his father was an Afghan, and Kabir claims he has taken the job to honour his father's memory. He is cool, calm and unflappable.

His first language is Pashtu and this helps him immediately bond with the players.

It is unclear how many people were in the running for the Afghan job but it can't have been many. The ACF has just changed hands and is in a state of flux, the country is at war, the team is in the second lowest division of world cricket and the pay isn't great. But for Kabir the job is just right. He sees an exciting project: coaching players with real potential that he can help develop and craft into a strong international cricket team.

Kabir is not intending to manage this alone. One of his conditions on taking the job was that he was allowed to bring an assistant with him. He has chosen Fazal Azeem, a trainer and physio who owns a gym in Peshawar and has worked with the Pakistan national team. Kabir and Azeem are a perfect double act. Kabir plays the serious, retiring intellectual and Azeem the ever-smiling joker. The coach, who has a beard with the moustache shaved off, has a few specks of grey in his hair that emphasise his studious demeanour. He is trim and in shape. Kabir's standoffish manner hides a warm, good-natured personality. He is always polite but takes a while to open up to people. Azeem by contrast is a bundle of energy, has a quick smile and an easy laugh and always has a ready high five and a hug.

In Tanzania for the Division Four tournament it is immediately clear the team is playing at a higher level by the class of hotel it is staying in. The Golden Tulip hotel, about a 20-minute drive from the centre of Dar-es-Salaam, will house the team for its stay. Gone are the communal toilets, the numerous players to a room and the mattresses on the floor of Kabul, gone also are the dancing pensioners, bad, stodgy breakfasts and tired-looking furnishings. They are replaced by infinity pools, sea views, tropical gardens and trendy minimalist furniture. In the lobby they can check their e-mails and one or two of the players have purchased laptops. There seems to be more money around. Players are cagey about what they have received and from whom, very probably because much of it is given in the form of gifts and private donations from rich businessmen. In post-Taliban Afghanistan there is a lot of money swilling around, many of the wealthy view associating with successful sportsmen as another route to gaining power and influence. A few hundred or a few thousand dollars is seen as a good investment in case the Afghan team hits the big time.

The players have also started dressing in a more Western style: Nabi, Noor Ali and Raees wear jeans and T-shirts. Hamid, who picked up the style in England, has become even more of a fashion victim. He has a hands-free mobile phone receiver constantly plugged into his ear and has started wearing gaudy, tight T-shirts, baseball caps and sunglasses (even indoors).

No one is quite sure why the ICC has selected Tanzania as the venue for the tournament as the country is in the middle of the rainy season. Nonetheless, it is the team's first experience of Africa and, apart from playing Botswana in Jersey, they have had little or no contact with

African people. Some of the players are wary of black Africans; they call them 'danger men'. Their lives have been extremely isolated to date, and their touring experience has been limited to Asian countries and Jersey.

Tanzania is poor; the Afghans feel it is even poorer than their own country. The people eat different food, look different and the only common language they have is English, which only a few on the team speak well enough to hold a proper conversation. There are no black people, aside from soldiers, in Afghanistan. In Asia, and Afghanistan is no exception, many people believe the whiter the skin the more attractive the person is considered.

Many Afghan men find it shocking that anyone could find an African woman attractive. Asghar, the Adrien Brody lookalike, is amazed at the size of their bottoms and jokes about it with his teammates. However, as the days progress they befriend their bus driver, speak to other people in the hotel and discover the locals are warm and friendly, much warmer than in Jersey. It is amazing to see how quickly their prejudices dissolve.

When they arrived they were nervous and cautious but within days are taking photos with Tanzanians they meet on the street. On one trip Nowroz and Asghar marvel at a little boy's tight, curled hair. Asghar who has perfectly straight hair pulls out one of the boy's curls and watches, in amazed silence, as it curls back up when he lets it go. He then gets the child, who is only about six, to touch his own hair. Both laugh and pose for photos. It is a small moment but one that illustrates how little the players knew of the wider world and how quickly their minds are opening up to it. They are inquisitive, good-natured and sympathetic. They are still sportsmen, and are largely uninterested in seeing historical sights or learning about the history of the countries they visit, but they are becoming interested in the people.

Raees Ahmadzai, the former captain, is the exception: he takes himself off to the fish market to discover a bit about Tanzania. He mingles with local fisherman and in broken English tells them the Afghan team is going to win the tournament and beat the host nation. None of the people they meet give any indication they even knew Tanzania had a cricket team – a situation the Afghan players can empathise with – it wasn't so long ago that no one in Afghanistan knew that they played cricket.

The Afghan team's introduction to Africa is smoothed by the fact they find a south Asian restaurant in Dar-es-Salaam. The food is halal, the meat is cooked to their taste and they can get rice. The proprietor likes the idea of feeding an international team so gives them a discount. The players still aren't being paid or receiving match fees but they have been given some money for food, and Tanzania is much cheaper than Jersey.

The team has also been put in touch with a couple of Afghan businessmen who have moved to Tanzania. The businessmen bring the team rice and meat in huge vats to keep them going and keep the costs down. All in all their stay in Tanzania is more relaxing and they have many more home comforts than when they played in Jersey.

The composition of the tournament in Tanzania is also different to Jersey. In this qualifying round there are only six teams: Tanzania, Jersey, Italy, Hong Kong, Fiji and Afghanistan. All the teams play each other and the top two go through to a final and the next round. It is a much tougher test but will bring the victors another stage closer to the World Cup finals.

Afghanistan's first game is against Fiji. As befits the season, the day of the game is warm, wet and soggy. In the changing room before play starts, Kabir reminds them of the work they have been doing at a pre-tournament training camp at the National Cricket Academy in Lahore. Ironically, even in Pakistan, the war impinges when a bomb goes off nearby, and the camp is cut short by three days.

The new coach had decided to concentrate on an aspect of the team's game he felt would bring immediate rewards without the need for too much technical training, given they didn't have long to practice. In many of the games, he observed, the team panicked at the first setback – the momentum swung away from them if the opposition got on top. Kabir felt the Afghans had a tendency to buckle rather than steady themselves and fight back. He spends a lot of the training camp working with them on their mental strength – increasing their resolve and their resilience. Kabir wanted them to appreciate that a setback could be reversed, and that one of the most important aspects of any competitive sport is how to deal with the change of fortunes during a match. It proved to be a useful exercise in the first game of the tournament.

The other aspect they managed to work on was their physical condition. Although Azeem, the physio, has only had a few weeks with them in Peshawar before the tour they already look fitter, slimmer and healthier. Training sessions are disciplined and focused and the players are now also warming up and down properly before and after games.

Fiji win the toss and put Afghanistan in to bat. The wet, warm conditions are a fillip to the bowlers and Afghanistan struggle to find their feet with only four batsman getting into double figures: Ahmad Shah top scores with 34. They are all out for 132 in the 36th over. Kabir doesn't panic, reasoning that the wicket is poor and the conditions favourable to his team's seam bowlers. They can make Fiji's innings very difficult. His confidence transmits itself to the team and the players take full advantage of the moist air, swinging the ball expertly to skittle Fiji out for 52 runs in 21 overs.

Afghanistan have always been good with the ball but Kabir seems to have harnessed their raw aggression. Hamid, who gets Man of the Match, takes four for 22. Ahmad Shah also returns remarkable figures: in four overs, he bowls three maidens, taking two wickets for three runs.

The second game is against Jersey. On paper it will be an interesting test of the team's discipline as Jersey are desperate to avenge their loss in the final of the Division Five play-off. The match is played at the Dar-es-Salaam University ground in completely different conditions. The players are delighted to see a dusty weather-beaten pitch that wouldn't look out of place on the Asian subcontinent. The grass is scrubby and the wicket bare. The Afghans immediately feel comfortable. Around the ground a number of wooden shades have been erected to shield the few spectators from the scorching sun.

The team bats first, and their innings is suffused with control and patience, lasting the full 50 overs and ending on 203 for nine – a much better score than any they got in Jersey. The pick of the batsmen is Karim who top scores with 60. In reply Jersey start solidly but that all changes when Hasti Gul, their nemesis with both bat and ball in Jersey, comes on to bowl in the sixth over. With his final two balls he takes two wickets, and suddenly Jersey are 22 for two. This leads to a batting collapse – Jersey struggling to a humiliating 81 all out in the 36th over. Hasti Gul and Hamid finish with three wickets apiece.

Kabir has to take a lot of credit for both performances: he has changed the way the players think about the game and how they react to pressurised situations. While Taj was a master motivator, never short of words of encouragement, during matches he was sometimes lost tactically. Kabir brings years of international experience to the team – there's not a cricketing situation he hasn't personally encountered – and he reacts calmly to the ebb and flow of events on the pitch. The players have noticed the difference immediately and they are full of praise for the new coach and physio. The captain, Nowroz, believes the coach is making them more professional and, if he stays with them, they can reach their goal of the World Cup.

In order to try and calm players before games, Kabir forbids them from talking about cricket the evening before and on the morning of matches. He doesn't want them to think too much about their play and get themselves into a muddle. He wants them to go out and play their natural game without being weighed down by fears and worries. It is his job, not the players, to have a game plan. The Afghans have an incredible natural talent and he wants to enable them to express that ability at the highest level.

Kabir is also trying to instil in the players a sense that they are ambassadors for Afghanistan. Although Taj had similar ideas, Kabir feels that under the previous regime this may have been misdirected. Before he arrived, he says, all the team did was joke and brag about how they were going to win matches and get to the World Cup. This had a very negative effect on their opponents and what spectators there were. Kabir wants them to be aware that they are representing Afghanistan at all times – on and off the field.

The players become less rowdy and more respectful. They thank the bus driver and waiting staff and hold doors open for elderly hotel guests. It seems most likely that Kabir can get them to do this as he has played Test cricket for a Test nation – he has been where the players aspire to be. Kabir is confident he can coach the team to international standard by reining in the excessive ambition of the players and getting them to focus on what they have to achieve, rather than constantly chasing records and headlines. The team is now given a game plan for each match and the players are instructed to stick to it for the duration – regardless of events. This approach provides the framework the players need in which to use their talent effectively.

Their successes in the tournament so far reflect how well this change is working. After comprehensively beating Jersey their next game is against Tanzania, the home side. Before the game Kabir tells the team to 'have a big heart' and he makes it clear he expects victory. Nowroz wins the toss and elects to bat first. There seems to be a newfound faith in their batting – previously they would prefer to chase a total. Now they believe they can amass a big total and intimidate their opponents. And today the conditions are such that it makes sense to bat first: the pitch is dry with a good batting surface and it looks like it might rain later.

Despite their meticulous planning, the team makes a disastrous start with the first five wickets falling for only 69 runs. Karim is out for a duck, Nabi for seven and Nowroz for 13. Kabir's policy of encouraging them to react to setbacks in a positive way is put to the test immediately. They now know the problem is not that they have lost early wickets, any team can do that, it is their response that determines how big their heart is and ultimately how good the side is.

Afghanistan rally. Though they do nothing spectacular, the middle-order calmly adds runs, as does the tail. There is no panic, no flailing around with the bat and no pointless wickets. All the players contribute to the total as they are dismissed for 143 in the 47th over. Top scorer, with

25, is new squad member Shafiqullah Shinwari, or Shafiq Shafaq as he is known. He had also batted well against Jersey; it is an impressive start considering he is coming in to bat at No. 7 or 8. He has added some real steel and resolve to the tail. Much to his annoyance Shafiq has been given the nickname Shafaq, simply because it sounds good with Shafiq. The nickname has stuck and appears on all the ICC promotional literature for the tournament. His tribal name, Shinwari, seems to have been forgotten. He is worried that his tribe won't like it – and has already had complaints from his father and uncles.

Like many of the Afghanistan team, his progress has been astonishing. He's only been playing cricket with a hard ball for about a year, although he has played tennis ball cricket since he was five. Also in common with some of the other players is the fact that his exact age is a little unclear. He thinks he is around 21 or 22, and a full face of stubble and an abundance of chest hair suggest he may well be older than the 19 years claimed in his passport. Like Taj and his brothers, Shafiq had endured beatings for neglecting his studies in order to play cricket. He was undeterred and this resolve is reflected in his dogged resistance at the crease.

Tanzania warm-up for their innings in their dressing room by dancing to the beat of an African drum. On the pitch, they start slowly. When rain falls in the 27th over and play is briefly suspended, they are 71 for five, ahead of Afghanistan at the same stage, but only slightly. The players return amid mounting pressure. But whereas

Afghanistan might once have buckled under the pressure, this time they pull through – winning by eight runs with ten balls remaining. Three games, three victories: a perfect start for Kabir and his team.

Their next game is against Hong Kong, the toughest team in the tournament and one that a number of the Afghan players are starting to regard as their bogey team. A win will almost certainly guarantee them a place in the top two, and therefore promotion to Division Three.

Hong Kong win the toss and elect to bat. Afghanistan get an early wicket when Karim, the wicketkeeper, and Hasti, the bowler, combine to dismiss one of the openers for only five runs. But without doing anything spectacular, the batting side begins to accumulate runs. They close on 206 for nine, a higher total than any Afghanistan have achieved so far in the tournament.

In reply, Karim blasts 20 runs off 13 balls before he is clean bowled, Ahmad Shah scores a painfully slow seven off 46 balls before he is caught and, when Asghar is run out for 18, Afghanistan are 48 for three. Things are not looking good. Hong Kong had scored 152 runs when they lost their third wicket and their total now looks beyond Afghanistan. However, Nowroz and Nabi show some resolve, scoring 50 and 70 respectively in a fourth-wicket stand of 105. When Nowroz is out, stumped trying to hit a boundary, Raees joins Nabi at the crease and the two continue the scoring. In the final over Nabi is finally dismissed to leave them 204 for six. They need three runs off three balls as Sami walks to the crease to take guard.

Sami, who has matured since Jersey and is developing into a real all-rounder like Nabi, smashes his first ball for four. Afghanistan have won by four wickets. They have finally beaten Hong Kong. It is a performance of real guile, strength and maturity epitomised by Nabi's innings of 70 off 78 balls. He is also the best of the bowlers picking up five wickets for 32 runs. Unsurprisingly he is given Man of the Match.

Against Italy they win the toss and again elect to bat. This time it's the top order that does the damage – Raees Ahmadzai and Ahmad Shah both contributing half-centuries to a total of 234. The Italians struggle against the pace bowlers, in particular Hamid who takes three for 19, and are dismissed for 141. This run-of-the-mill victory ensures Afghanistan a place in the final and in the Division Three tournament. But there is little time to celebrate as two days later they face Hong Kong, again, in the final.

The momentum is clearly with Afghanistan. Despite struggling to a total of 179, Nowroz and Raees Ahmadzai leading the charge with solid 40s, they blow Hong Kong away with the ball. Nabi, again the pick of the bowlers, finishes with four wickets as Hong Kong are dismissed for 122. When Nabi takes the final wicket, the players gather together, wrap their arms around each other's shoulders and jump up and down. As they come off the pitch they surround Kabir, raise him into the air on their shoulders and shout 'Kabir Zindabad!' 'Afghanistan Zindabad!' 'Kabir Zindabad!' Long live Kabir! Long live Afghanistan! Long live Kabir! Leading the chanting, with one of Kabir's legs over his shoulder, is Karim. It seems the coach, with his quiet understated style, has won over even Taj's most loyal supporter.

Kabir is unused to such attention and emotion. He smiles shyly but is clearly touched. He has warmed to the players and grown close to them, he says he feels like their elder brother.

After the match the celebrations are more measured and respectful than in Jersey. Another trophy, but this time obtained with ease and quality. Revenge for the Afghan team is sweet, two victories over the Hong Kong team in less than a week have erased the hurt many of the team felt after losing to them in the Trophy Elite. They are worthy tournament champions and, incredibly, are now halfway towards their quest for World Cup qualification.

The day after victory and a day before they fly back to Afghanistan, the team celebrates with a trip to the beach where they have a barbeque provided by some Afghan traders who live in Tanzania. In the minibus on the way to the beach the team dances to Bollywood tunes, Karim twists and turns more than most. He flicks his hands like a female Bollywood dancer. They stop to pick up some coconuts for the feast.

To get to the beach they need to take a ferry. The ferry is small, carrying some 20 cars and 200 passengers. One of the players compares it to the *Titanic*, the only ship he has ever heard of. Two of the players re-enact the famous scene where Kate Winslet and Leonardo DiCaprio stand at the front of the boat with their arms spread out. They are relaxed and happy, although Ahmad Shah is worried that, like the *Titanic*, the ferry might crash: he spends the whole journey clinging to his seat and muttering prayers to himself.

When the team arrives at the beach and the minibus is unpacked there is a huge feast to enjoy (including eight chickens, a cow and a goat). Their business connections have rewarded the team's great performances in some style. The players make kebabs, curry and cook whole chickens. The squad, many of whom haven't seen the sea before, are ecstatic. They build sandcastles, dance the traditional Attan and splash around in the surf like children. Nowroz, ever the organiser, is scared some of his players might drown and spends most of his time standing chest deep in the sea calling them back if they go out too far.

As darkness falls, the team board the minibus to return to the hotel. In the bus there is a microphone, which Hasti Gul is quick to pick up. He starts his routine. He pretends to be a news reporter, a religious leader and then impersonates other team members. The players howl with laughter.

It is on this happy note that the team heads back to Kabul. The team has now won two tournaments and suddenly Taj's boast that they will make it to the World Cup is not looking so fanciful. With Kabir as coach they look more settled, mentally stronger and sharper – can the new coach transform Taj's greatest ambition from dream to reality?

Chapter 10

A Golden Day

PESHAWAR, OCTOBER 2008

Now back in Pakistan, Taj is watching the progress of his team with mixed emotions. He is, of course, proud of their achievements – and the ongoing success of his brothers in the team – but he is also bitter about the way his life's work has been cast off so easily. Infrequent but expensive phone calls from his brothers don't help his mood. They are difficult for him to handle emotionally and hampered by the technological obstacles of a poor electricity supply and haphazard telephone connections.

Since he resigned as coach and was then unceremoniously dumped as general secretary he has moved out of the Kacha Gari refugee camp to a village six kilometres away. His new house is located in the village of Shah Kaz in the tribal areas and the territory is increasingly coming under Taliban control. Taj views the success of the team in Africa as partly his own and his bitterness reaches its peak when all of those who return from Tanzania are rewarded by the Afghan government with a trip to the great Muslim pilgrimage of Haj.

It is journey Taj has always wanted to make. And when he hears Hasti and Karim talk about the trip he wishes he could have been there. As the weeks pass, though, he starts to enjoy the freedom of not being the coach. He no longer feels stressed, he isn't worried and he enjoys spending time at home with his two wives and their five children.

For the players, the trip to Saudi Arabia is one of the highlights of their lives so far. Haj is obligatory for all able-bodied Muslims who can afford it, and the players all agree it is a special moment in their lives. Millions of Muslims converge on Saudi Arabia to carry out the annual pilgrimage, which is a declaration of faith and solidarity. It bonds the team as part of something larger than the cricketing fraternity. Muslims from all over the world attend and the players take great pride in telling their fellow worshippers what they are trying to achieve. The reaction from other Muslims is overwhelmingly positive. Everyone they meet says they will pray for the team and this gives them strength.

During Haj many of the players experience a feeling of extreme well-being, some cry uncontrollable tears, others feel guilty for the mistakes they have made, but all leave with an enhanced sense of togetherness and an increased religious belief. Ahmad Shah, who is on his second Haj, is particularly touched. He stops wearing Western clothes and replaces his moustache with a beard.

The cricketing reward for their tournament win in Tanzania is a place in the Third Division tournament in Argentina – a culture at least as alien to the Afghanistan team as Jersey and Tanzania. Kabir is lying in a hospital bed in Peshawar recovering from minor surgery when Allah Dad calls, asking him to pick the team for the trip. He tells Allah Dad he will be unable to do it for a few days. He needs to rest, reflect on Tanzania and scout for players.

Three days later, when Kabir is at home recovering, he gets a visitor who has some surprising news. The visitor, someone who Kabir has never seen before, tells him he is the chief selector. He presents Kabir with a team sheet and asks him to sign it.

The coach, bewildered, glances at the names on the sheet. He immediately notices two surprising omissions. Neither Sharpour, the tall, fast bowler who had missed out on the trip to Jersey and a number of games in Tanzania through injury nor Noor Ali, the stylish batsman whose brother provided funds for the team in Jersey, are on it. For Kabir both of the players are rising stars and need to be nurtured not dropped, especially as Sharpour is just returning from injury and Noor Ali, who is a real confidence player, is struggling for form. Neither has played particularly well to date but Kabir has seen something in both of them. In practice Sharpour is fast and accurate, but is said to choke in big matches. Kabir thinks he can work with him and help him develop and calm his nervousness. Noor Ali is the most naturally gifted batsman in the squad but he has yet to find his feet in international tournaments. These players' places are filled by Khaliq Dad and Assadullah.

Kabir has heard of Khaliq Dad, though he hasn't played for Afghanistan since their 2006 tour of England, after which he had claimed asylum. He is the new president's brother and, though Kabir has no knowledge of it, has been promised a place in the squad if he returns from England. The other name on the list, Assadullah, is new to Kabir. When he asks who it is, the chief selector points to himself. He promises Kabir he is a great player and deserves his place in the squad on merit, but Kabir is understandably suspicious.

Assadullah tells the coach that he had played for Afghanistan in their first ACC tournament in Malaysia in 2004 and was named Man of the Match with an unbeaten 45 in the match against the home team. The coach is astonished at his inclusion as he immediately feels that the player has been out of the game for too long and has no right to a place in the squad.

Kabir is immediately thrust into a crisis of conscience. He has deliberately developed a policy of bringing in young players and nurturing a squad through togetherness. He has never seen these men play and is deeply uneasy about two new names arriving untried into a winning team while two potentially very talented players, already integral to the group, are dropped for no good reason. Picking players who have once played for the team but have since been dropped, who were getting older and have no potential for improvement is not the road Kabir wants to go down.

He is also dismayed by the nepotism. As if picking the brother of the president isn't bad enough, he can scarcely believe the chief selector has picked himself. He refuses point-blank to sign the team sheet, barely able to disguise his fury, and sends Assadullah on his way.

Kabir is distraught. He can't believe that with all the obstacles standing in the way of success – war, a lack of funds, a lack of facilities and a very young, raw team – the biggest problem might now come from within. He is stunned that Allah Dad, the new president, is insisting that the selector and his brother be included in the team, even though it could cost them the tournament.

Matters then take a turn for the worse. As it turns out, his refusal to sign the team selection is nothing more than a symbolic act. During a press conference held in Kabul ahead of the tournament and while Kabir is still recovering in Peshawar, Allah Dad pretends to the media that Kabir has signed the sheet. And if that wasn't enraging enough, it transpires that the ICC only requires the president's signature on the team sheet anyway.

When the news of the selection gets out, the players are furious that Allah Dad has meddled in team affairs and threaten to pull out of the tour. Despite being angry himself, Kabir insists they have to carry on. He persuades the team that they themselves are the only people who will suffer from withdrawing. He decides if he has to have two members in his squad picked by Allah Dad and Assadullah, that is the price he has to pay. He still feels his squad is good enough to compete.

His scepticism about Assadullah and Khaliq Dad doesn't change when he sees them play: they are unfit and not as talented or hungry for success as the players that have been dropped to make space for them. Despite his confidence in the players, he does have doubts. He sees irony in the fact that the influence of nepotism that helped found the ACF in 2001 now threatens to destroy it. One thing he had always been impressed by has been the togetherness of the team, the players seemed like brothers. Everyone supported each other and backed each other up. His worries centre on the possibility that Assadullah and Khaliq Dad might change the dynamic of the squad.

Despite this behind-the-scenes drama, the team sets off for Argentina in January 2009 knowing that a win will take them to South Africa and the actual World Cup qualification tournament. Suddenly no one is laughing at the Afghans anymore, they are seen as a real threat, cricket websites and newspapers even label them the favourites and Kabir remains unsure how the players will react to this. The Afghan team has become used to playing in unusual places; Jersey and Tanzania were a world away from Afghanistan. But Buenos Aires is a step further.

The journey to Argentina is the most arduous they have undertaken. From Kabul they fly to Dubai, from Dubai to Johannesburg and from South Africa on to Argentina. It takes over a day and a half.

At the opening ceremony the players' feelings of isolation increase: they have never felt further from home or more out of place. As part of the ceremony all the teams are invited to watch a performance of the famous tango. The Afghans have never seen anything like it. A lithe, busty, dark-haired woman in a skin-tight red dress with a slit right up the leg dances with a long-haired, swarthy man with a goatee beard and the top four buttons on his shirt left open. The dance is erotic; the lady grinds into her partner who flings her around, raising one leg into the air. Some of the players, like Karim, watch the dancing with nervous smiles. Others, like the devout Ahmad Shah, retreat to their bedrooms in disgust. But the performance shocks them all. Despite the fact that they are now seasoned travellers, in Jersey it was often too cold for girls to wear skimpy clothes, although at times the players were still stunned by what people wore; in Tanzania the women normally dressed in long skirts, but in Argentina flesh is on display everywhere. Every time the players go out of the hotel they are confronted by girls with exposed arms and legs.

Some of the more devout members of the team can't believe it when they see girls in shorts kissing men in the streets. Ahmad Shah is growing a thick, long beard with the moustache shaved off to imitate the style favoured by the very religious – this he hopes will serve as a reminder to the others not to be tempted by these provocative sights. It isn't just the girls' clothing that proves problematic for the team. Once again, they find it almost impossible to find halal food or anyone who speaks enough English to understand what it is. Most Argentinians have no idea what halal food is, there are no Indian restaurants and in desperation the players persuade the hotel they are staying in to let them cook their own food in the kitchen. Azeem, the physio, and Hasti Gul do most of the cooking.

Despite the distance, the food and the half-naked women, things start well on the field. They beat the Cayman Islands by 105 runs in a warm-up game. But even after this comprehensive victory, Kabir warns the players that getting through this division is going to be tough. The tournament is structured like the one in Tanzania: there are six teams and all play each other on a mini-league basis, with the top two going through to the World Cup qualification tournament proper in South Africa. The standard of the teams is a step up again from their last tournament. Their opponents include Uganda, the rising stars of African cricket who have recently defeated Kenya and had come close to upsetting Bangladesh; Papua New Guinea and Hong Kong are also strong and although Argentina are not as strong as they had once been, they have home advantage. Despite their poor performance in the warm-up game the Cayman Islands have beaten Hong Kong and Canada, who have played in Division One, before and so are used to playing at this level.

In their first game, against Uganda, the Africans win the toss and elect to bat. They open well, their first two batsmen posting 88. Afghanistan are solid in the field, but Nabi and Hamid don't bowl well and the other bowlers seem unable to take hold of the game. Uganda finish their 50 overs with a decent looking 216 for eight. Kabir worries that the enforced changes have upset the balance of the team. His fears increase when Afghanistan go into bat. They start badly, showing abysmal shot selection: Shafiq, who made his debut in Tanzania, makes 18, Ahmad Shah is out for one, Asghar for three, Nowroz and Nabi for ducks. The top five batsmen are back in the pavilion with only 22 runs on the board.

Karim comes in at No. 6. He has been dropped down the order, mainly because Kabir feels that he doesn't have the right temperament to be an opener. Openers need to work for the team, see off the shine on the ball and establish the innings. Karim tries to make a name for himself with every shot. He scores 17 but the Afghans are still desperately behind. They need runs and they need someone to steady the ship. With Raees Ahmadzai, the former captain and elder statesman of the team, and Sami, the player who has aspirations to be a male model come in, at the crease the situation improves. Raees plays the innings of his life and scores a brilliant 78, including six fours and three sixes, and Sami scores 52 during their 121-run stand. But Raees is finally dismissed, caught behind, with the score on 174. Despite more runs from the tail, Afghanistan are all out for 202 in the final over and Uganda win by 14 runs.

Kabir remains upbeat. After such a disastrous start the team rallied and came close to victory. He is happy with the effort put in by Raees and reminds the team they are not out, they need to remain calm. The thing that cheers him the most is the spirit the team shows, despite all the problems leading up to the tournament the squad has pulled together. Significantly, neither Khaliq Dad nor

Assadullah played in the game: just because they are in the squad doesn't mean that Kabir has to pick them.

Despite his outward confidence, Kabir knows that if the team is going to qualify for South Africa, it can't lose again. The pressure is tremendous. The players respond and Afghanistan win the next match, against Hong Kong, by 13 runs, and the next against the hosts Argentina by 19 runs. They continue their winning streak with a nine-wicket victory against Papua New Guinea, in which Karim deputises as captain after Nowroz has been suspended for a slow over rate against Argentina. Karim takes six catches behind the stumps and scores a half-century – making him Man of the Match. Confidence throughout the team is suddenly riding high.

Despite Afghanistan's impressive sequence of wins, they are by no means certain to qualify. Results in other games work against them. Papua New Guinea beat Uganda and, going into the final round, the top spot is jointly held by Afghanistan, Papua New Guinea and Uganda. The last games will decide which two teams go through. What is certain is that Afghanistan need to win.

Afghanistan face the Cayman Islands, whose only victory had come against the hosts. The Afghans are confident following their victory in the warm-up game, but this time the weather is against them. Rain disrupts play all day and Afghanistan only get to bat for 31 overs, putting a miserly 68 on the board. Because the weather is so bad the Cayman Islands are set a target of 63 runs from 20 overs. They start well. After seven overs they are on 35 for two. Afghanistan are going to lose and with it will go their chance of qualification. Their only hope is more rain. It's getting late in the day, the outfield is wet and Kabir can't believe the match hasn't already been called off. The Afghans are furious and becoming paranoid. Forgetting for a moment that the weather has played a part in them getting to this stage by saving them in Jersey, they convince themselves that the ICC doesn't want them to reach the World Cup and are trying to sabotage their qualification by making them play in bad conditions.

Kabir paces the outfield dragging a photographer with him; he orders her to take pictures of pools of water. These, he says, prove the game should be called off. At one stage some of Allah Dad's cronies, a number have come over on a junket, argue with Argentinian spectators. The mood is ugly. On the pitch the players are told that if the game is stopped one more time then it will be cancelled. Karim can see a raincloud in the distance, he has no idea how long it will take to arrive overhead, but it looks like the Cayman Islands will score the runs before it arrives. He's keeping wicket and after another particularly wayward delivery, the Afghans have been bowling poorly today, he dives and stretches. As he hits the ground he screams and rolls about dramatically. It is obvious to all watching that Karim is faking an injury. Journalists watching audibly exhale; one accuses the Afghans of copying the antics of the Pakistanis. As Karim writhes in mock agony even the ICC officials start to voice concerns about Afghanistan's sportsmanship. Karim, slowly and gingerly, gets to his feet and only minutes later the raincloud is overhead, the rain begins again and the game is called off. It rains for only a few minutes but it has saved Afghanistan.

Despite the reprieve, the coach is furious. The players have never seen him so angry. He gathers them around him and launches into a withering tirade: they are not fit to play for their country, how could they throw away this chance having worked so hard, had they forgotten all they had learned from him? Some of the players are shell-shocked. Hamid crouches on his knees – head in hands. He can't believe how close they have come to being eliminated. But Asghar is more philosophical about the game. He believes that the team was over-confident and that God is teaching them a lesson.

Whatever their individual reactions, the tirade has the desired effect on the team and the following day they sweep aside the Cayman Islands by a margin of 82 runs. Batting first, Afghanistan rack up 230 for eight, Nowroz hitting seven boundaries in his 89-ball 70 and Asghar contributing an unbeaten 66. The Cayman Islands are bowled out for 148. Nabi strikes twice in the first 15 overs to rip the heart out of the innings and finishes the match with four for 23.

The division finishes with three teams on eight points: Afghanistan, Uganda and Papua New Guinea. The order is decided by net run-rate, with Afghanistan on top, Uganda second and also through to South Africa and the unlucky Papua New Guinea eliminated.

The press gathers round the celebrating Afghan players.

Kabir is delighted. He expresses his pride, calling it the happiest day of his life and a golden day in the history of Afghanistan cricket. He is used to dealing with the press attention and makes all the right noises, acclaims their great achievement and explains that his players should enjoy their victory. Captain and Man of the Match Nowroz also enjoys his moment in the sun in front of the reporters. He expresses his pleasure at winning the Division Three tournament and making it to the World Cup qualifier.

Away from the spotlight Kabir knows that his experience of world cricket is about to be put to the test. He is already planning a training camp in either Pakistan or India ahead of the upcoming challenge. Nowroz too is realistic. He knows that it has been a big day in the history of Afghanistan cricket but that the hard work is still to come. The teams competing in South Africa will be a step up again. For now, though, captain and coach are happy. Amazingly, and against all the odds, the Afghans are only one tournament away from the World Cup.

Chapter 11

Rubbing Shoulders

SOUTH AFRICA, APRIL 2009

The team hotel for what Kabir hopes is the final stage in the journey to the World Cup finals is in the upmarket district of Sandton, just outside Johannesburg. The five-star luxury accommodation couldn't provide a more marked contrast to the place that many of the squad set off from on their way to Jersey almost a year ago. The hotel building – a study in glass, chrome and marble with swimming pool, gym, fine dining and shopping mall – belongs not just to a different continent, it belongs to a different century to the run-down, windowless, dirty and disease-ridden shack the team had stayed in before the trip to Jersey.

The Afghan team is staying on the top floor, which they reach by a glass elevator that looks out onto the hotel's imposing courtyard. The rooms, which cost hundreds of pounds a night, all have views over Johannesburg, and the clientele is the rich, well-travelled executives of the global banking business.

The Afghans have overcome enormous odds to reach South Africa. They are the only nation ever to win three World Cup qualifying rounds in a row, the only nation to have ever risen from the lowest division to the verge of qualification and among the nations left in the tournament they have by far the shortest history. Whereas the quality of teams in previous tournaments increased slightly with each round, in South Africa Afghanistan face the best non-Test-playing nations. This time the leap in standard is huge.

Before the tournament the team has its best training camp to date. The players spend four weeks solidly preparing: two weeks in the National Cricket Academy in Lahore in Pakistan and two weeks at the Sharjah cricket ground in the United Arab Emirates. The squad arrives in South Africa fit and ready for action.

The tournament consists of two groups of six teams who play each other in the first round. The top four from each group go through to a second round called the Super Eights. The teams are given an extra incentive in the first round because they carry forward any points they gain against other teams who qualify for the Super Eights. In other words if, for instance, Afghanistan beat Kenya in the first round and both teams go through, then Afghanistan will take those points with them. The top four teams from the Super Eights will make it through to the World Cup.

Afghanistan's group is tough: they will play Kenya, the Netherlands, Denmark, UAE and Bermuda. All of these teams, except Denmark, have played at the World Cup and all have made an impression on world cricket.

Kenya has a long cricketing history dating back to the end of the 19th century. Colonial settlers originally brought the game with them but the Kenyan Cricket Association (formed in 1953) has since put the game on a solid platform and it is now widely played throughout the country. In fact cricket was the first inter-racial sport to be established in Kenya. The Kenyan team is recovering from a turbulent period in its cricketing history. It reached the semi-finals of the World Cup in 2003 but in the aftermath of that achievement, Kenyan cricket was nearly destroyed by a series of crippling scandals: player strikes, huge debts and match-fixing allegations all led to the suspension of its official One-Day International status by the ICC. It was not until 2006 that the Kenyan Cricket Association re-launched as Cricket Kenya and the team regained its ODI status.

The Netherlands have one of the longest playing traditions in Europe – the first Netherlands Cricket Association was formed in 1883 though it was not accepted into the ICC until 1966. At one stage cricket was one of the most popular sports in the country. Today it's nowhere near as popular as football but the country still has around 6,000 registered cricketers. They have some players of real ability, many of whom play first-class cricket in England: Alexi Kervezee, their Namibian-born attacking batsman and medium pace bowler, plays for Worcestershire; Bas Zuiderent, a batsman, has played for Sussex; and Ryan ten Doeschate, a South African-born all-rounder, plays for Essex. The Netherlands played in the 1996, 2003 and 2007 World Cups and were due to take part in the World Twenty20 to be held in England later in the year.

Bermuda had also been to the 2007 World Cup, where they unfortunately recorded the largest ever World Cup defeat. India beat them by 257 runs after posting a total of 413, the highest ever total in the World Cup. The only bright spot for Bermuda was an unbeaten 76 by David Hemp who had played for and captained Glamorgan.

Denmark has a history dating back to the mid-19th century. Although they have never been to a World Cup, they have played high-level cricket against tough European competition for a number of years. Their wicketkeeper, Frederick Klokker, is, like Nabi and Hamid, a former MCC Young Cricketer and has played for a number of English county sides.

The United Arab Emirates are the final team in the group. The UAE have been a member of the ICC since 1989 and appeared in the World Cup in 1996. They are considered one of the strongest non-Test nations in Asia. They have the best facilities of any non-Test nation including three international quality stadiums in Abu Dhabi, Dubai and Sharjah, and Dubai is also home to the ICC. The UAE squad are all south Asian ex-pats and are mainly Pakistanis or Indians, a number are second generation and were born and brought up in the UAE. And Kabir knows them well: he coached them for a few months in 2007.

The Afghans are set to play teams brimming with talent and experience and are widely considered the weakest in the group. Even to qualify for the Super Eight, they will, once again, have to battle against the odds.

A change is noticeable in the team since the pilgrimage to Haj. Kabir has developed the team by introducing some new players and has redeployed others in new and useful roles. Ahmad Shah is one example. Since Haj, his religious devotion has increased, perhaps to the detriment of his passion for cricket. He has gained weight and lost form, but Kabir recognises his contribution to team spirit and retains him as assistant coach. It's an important role – Shah helps some of the more devout players deal with the extreme luxury and temptation the South African trip offers.

One of his first acts as assistant is to clear all the furniture out of one of the bedrooms to make a prayer room. His second act is to cover all the African art in his room and the prayer room with towels, as the carvings depict people he says are idolatrous. It is acts like this that illustrate just how far out of their comfort zone the players are.

A further problem arises because both the Australian team and those players taking part in the Indian Premier League (which has recently been moved here from India because of security concerns) are also in South Africa during the tournament. All the players appear to be staying in the same hotel and the Afghans cannot believe their luck. For years they have idolised international players and now they are brushing shoulders with them in the pool, the gym and the restaurant. Though the Afghans are awestruck they think nothing of knocking on the players' doors and introducing themselves, often inviting themselves in and outstaying their welcome. Some of their behaviour prompts a complaint to the Afghan Cricket Federation and Kabir has to issue a stern warning.

All this presents Kabir with a new problem. The team's rise has been so meteoric (it's only 11 months since they played the Division Five tournament in Jersey) that new experiences are coming thick and fast. It is taking the players time to adjust to their new lifestyles. The only celebrity cricketer they met in Jersey was Geoffrey Boycott, who was presenting the winners' trophy; now the team is in a five-star hotel surrounded by the world's cricketing elite.

Despite rebukes and warnings the players can't stop themselves. Noor Ali, who has been recalled to the team after losing form, is delighted to find that Ricky Ponting is staying in the same hotel. They swap shirts, take photos and Noor Ali asks for some advice. Many of the players have just signed up to Facebook and soon photo albums dedicated to the players they meet start appearing on the website. Ponting fires Noor Ali up, he can't wait to start batting and many of the other players who encounter their heroes are similarly inspired. Other players are bewildered by the star treatment they receive themselves. The tall and handsome fast bowler Sharpour is also back in the squad. When he walks through the hotel's shopping mall he attracts the attention of girls who stop and stare at him.

But Kabir has done good work. The set-up behind the Afghan team is starting to look more professional. Under the new coach everything has become better organised: the players dress smartly, attend the necessary functions and press conferences and they all eat together. They travel around in a bus provided by the ICC. One evening they are taken to a restaurant in Mayfair, the Muslim quarter of Johannesburg. Kabir knows the place because he had been here when he toured South Africa with Pakistan. On the way the players are excited to learn that the Indian cricket team eats there.

The outing is a great success. The chicken is halal and cooked just right, they eat Peshawari naan and the rice is served with butter and burnt on the bottom, just the way they have it at home. Hasti is delighted that at last they have found somewhere abroad that suits their palate. The waiting staff speak Urdu so communicating is easy and they can eat with their hands and no one looks at them in astonishment. In the restaurant the team has never looked more at ease: the players smile, laugh and joke. The contrast with their behaviour in the hotel couldn't be more apparent.

While the players eat, coach Kabir considers his options on the playing front. Khaliq Dad, Allah Dad's brother, is still in the team, but there is some lingering tension between him and the other players. Since arriving in South Africa he has visited a trendy hairdresser to have his hair bleached and bought a ridiculously expensive pair of Italian leather shoes. Neither action has gone down particularly well with the others. Assadullah, however, has been dropped. In his place is Mohammed Sherzad, an elfin, five foot five-inch wicketkeeper and batsman. Taj had tried to persuade

Sherzad, who has a Pakistani mother and Afghan father, to play for Afghanistan when he was coach. Sherzad resisted as he thought he was good enough to play for Pakistan, but when the call didn't come and Afghanistan made it to the qualifier, he decided to play for his father's nation. It says something about Kabir and how far he has brought the team that Sherzad made that decision. Sherzad is the new wicketkeeper, allowing Karim to bowl more. Sherzad idolises the Indian Twenty20 captain MS Dhoni and calls himself MS Sherzad in homage to his hero.

Before the tournament starts, the ICC makes a big point of telling everyone they will be carrying out random drugs tests. In the past some of the Afghans have smoked marijuana; it is as common in Afghanistan as beer in the UK. It is hardly a performance-enhancing drug but it is on the list of banned narcotics issued by the ICC. Those players who have smoked in the past wonder how long it takes to get out of their system and how accurate the tests are; fortunately as their first match arrives no positive tests are returned. For the Afghanistan players the world of drugs testing is very new. Before the tournament, many of them weren't even aware marijuana was a banned substance.

Afghanistan's first match is against Denmark. Kabir is right to warn the players against complacency. Although not a traditional cricketing powerhouse, in 2008 Denmark had finished third in the European Championships, ahead of the Netherlands. They have potential. But, aside from wanting to start with a win, the Afghan team also wants to beat Denmark for political reasons. In 2005 a Danish newspaper published controversial cartoons of the Prophet Mohammed, depicting him as a terrorist. The cartoons drew widespread protests across the Muslim world. Afghanistan was one of the countries where the protests were the most violent; a number of protestors were killed in clashes with the police and Danish troops in the country were told by the Taliban that they would be specifically targeted. Losing to Denmark, the players say, is unimaginable: their countrymen would never forgive them. They need to win this game: victory would go some way to righting a wrong.

Afghanistan win the toss and put the Danes in to bat. The Danes score 204 for nine in their 50 overs. Free from his wicketkeeping duties, Karim bowls eight overs, taking four for 27. Karim has, as usual, predicted the Afghans will crush all their opponents in this tournament and he is doing his best to uphold his end of the bargain. It is also his mission to finish the competition as the Player of the Tournament, something he has aimed for and not achieved in every other of the qualifying tournaments.

Afghanistan's reply begins with a setback as two wickets fall quickly: Shafiq is out for six and Noor Ali, despite his inspirational chats with Ricky Ponting, for one. But Karim scores an impressive 39 off 40 balls, including seven fours, and Sherzad, on his competitive debut for Afghanistan, scores 55 not out. Nabi fires 47 from 51 balls and Afghanistan reach 205 for five in the 47th over, giving them a comprehensive five-wicket victory.

Next up for the Afghans is Bermuda. The game is played

at Senwes Park in Potchefstroom, an impressive Test and one-day ground. Despite the free admission there are no more than 20 spectators in attendance. Since Bermuda qualified for one-day status in 2005, they have reportedly been given almost US$3 million by the government for the development of the game there. Though their star player is batsman David Hemp, perhaps their most recognisable player is 20-stone, left-arm spinner Dwanye Leverock. He took the wickets of Paul Collingwood and Kevin Pietersen at the 2007 World Cup and took an incredible (largely because of his weight) one-armed, diving catch at slip to dismiss Robin Uthappa of India. He is as famous for his cricketing as his unusual style of celebrating; he marks catches and wickets by bouncing his ample belly.

Afghanistan win the toss and elect to bat. Karim and Shafiq open the innings but Shafiq, who is struggling for form, fails again and is caught behind for two. Karim and Asghar take the score to 128 before Asghar is caught for 38. Karim, who is on form and playing with real freedom and aggression, smashes ten fours in his innings. He is desperate to score a century to prove he belongs on this stage. When he is caught on 83, the pain etched on his face is clear to see. He looks to the sky, pulls his baseball cap down over his eyes and lets out a pained cry. Nevertheless, as he leaves the field Afghanistan are 147 for three and in a good position after 32 overs.

But wickets fall quickly as Sherzad is out for a duck, Nabi for one and Raees for one. Despite the collapse, captain Nowroz holds the innings together and hits 71, including six fours and two huge sixes, and Afghanistan finish their 50 overs on 239 for nine.

Afghanistan take two early wickets to leave Bermuda reeling on seven for two with both openers back in the pavilion. Dawlat, who has taken a wicket with his third ball, continues to bowl fast and accurately and in his opening five-over spell he concedes just five runs. The next two batsmen put decent scores of 68 and 62 on the board but once they are out, there is only one team in it. Bermuda need 115 from the last 16 overs and don't even come close with the final seven wickets falling for only 35 runs. Afghanistan win by 60 runs. They have shown guile in the field, discipline with the ball and aggression and skill with the bat.

Afghanistan have three more group matches to play, although by winning two they will almost certainly be guaranteed a place in the Super Eights. But with the points counting in the next round, they need to keep on winning. It is unlikely either Denmark or Bermuda will qualify, so the next matches, against the strongest teams in the group, are the all-important ones.

Predictably the Afghans lose all three. They are hammered by Kenya, losing by 107 runs and then lose to the Netherlands by five wickets. The match against the Netherlands is a bad-tempered affair. Two players show a complete lack of discipline. Karim attempts to trip up the non-striking batsman when he goes for a run and Mohammed Sherzad is given a warning for pointing his bat at the umpire after he has been given out. Though their actions might be said to illustrate their desire and competitive spirit, it is also clear that they lose their hard-won self-control in the face of seeing their World Cup chance slipping away. At a lower level they might have been able to get away with such a display of petulance, although Karim had been warned about his conduct in Jersey, but this is non-Test cricket at its highest level – they need to keep their heads and stay calm. The consequences though are a lesson in themselves as Karim is banned from the next match and Mohammed Sherzad is given an official warning.

With Karim banned, Afghanistan slump to a five-wicket defeat against the UAE, a match they should have won. Despite this, somehow they scrape through to the Super Eights by finishing ahead of Bermuda and winless Denmark.

Celebrations are subdued, however. Three defeats on the trot have not been good for their confidence, and the never-say-die attitude that Kabir has drilled into his players is being severely put to the test. The Afghans go through with the Netherlands, Kenya, the UAE and Namibia. However, with no points to take through from the group stages, Afghanistan are in a weak position. Kenya, the Netherlands and the UAE all take four points through with them, each having beaten two other qualifiers. Before the first match is played, Afghanistan sit at the bottom of the table alongside Namibia, who also go through with no points.

If Afghanistan stand any chance of making it to the World Cup, they need to win at least three of the next four games and even that might not be enough.

Chapter 12

Phoenix from the Flames

The pressure is intense. Following qualification for the Super Eights, the situation becomes clearer. Joining the teams from Afghanistan's group are Ireland, Canada, Scotland and Namibia. The new round requires that each team plays each other once with a series of play-offs to decide the final order. The top four teams will qualify for the World Cup in 2011, to be played in India, Sir Lanka and Bangladesh. Their first game is against Ireland – the form team of the tournament.

The players are beginning to feel the strain – with each qualifying round the World Cup gets closer but the standard of opposition is getting correspondingly higher. Even with the vastly improved coaching and fitness routines, the players are having to learn a lot while trying to maintain their progress. Kabir is sanguine about this, as he is about their chances of reaching the World Cup. As long as they develop their talents, and grow as a team of players, he is happy.

To alleviate some of the pressure, the team decides to go on a safari. The safari park is near Johannesburg and, unlike the larger reserves further out in the bush, the animals are restricted – penned in by fences. In practice it is more like a large zoo.

The players load up in two open-back 4x4s for the tour. After the beach party in Tanzania, this is another new experience – of African wildlife. As the tour guides point out animals, the players repeat the names totally in awe. Asghar and Hasti find the emu particularly amusing – they have simply never seen anything like it before.

Whenever the vehicles slow down, Hasti jumps out and runs alongside. Despite the protests from the guides and the threat of wild animals on the loose, he keeps doing it until someone tells him there are snakes in the grass. When the team comes across two rhinos they laugh, giggle, wave, generally making a nuisance of themselves. The guides explain that the rhinos are a mother and daughter and not to make too much noise as it might make them aggressive. The players don't seem concerned by the pleas for quiet. Raees hangs out the back of the jeep and other players continue to laugh and joke, until the mother rhino turns and starts walking slowly and menacingly towards the jeeps. Karim, who is sitting on the open side nearest to the rhino, turns sheet-white and starts panicking. He starts screaming at the driver to drive and curls up next to Asghar. The other players start laughing.

The jeeps pull away and Karim quickly removes his head from Asghar's shoulder. The team have a good laugh at his expense. He always likes to make out he is the tough guy and on the pitch he is a brawler, but the rhino had him scared.

Back at the hotel the Afghan team holds a training session in the pool. They are surprised to find the Irish players' girlfriends, who have travelled with the team, sunbathing in bikinis. Although the Afghan men have become better at talking to and interacting with members of the opposite sex, they are still taken aback by the sight of them in a state of undress in public.

But it's not necessarily outrage they feel. When they played the Netherlands, the Dutch team had two female physios who wore impossibly short shorts and tight figure-hugging T-shirts. The girls would massage the players before they went into bat and the Afghans, as one, audibly gasped when they first saw this. Once they had composed themselves, they wanted Karim to explain why the Dutch got two attractive women and they only got Azeem?

For the Afghan team, seeing women in bikinis or tight shorts massaging men is just totally foreign. Most of the team are married but they never discuss their wives, and as Pashtuns the women aren't even allowed to leave the house without a relative and most wear the traditional figure-covering blue burka. The players are still finding it difficult to come to terms with the way things are done in the Western world.

The match against Ireland is to be played in Krugersdorp, a gold-mining town about an hour outside Johannesburg. A crowd of around 150 has come to watch, not a bad number for one of these qualifiers. The Irish have played here a number of times and have developed a small local following. A group of Irish fans have also travelled from home to watch their team and have a holiday at the same time.

Ireland win the toss and put Afghanistan in to bat. The Irish are fairly confident of victory: they have won every game so far and qualified top of their group. One of the Irish players jokes about where the Afghans have hidden their suicide bombs and, as the openers Nowroz and Karim head out onto the pitch, the announcer mispronounces Karim's full name, Sadiq becomes 'Sad Dick' and the crowd chortle. The Afghans are less amused.

There has also been high drama in the Afghan camp. Allah Dad has flown in from Afghanistan and has started making a nuisance of himself in his capacity as president. He imposes his will on Kabir, much to the team's disgust, forcing him to pick his brother Khaliq Dad, or KDN as he is known, for this crucial game. KDN has only bowled once since being in South Africa, against Kenya. He returned the rather unimpressive figures of no wickets for 29 runs in three overs and was largely blamed for the humiliating nature of the defeat. To pick him in the team's toughest match to date makes no sense, shows no understanding or respect for Kabir's management and upsets the team. Hasti, who has been dropped for KDN, publicly expresses his concerns with the situation via a telephone interview with a radio station back in Jalalabad.

Taj hears the report on the radio and can't help but laugh. After moving out of Kacha Gari, the family's yearning for home had increased. They decided it was time to move home. His decision was based on a number of reasons: the area around the new family home was becoming increasingly lawless and Taj concluded that he was probably as safe back in Afghanistan as he was in Pakistan. He and his family had grown sick of life as refugees and, despite his ignominious exit from the Afghan cricket team set-up, he had gained a certain celebrity in their homeland for his efforts on their behalf. Taj had done occasional commentary and punditry on the radio and decided to see if he could capitalise on his status by setting up a cricket academy and earning some money that way.

There is also a renewed air of optimism and hope that with Barak Obama taking office in the United States in January 2009, things in Afghanistan might change. In one of his early speeches on the matter the new US president promised to support the people of Afghanistan, pledging diplomacy as well as more troops to fight the insurgency. When he took office there were around 35,000 troops in the country, Bush had already promised 10,000 more and these arrived as Obama was being sworn in. Shortly afterwards Obama announces an extra 17,000. Eventually American troop numbers in Afghanistan will reach 100,000.

*

Back in South Africa, the Irish start well, taking Karim's wicket for six. It's a big wicket – Karim has performed well in the tournament. Aside from a poor innings against Kenya, his scores have been impressive: 83 against Bermuda, 72 against the Netherlands and 39 against Denmark. He is bitterly disappointed to get out so early and sits, shoulders slumped, on the edge of the field next to his brother Hasti. Noor Ali is out shortly afterwards for 18 – another disappointment. Even though he has Kabir's support, if he is to keep his place in the side he needs to start scoring big soon. After 11 overs Afghanistan are 46 for two.

Once again the middle-order batsmen steady the ship. Propped up by Mohammed Sherzad, who scores 46 before a misunderstanding with Nowroz sees him needlessly run out, Asghar with 47 and Raees Ahmadzai who hits an unbeaten half-century, Afghanistan close their innings on 218 for seven.

It's a good total against a strong team but the players are worried that it won't be enough. As usual Kabir gets them to focus on the game plan – to think about how to bowl to each of their opponents and, above all, to maintain their discipline while bowling or fielding. As the Irish innings begins, Kabir wanders around the boundary away from everyone else, he tugs at his beard as the stress finally begins to show. Hasti sits on a chair muttering to himself, he is asking God for help and reciting an old Pashtu proverb that wishes blindness upon one's enemies.

Hamid, who normally comes on as first change, this time opens the bowling. His line and length are perfect and in the third over he gets a wicket. Khaliq Dad surprises everyone and takes a wicket in the fourth over and suddenly Ireland are six for two. It is a fantastic start. Khaliq Dad's bowling starts to slip and before long he has bowled five overs for 20 runs. Although it's not a disastrous rate, there is a sense that he is struggling to hold it together. Between overs he falls in the field and signals that he needs to come off. He doesn't look injured and indeed he's not. Embarrassed to be picked because of his brother and not his talent, and aware he isn't playing well, Khaliq Dad has faked an injury so another player can play. It is a gesture that doesn't go unnoticed among his teammates.

Ireland have already shown grit with the bat in this tournament. Three days before they had chased down Namibia's 213 in 43 overs, losing only 3 wickets. Before that they reached 223 in 41 overs to overhaul Canada's 220, they ran down Uganda's score of 159 in 31 overs, and posted winning totals of 283 against Oman and 233 against Scotland. They deservedly topped Group A, which was considered the tougher of the two groups.

But Afghanistan continue to apply the pressure. By the halfway stage they have taken five wickets and Ireland have only scored 73 runs. Behind the stumps Sherzad celebrates each wicket with a little bow and curtsey, which draws laughs and alleviates the tension. Few people in the crowd seem to support the Afghans although one, a Scot, who everyone refers to as 'Mr Taliban', cheers each time they take a wicket. The groundsmen, the only black people present, are also rooting for them.

Batsmen six and seven lift the total from 73 for five to 186 for five. Suddenly Ireland are in control: they have five overs left, five wickets in hand and only need 32 runs. As Afghanistan have done so many times before in their time of need they turn to Hamid, who tosses the white leather ball between his hands as he organises his field.

Hamid is full of confidence but he knows that to realise his real potential he'll have to perform in situations like this one. He licks his finger and runs it along the seam, then he rubs the ball against his trousers, urging himself to stay calm and focused. He is nervous, feeling the pressure. He knows that if Afghanistan are going to win and stand a chance of qualifying for the World Cup he's going to have to take the wickets.

The time has come.

Four balls later, he clean bowls one of the two stubborn Irish batsmen. In his next over, incredibly, he bowls the other one, following that with two more wickets. He marks each wicket with increasingly elaborate celebrations. After the first he raises his arms out and runs around like a footballer, after the second he picks up the ball and throws it at the floor in celebration, for the third Hamid performs a cartwheel.

When Nabi takes the final wicket, all Hamid can do is fall to his knees and kiss the ground. Nabi, his best friend, stands rooted to the spot his arms thrust into the air. Sherzad dances and Karim runs around like a lunatic. Hasti Gul and Ahmad Shah fight over who gets to wrap the Afghan flag around their shoulders and the two end up charging around the pitch pulling it between them. All thoughts of decorum, of the need to be dignified in victory and defeat, go out of their minds. It is a purely emotional reaction to what has been a very tough contest against one of the strongest non-Test playing teams in the world.

After the excitement of the win, heightened because Ireland have once beaten Pakistan and therefore the Afghans now think they are better than their neighbours, the team gathers in front of the scoreboard and lines up to pray. Ahmad Shah stands at the front and the other players feather out behind him as he leads the call to prayer. For ten minutes, while the Irish, still shell-shocked by defeat look on, the Afghans rise and fall in prayer. As the players board their respective buses back to the hotel, the Irish players make sure they shake the hands of the Afghan players.

Afghanistan have still not qualified for the World Cup, but it feels like it. The team celebrates this time with a swim in the pool and some Nando's chicken in the local shopping mall. They've had enough of safaris for the time being.

The following game is against Canada in Pretoria. Going into the game Ireland and Canada are on six points, Scotland, Kenya, the Netherlands and the UAE are on four. Afghanistan and Namibia are on two.

The captains toss up, Afghanistan lose and are put in to bat. Noor Ali has been told he is opening the batting with Karim. He hasn't impressed yet and this has made him more superstitious. He has scribbled the name 'Ricky' in biro onto the top of his bat to remind him of his idol and to try to help him focus. He has also, for some unknown reason, developed a strange habit of dressing right side first. He makes sure he puts his right sock on before his left and his right shoe before his left and works his way up, finally he puts on his right glove before his left. The other players find Noor Ali's superstitions amusing, they don't have time for such frivolities, the most they do is offer a prayer before they step onto the pitch.

Noor Ali has also shaved his head to try and hide an increasing bald patch and, as he kits up, he ties a bandana made from an Afghan flag, around his head. On top of this he places a helmet. Before he walks out onto the pitch, he sits on a chair, staring ahead deep in thought. He sits there fully kitted-up for ten minutes of silent reflection, holding his bat in his hands. He feels its familiar shape and weight and this comforts his nerves. He thinks back to Khost and his friends back home, he reflects on all the troubles his country has endured and he thinks that despite his run of poor form he can turn it around.

Like all the players, Noor Ali has become increasingly troubled by the violence at home. The day before their first game militants attacked the Police Academy in Lahore – 16 people died and over 90 were injured; the team had been at the nearby National Cricket Academy only a few weeks before. In April, when the group matches began, US forces had raided a home in Khost, the home province of Noor Ali and Nowroz, and killed four innocent civilians. President Hamid Karzai criticised the raid and urged international troops not to carry out raids that harm civilians. He said an investigation would be launched into the attack, which killed two men, two women and a baby inside a pregnant woman who survived. The attack brought back memories of Rahmat Wali and reminded the players of his death.

In this moment of need he asks himself what Ricky Ponting would do, and he knows the answer. Ricky would go out and score a century. Ricky would show all the doubters what a great player he is. Noor Ali is more focused than he has ever been.

Canada had only lost one game in the group stages, against Ireland. In their last game they beat Kenya, who had thrashed Afghanistan by seven wickets. They were a tough team. The only positive for Afghanistan is the news that John Davison, a hard-hitting batsman, who played state cricket in Australia, is out injured.

The match is played in Pretoria at the LC de Villiers Oval and, unlike the Ireland game, there are very few spectators. A number of journalists have come to watch and the MC plays loud trance music, which reverberates around the empty stadium.

When the Afghanistan innings begins Noor Ali looks more confident than he ever has before. Always stylish and technically good, it is sometimes his shot selection that lets him down, though people have also questioned his mental strength in big matches. Today he looks invincible. He repels everything the Canadians throw at him. When the balls are loose or wayward he strokes them away with apparent ease, when they test him he blocks or leaves them. When Karim is caught and bowled for 13, Afghanistan are on 39. Sherzad falls for ten but when Nowroz comes in at No. 4, the pair add 118 runs to take the score to 187 for three and things start to look up. Afghanistan then have a wobble as Asghar and Nabi both fall for ducks to leave the total at 189 for five. But Noor Ali, compact, neat and focused, bats on. His century finally arrives. He lifts his bat in celebration and savours the moment. But he doesn't have long – Afghanistan need more runs.

He's finally run out for 122. The tail fails to wag and they finish their 50 overs posting 265 for eight. It's a good score, but it's on a really good batting wicket and scores of over 300 are not uncommon.

Canada, led by Ian Billcliff who scores an unbeaten 96, are just too strong for Afghanistan. They reach the winning total of 268 for the loss of four wickets in 39 overs. The Afghan bowlers had been on fire against Ireland two days before, particularly Hamid, but today they have struggled. Hamid gets smashed for 32 off three expensive overs. Nowroz, who doesn't normally bowl, goes for 19 in two. Karim was bowling too short and was smashed all over the ground.

The players leave the pitch shattered. The news gets worse. The Netherlands, Ireland and Kenya have all won. This means that Ireland and Canada now have eight points, Kenya and the Netherlands are on six. The UAE and Scotland are on four and Afghanistan and Namibia are still on two. With only two games left any chance of finishing fourth depends on winning both their own games and on the Netherlands or Kenya losing both theirs, though even then Afghanistan's run-rate will probably be inferior.

The World Cup dream is all but over for Afghanistan; although there is still a mathematical chance they can qualify, all the players know that won't happen. They realise too that if they had played better in the group stages, then this loss wouldn't count so much. As Canada celebrate their World Cup berth, the Afghan players slump, despairing in the knowledge that the dream they've held and, extraordinarily nearly achieved, is over. Some are close to tears; no one speaks for several minutes. Everything they have worked towards is over; their dream of playing at the 2011 World Cup has been cruelly taken away from them at the final stage. They really were that close.

Kabir is the only one who doesn't look heartbroken. His boys are heroes and have achieved much more than he had dared hope. But he also has a masterstroke up his sleeve. He has something to divulge which he has been keeping to himself. Kabir's focus coming into this tournament was not just to get a place in the World Cup, or even to play well; he knew that a top-six finish would see them qualify for ICC ODI status. He chooses this moment to tell the players.

Kabir explains that he hasn't spoken of this publicly because he didn't want to distract the players from their World Cup dream. He had been doubtful all along that they could get to the World Cup in, effectively, one year and that, even if they did, they would be ready for the challenge. In his back pocket, all the time, though, he kept hidden the knowledge that if they finished in the top six in this tournament, they would qualify to be ranked alongside the ten Test-playing nations in the world.

Hope immediately rises in the players' minds, like a phoenix from the flames. They immediately realise that if they can beat Scotland and Namibia then they will make the breakthrough. They will get official ICC ODI status for four years and with it will come all the sponsorship money, investments, endorsements and international tournaments and other fixtures that they desire. Suddenly, the two remaining matches have become the most important of their lives.

Excitement immediately infects the team. Against Scotland they look freer, the weight of expectation has been lifted off their shoulders and replaced with a tangible confidence. Afghanistan put 279 on the board; it's a challenging total. Karim leads the way with 92, and Nowroz provides the backbone with a solid 72. Scotland, one of the tournament favourites, had struggled so far. If they were going to beat the Afghans they would have to score higher than they had in any of their other games. However, at 200 for five with eight overs remaining, the match is finely balanced. But Nowroz rallies his men. The bowlers respond to the pressure and tighten their line and length, taking the last five wickets in five overs and reducing Scotland to 237 all out. Sharpour is the pick of the bowlers, returning figures of 9.1-2-36-3, and Karim is made Man of the Match for his powerful innings.

As they leave the pitch, the Afghans' mood is lifted further. The Netherlands and Canada have both lost their matches. The league table looks much better: if they lose again and Afghanistan win, they will all finish on the same points. Honours will be even despite their superior run rates.

Two days later they're back at Krugersdorp, where they had beaten the Irish. They hope it will prove to be their lucky ground. Afghanistan v. Namibia. At stake is over US$2 million in funding. Understandably, nerves are a little frayed before the match starts. The Namibian team is mainly made up of blond, beefy Afrikaans speakers, many of whom play their club cricket in South Africa. Kabir underlines the fact that this team had made it to the 2003 World Cup and is certainly not to be underestimated.

Afghanistan win the toss and elect to bat. Noor Ali and Karim open the innings. Noor Ali's century against Canada and Karim's consistently high scores mean they are the two in-form batsmen. Both fall early. It is left to Sherzad and Nowroz to take control. Coming in at Nos. 3 and 4, the pair takes the innings by the scruff of the neck and adds 87 runs to the total before Sherzad is caught on 73, Nowroz goes for 78 and Asghar adds 27. After 50 overs Afghanistan have posted 243 for seven wickets – it's another good score.

Sharpour opens the bowling and continues his impressive form, taking a wicket with his third ball. By the 25th over Namibia are in real trouble at 79 for five. Afghanistan smell victory. Kabir and Azeem laugh and relax on the sidelines. A sixth-wicket partnership briefly threatens a revival, adding 78 runs, but once that is broken in the 37th over Afghanistan are in complete control and Hamid takes the final wicket to win the game for Afghanistan. Namibia are all out for 222 in the 49th over.

They have done it. After only eight short years of international cricket, Afghanistan has become an ODI nation. Not only that, they have also come within a whisker of qualifying for the World Cup, finishing only two points behind Kenya and the Netherlands who both won their final matches today. They have risen from the lowest division in world cricket to the top in a year, something that has never been done before. Afghanistan are also the first ICC affiliate nation ever to gain ODI status.

On the pitch after the match Hasti sums it up in a phone call home: he tells a friend the team have gone from the refugee camps to the world stage. Who, he asks, would believe it if it wasn't true? He passes the phone to Karim and begins to recite a Pashtu poem that says happiness in a poor man's life is rare, when it comes you go out onto the street and start dancing.

Afghanistan play Scotland for fifth place. This game also marks Afghanistan's first ODI. The Afghans run out easy winners. They score 295 for 8, Nabi top scores with 58 and they skittle Scotland out for 206 in 40 overs. Hamid takes 3 for 33.

The victory has an immediate impact on cricket in Afghanistan. In 2003-04, the cricket board was given US$46,294 by the ICC and ACC, the year before the qualifier they had received US$253,213, now thanks to their ODI status they will get US$826,463 and the funding and sponsorships will keep increasing.

This, however, is not the best news. The team finds out that all the ODI nations will be entered into an eight-team qualifier to be held in Dubai in February 2010 for the 2010 World Twenty20 tournament. The top two teams will make it to the finals, which are to be held in the West Indies in May. The World Twenty20 is, by another name, the World Cup for the shorter format of the game. It is amazing news for the team – the bitter disappointment of failure to qualify for the 50-over World Cup has been wiped out by the prospect of making it to the World Twenty20 finals. Two years ago in Kabul they had set out to reach the World Cup and they have, albeit in a different form of the game. Kabir is delighted; he feels Afghanistan can achieve qualification at Twenty20 in Dubai, and that it will be easier to adjust to 20-over cricket at the top level than 50-over.

Cricket purists often deride Twenty20 cricket as a slog-fest with no tactics. But for its supporters it is fast paced, exciting and hugely good fun. In only 20 overs batsmen can take more risks and hit harder; and for bowlers and fielders it is a stern challenge. For the Afghans, who are still learning the nuances of the game, it is the perfect match-up. At this level they can hit harder and bowl faster than almost anyone. The Dubai qualifying tournament should be fun as there is a large expat Afghan community living there – for once, the team will have some vocal support.

To put the cricket team's achievements into perspective, Afghanistan is not a nation awash with sporting heroes. At the 2008 Olympics they won their first and only medal with a bronze in taekwondo. In 2008 their football team played a number of games: losing 0-5 to Turkmenistan, 0-4 to Tajikistan and 0-6 to Malaysia. They salvaged some pride with a 2-2 draw against fellow minnows Nepal and upset the form-book with a 1-0 victory over India. In 2010 the football team were ranked 195th in the world out of 203. Taj had said in 2008 when they set out on their World Cup journey that it would take the football team fifty years to be able to compete on the world stage and the cricket team just ten. At the time it seemed ridiculous that this would happen so quickly but for once he had underestimated the team's potential. They had gained one-day international status the following year and in February, less than two years later, would find out if they were going to the World Twenty20.

When the team arrives back at Kabul Airport, the players are welcomed as heroes; politicians, heads of various governmental agencies, sponsors and hundreds of fans greet them as they land. They are promised money, land, houses and sponsorship. The team is now big news; it is getting money from the ICC, beating established teams and will soon be playing matches all over the cricketing world.

A day later they head to Jalalabad, a city in the east near Pakistan, where most of the players originally come from. It is also the main cricket-playing region in the country. The players travel in two mini vans, Allah Dad Noori and his cohorts travel in a separate car and Taj also goes, travelling in a 4x4.

Allah Dad and Taj don't talk; they can barely look at each other. Allah Dad is already worried about his position, now so much money is coming in his worry has increased. He has been accused by many of the players of misusing money that the ACF has received and they are angry that he meddled in team affairs and selection. To add to his woes, they are all heading towards Taj's home city, and he is worried that he might not receive as warm a welcome as his rival.

The road to Jalalabad has been upgraded since Taj travelled it in 2001 and now the journey takes only two hours. Or it should, but for all the right reasons this time it takes much longer. Every time the convoy reaches a village the road is blocked by fans who shower the players with confetti, drag them out of the vans and hoist them on their shoulders. At one village a soldier fires his machine gun in the air in celebration, at another a group of men bang drums and dance. By the time the team reaches Jalalabad it is getting dark, the journey has taken double the time. Here the streets are teeming with fans, and it is quicker to walk than drive. Men have hooked up ghetto blasters and are calling out praise to the team and Taj; noticeably Allah Dad receives no praise. Some fans have fashioned homemade flamethrowers out of aerosols; they fire the gas into the air and light it, sending flames shooting five feet into the air. The players are adorned with garlands of fake flowers. They are invited to the governor's house and presented with a feast.

For Allah Dad the celebrations don't last long, within the month he has been replaced as president. The players have become increasingly frustrated with him and take matters into their own hands. They approach Omar Zakhilwal, the country's finance minister, and persuade him to become the new president of the ACF. Zakhilwal is universally seen as a good man and one who is fair and impossible to corrupt. Under him a CEO and a new three-man selection committee is appointed. Sherzada Massoud is back in a largely ceremonial role and Hamid Karzai, the Afghan President, is Patron in Chief. Many other changes are made too. The Afghanistan Cricket Federation becomes the Afghanistan Cricket Board in a move to try and stop nepotism and corruption. They break away from the Olympic Committee, which means they have more autonomy over their funds but they lose their academy because it was built on land donated by the Olympic Committee. The foundations for further progress and professionalisation of the sport have been laid.

Chapter 13

The World Cup Dream Comes True

DUBAI, FEBRUARY 2010

T he World Twenty20 qualifier is an eight-team tournament played in the United Arab Emirates. The teams
are divided into two groups with the top two teams from
each group going through to the Super Fours. Two teams
from the Super Fours qualify for the World Twenty20
competition proper to be held in the Carribean in May.
They will play each other in the final to decide which
group they enter in the main tournament.

Ahead of the qualifiers in Dubai, the Afghans play some
warm-up games in Sri Lanka. Kabir is happy for once
because he has had the team for a significant amount of
time, and gets to know the players' individual strengths and
weaknesses. They are fitter than they have ever been and

they are properly prepared for the tournament – another example of the way the team is progressing.

There is a welcome surprise for the players: Taj is back as an assistant to Kabir. Taj hasn't been a particularly keen supporter of his replacement. Only recently Taj was heard accusing him of being too defensive and not adapting his team's play with the Twenty20 format in mind. However, Kabir needs Taj as back-up for this new stage in the team's development. There will be a lot more individual coaching and morale boosting needed, and for all his faults no one knows the players better than Taj.

For Taj it is a vindication of sorts. After being dumped out of Afghan cricket it is a proud moment when he is invited back into the fold. It is reassuring to know he is still needed in some capacity. Taj has lost none of his bustle and arrogance. He will tell people that although he is an assistant coach this is just a title, in practice, he brags, he is actually the man in charge.

With improved resources, scouting has been made easier, resulting in some interesting additions to the pool of players. One new recruit, from northern Afghanistan, is Mirwais Ashraf, a blond-haired, blue-eyed man who the players call 'Flinty' after the English cricketer Andrew Flintoff. Another player that has been drafted in is Aftab Alam, yet another of Taj's brothers. Hasti Gul has retired from international cricket and has taken up a position on the new cricket board. Kabir feels there is enhanced competition for places now, making the team stronger than it's ever been. From his experience of international cricket he knows that the spirit of competition is important in bonding the squad – the top players are always playing for their places as well as their country.

Dubai is a city of contrasts: there are the obscenely rich, who earn massive, tax-free salaries and live a life of pampered luxury; and the poor manual labourers, who live in virtual slavery but keep the city functioning. They build the skyscrapers, drive the cabs and pick up the rubbish. Many of them come from Afghanistan and, as it's free to come and watch the cricket, they will be out in force to support their team. The fixture list is given some added spice as the third group game is against the USA. But before they meet cricketers from the world's most powerful nation, they have to face Ireland and Scotland, both out for revenge after the 50-over World Cup qualifiers in South Africa.

Only two of the eight teams will go through to the World Twenty20 finals but Afghanistan, given their unshakeable self-belief, feel that over 20 overs there is no one as good as them. Despite losing a couple of the warm-up games in Sri Lanka they are confident. So far they have done well in every Twenty20 competition they have entered: their first was the ACC Twenty20 Cup in 2007 where they finished joint winners with Oman, they went on to win the tournament in 2009. Now they want to prove themselves in this format against the world's best non-Test nations.

Despite their relative lack of Twenty20 experience, Afghanistan start well and beat both Ireland (by 13 runs) and Scotland (by 14 runs). Noor Ali scores 42 against

Ireland and Nabi 43 against the Scots. With the ball Karim returns figures of three for 17 in the first match and Hamid three for 32 in the second.

The conditions suit the Afghans. The temperature never drops lower than the high twenties and the air is dry. The wickets, baked by the sun, are hard. The Afghans have grown up playing in these conditions. The thousands of Afghans who call Dubai home have come out to support their team and the support is particularly vocal for their third and final group match against the USA. Afghanistan have yet to feel the pride of walking out to play a game in front of their home supporters, but this is what it might be like.

The two teams meet at Dubai Sports City cricket stadium, a 25,000-seater arena in the middle of the desert – one of four purpose-built stadiums which will make up a futuristic 'sports city' when completed. Although the stadium is modern – and has an impressive, space-age design – it is underused and the outside looks unfinished. Turnstiles are off their hinges or locked shut, metal gates sit in stacks, waiting to be installed, and the stairway up to the stadium trails off into a dusty patch of car park. Inside the stadium though the conditions are perfect and the pitch immaculate.

There has been huge interest in the fixture in the international media, for obvious reasons. The match has really got the Afghan players fired up. Publicly, they maintain decorum, saying it is no more than a cricket match; privately they say they want to beat the USA more than any other team they have ever played.

The two sides almost met in Jersey but the USA lost to Nepal and were eliminated at the group stage. The USA are only in the World Twenty20 qualifiers because the ICC is determined to encourage cricket to grow in America and they thought a place in the competition would help. The sport is still very much on the fringes of the American sporting psyche, none of the players on the national team is American-born and the vast majority of the squad learnt their cricket in the Caribbean. But they are no mugs as they have already shown at this tournament, cruising to a six-wicket victory against Scotland in their opening game.

None of this means anything to the Afghans; they want to beat the USA to show the world that, despite or perhaps because of everything going on in their country, they are capable of beating a superpower. Cricinfo, the popular cricket website, calls the game 'a politically charged encounter' and compares it to the USA soccer team facing Iran (as they did in the 1998 World Cup in France) or the baseball team playing Cuba. The Afghan players also want revenge for Rahmat Wali, the former player, killed by American troops.

The tie is given more spice, as if it needs it, because if the USA don't win they are out of the tournament. A win for Afghanistan will not absolutely guarantee them a place in the Super Fours but their run-rate at the moment makes it look pretty likely.

The game starts at noon; as it is February the temperature is a pleasant 25 degrees. It is a calm, sunny day and Afghanistan win the toss and choose to bat. As soon as the

Americans bowl the first over it is clear that the pitch is giving a lot of help to the seamers. In the third over with the score on five, Sherzad is back in the pavilion for a duck and batting first looks like a disastrous decision. When Noor Ali is run out in the eighth over things start to look bleak. Both batsmen have been in great form but here, in this politically important match, they are out before Afghanistan reach 40 runs.

Taj paces the boundary sweating, staring at the scoreboard and shouting orders. Kabir remains unflustered, sitting resolutely in the players' area. Despite the loss of the openers Afghanistan start to pile on the runs. Nowroz top scores with a steady 30 off 48 balls. Karim is stumped on 25 but it is Nabi, after impressing against Ireland, who saves the day again with a quick-fire unbeaten 26 off 26 balls, including one six and two fours. Afghanistan finish on 135 for four, not a monumental score but one they are confident of defending.

Sharpour opens the bowling. He had been dropped for the trip to Argentina as certain members of the Cricket Federation felt he choked in important games. Against the USA, probably the most important game of his life, there is no sense he is bottling it. As he runs in from his marker the crowd of around 2,000 Afghans bang drums and wave flags and homemade signs. One group of supporters has printed out all the letters of 'Afghanistan', each one coloured black, green or red after the national flag.

Opening the bowling with Sharpour is new recruit Mirwais Ashraf. Their first six overs yield only 20 runs, and their stingy spell sets the tone. In the eighth over, Mirwais' tight bowling is rewarded with a wicket. In the 12th and 13th overs two more wickets fall, one to Nabi and one to Hamid from the first ball he bowls. Hamid takes two more wickets, including one with a beautiful yorker that uproots one of the stumps and sends it tumbling across the field. In the final over the USA require an impossible 38. Sharpour has no inclination of letting them even get close. They take eight runs from the over, but have a batsman run out. Afghanistan win by 29 runs. Taj, Kabir and the players are jubilant. They have beaten the USA and qualified for the Super Fours.

Going through with them into the next stage of the competition are the favourites Ireland, the Netherlands and the hosts the UAE. First up for Afghanistan are the Dutch – but it's the same old story. Put in to bat, Afghanistan never really get going. They scrape to an unconvincing 128 for nine. The Netherlands, who beat Afghanistan in South Africa, again prove too strong, and reach a winning total in the 19th over. Sharpour, who has bowled so well against the USA and Scotland, is partly to blame, his two overs go for 20 runs and he drops a catch.

The defeat has sharpened their focus. Victory in their next match, against the UAE, a team who had also beaten them in South Africa, is essential to get into the final and get their coveted place in the West Indies. The contest will follow the only other remaining game in which Ireland face the Netherlands. Both matches are in effect semi-finals, the winner of each qualifying for the final to be played later in the day.

A crowd of over 5,000 has assembled at the Dubai Sports City. It is the biggest of the tournament, partly because it is held on a Saturday – for many in the city, a day off. Adding to the numbers are various dignitaries. Zakhilwal, the President of the Afghan Cricket Board, has flown in for the final, as have a number of politicians and businessmen. It is a big day for everyone. The authorities are wise to the possible problems the match might bring. The Afghan supporters have been put in the upper tier of the stadium to stop them running onto the pitch. And it's a sensible precaution. The crowd goes wild from the start. Some people have taken off their shoes and sandals and are banging them against the plastic seats; others jump up and down, out of control and beside themselves with excitement. Men bang drums, play toula flutes and a small section dance the free, floaty Attan dance, non-stop. They spin maniacally, flicking their long hair with each rotation – twisting and turning their hands in small precise circles.

The noise from the Afghan fans is, at times, deafening. The air is thick with the smell of sweat and tobacco smoke and heavy with anticipation. 'Afghanistan,' one cries; 'Zindabad,' hundreds reply in unison. Long live Afghanistan. 'Shabash. Shabash.' Come on. Come on. Most of them are dressed in the long shalwar kameez robes. Several have made outfits out of black, red and green material. One has fashioned a top hat out of the national colours. The older men wear turbans; many of the younger ones have mullets or heavily styled, gelled hair, in the Bollywood style. All the older men and most of the

THE WORLD CUP DREAM COMES TRUE

younger ones have beards, one or two have magnificent handlebar moustaches, drooping down below their chins. There are no women in the crowd.

Some supporters just scream, piercing and high pitched as if they are in pain, but it is a scream of unadulterated joy. It's a hard life for many of them in Dubai. It's not often they will get to see their national team playing cricket in front of them and what's more a win would see them go to the World Cup. They are ecstatic. Every few minutes someone screams, 'Allah Akbar.' God is great.

Twenty20 cricket seems like a perfect fit for the Afghan crowd. They love the big hits and the fast bowlers. They 'ohh' and 'ahh'; cheer and scream. If the ball is hit in the air they shout and whoop, sometimes right up until a player catches it. If the player drops it the cheers resume again, louder than before. If the ball hits the boundary the whoops are ratcheted up even higher. The crowd also celebrate the opposition's misfortune, not just dropped catches, but misfields, players who trip up and batting mistakes. The Afghan fans also cheer the opposition when they hit big. They really like the big hits.

Those that know a bit about cricket chant for wickets, fours and sixes. Afghan flags, some measuring three metres wide, hang everywhere. When a player does well, the flags are lifted into the air and shaken furiously.

Far below on the perfect grass pitch – Hamid Hassan, the tall, well-built fast bowler from Nanghar in eastern Afghanistan, is pumped up. Around his head he has a blue headband, around his wrists two sweatbands and on his cheeks he has painted the Afghan flag. If he looks like a soldier it is no coincidence, he has modelled himself on Rambo, the renegade super-fighter played in the films by his hero Sylvester Stallone. He is ready for a fight.

The Afghan bowling attack is electric. They pummel the UAE batsmen, reducing them to 100 for nine. The wicket is flat and slow but it is still an amazing achievement. Hamid takes two wickets and a catch. His best friend, Nabi, takes three wickets with his off-breaks. The 25-year-old father of two is modesty to Hamid's arrogance. Hamid celebrates his wickets by falling to his knees, cartwheeling or thrusting his arms into the air and letting out a scream; Nabi celebrates with a high-five and a hug.

Afghanistan chase down the runs but make hard work of it. Noor Ali top scores with an unbeaten 38 but there are scares aplenty along the way. Asghar and Noor Ali stitch together a partnership of 40 for the fourth wicket but when Asghar is out, caught on the boundary, with the score on 88 and two more wickets fall quickly, Taj's fingernails get shorter by the minute. They get the runs, but only with three balls to spare.

The Afghan fans flood onto to the pitch, having found a way from the top tier down, to celebrate with the players. They hoist them on their shoulders, dance in the outfield and charge around dancing. Taj joins them in celebration, not only is he overjoyed to be back with his team, but the team he raised in the refugee camps will be playing in a world final. It is hardly possible to understand how much this means to the players and the nation. For the first time ever an Afghan team is going to a world sporting finals competition – no one would have predicted that the sport would be cricket.

There is little time to celebrate. The players have to return to the pitch moments later to face Ireland again in the final. The players are all feeling good. Both teams are through to the World Twenty20 competition, but Afghanistan want to win. The winner of the UAE event will join South Africa and India in Group C while the losing finalist will join Group D, which includes the West Indies and England. Afghanistan want India.

They get their wish. Ireland win the toss and choose to bat. They score a decent 142 in their 20 overs, losing eight wickets. But the Afghans are on fire and chase the score down in 18 overs, Karim hits 34 and Sherzad an unbeaten 65. When it's over Taj, who once again is in tears, grabs the stadium microphone. Firstly he warns the fans not to invade the pitch, which they don't (there are rumours that security made an announcement saying anyone on the pitch would be deported) and then he presses his phone against the microphone and plays the national anthem. It is a scratchy recording but it silences the crowd. Taj stands hand on heart, tears streaming down his face. Kabir, normally so cool and emotionless, also looks close to tears. It is a priceless moment.

But for all Taj's bluster and belief it is Kabir who has masterminded the team. He has taken them from a ragbag collection of refugee players and forged them into a professional unit. Even in victory Kabir remains modest. He keeps saying how proud he is of his boys, but without him, of this the players have no doubt, they wouldn't be on the way to the World Twenty20 finals. Kabir encouraged the boys, helped them grow, supported them and believed in them. His belief has been rewarded.

After the anthem Sami, who has a smile as wide as his face, starts running around the players screaming 'zero kilometre' and 'Toyota Corolla' because an Afghan businessman has promised every player on the team a brand new Toyota car – hence the zero kilometres.

The Afghan players are treated to dinner. It is a superb Afghan feast of kebab and rice. Karim, who has made friends with some of the Irish players, takes food down to them in the lobby. In South Africa when they met, one of the players had wondered where the suicide bombs were, today they are equals and chat like old friends.

There is more good news. Before they return home the ACC announces that as soon as arrangements can be made Afghanistan will use the Sharjah cricket ground as their home ground. This means they will have a top-quality ground to play on, one in which they will be guaranteed a good, partisan crowd similar to the one they have just entertained in Dubai. Things are changing fast.

The next stop for the team is the West Indies and the World Twenty20. That will take them to almost exactly two years after they opened their World Cup qualification campaign against Japan in Jersey.

Chapter 14

On the World Stage

ST LUCIA, MAY 2010

En route for the West Indies there is something they need to do. The team has been asked to appear in a photo shoot and video for a mobile phone company. The players are to be the faces of the company's new Afghan-wide advertising campaign. This is big news. For the shoot, which takes place in a warehouse in Dubai and on the cricket pitch in Sharjah, a director has been flown over from Bollywood and the make-up lady is from Argentina. For the photos the players are required to hit a ball strung from the ceiling on a piece of string, mocking the movements they make on the pitch. Hamid is undoubtedly the star. He had to do a separate video in which, dressed in a tracksuit top, sweatbands, tracksuit bottoms and a trendy pair of Nikes, he carries out a warm-up routine to a Bolly-wood song then tries to catch a psychedelic, computer-generated, ball. He finishes the advert with a dance.

The players are delighted to find out that for the last part of their journey to the West Indies they are flying business class. It's the first time any of them has flown anything but economy. With the advert completed and the increased comfort, the players really feel like stars. They might not have the millions that the India players are getting paid, but they are finally being given a salary of a few hundred dollars a month, and they are, in Afghanistan at least, becoming stars. They no longer feel like imposters. They feel like they have proven themselves and can now compete both on the pitch and in the glamour stakes.

Taj Malik hasn't slept for days. He's jetlagged, nervous and very, very late for the most important event in his life. He bustles out of the tiny George Charles airport in St Lucia, a rucksack slung over his shoulder and a laptop bag in his hand, and jumps into the waiting car, which speeds off with the police outrider's siren blaring. There is half an hour to get to the stadium before Afghanistan line up against India in the first match of the World Twenty20 finals. It's a moment he has waited for all his life – his country, playing cricket, his sport, in a world-class tournament. The fact that the match is against India, one of the best teams in the world, is just the last piece of the beautiful jigsaw. He's dreamt about it and pictured it in his mind, but now it is really going to happen. And if people don't hurry up and get out of the way of the speeding car, he is going to miss it.

Getting here has been one hell of a journey. His unshaven

face, unwashed body and the anxious sweat infusing the crumpled clothes and ruffled hair attest to that. A pair of flash, sporty, mirrored, wrap-around sunglasses, the type cricketers favour, cover the bags under his eyes. He has flown from Afghanistan to St Lucia via Dubai, London and Barbados. But he very nearly didn't make it.

First his visa was held up at the British embassy in Islamabad. Then, due to the volcanic eruption in Iceland, an ash cloud grounded his flight from Dubai and finally when he arrived in Dubai ready to catch a flight to London, where he would transfer to the Caribbean, he stepped outside for a cigarette and lost his passport. To this day, he has no idea how he came to lose it but luckily someone handed it in to the police, unluckily not in time for him to make his connecting flight to London.

By the time he arrived in London he had missed his flight to Barbados and when he finally arrived in the Caribbean, it was the day before the match, and all the flights from Barbados to St Lucia, where the first game was to be played, were fully booked.

Friends sent him messages and emails telling him to take a taxi. He sent increasingly furious responses telling them there was sea between Barbados and St Lucia. A taxi was impossible.

Finally he managed to get on a flight on the morning of the game, and here he is – at 9 a.m., with the anthems set for 9.30. He has to hear his national anthem. The hairs on the back of his neck stand on end every time it is played and he has to fight back tears. Today it will be extra special, not only will everyone in the stadium hear it but it will be broadcast on television and heard across 181 countries. 181! At last, Taj thinks, people will hear about Afghanistan and think of something other than war.

Today is a day of many firsts. It is the first time any Afghan team has appeared on television across the world. It is the first time any team from the country has played in the finals of a major sporting event and it is the first time the team has played a top Test nation. But it is not the first time the Afghan national anthem has been played in St Lucia. Yesterday, while the team practiced at the stadium, the steel band practised. Some of the players sung the words:

Da Watan Afghanistan dai (The land is Afghanistan)
da izat de har Afghan dai (it is the pride of every Afghan)
Kor de sul, kor de ture (The land of peace, the land of the sword)
har bacai ye qahraman dai. (each of its sons is brave.)

When they finished, the players, some of whom seemed to be crying, took a moment to applaud the band. The tears are understandable. Emotions are running high. Two years ago they opened their World Cup qualification campaign against Japan in Jersey; today they face India, winner of the inaugural World Twenty20 in 2007.

The police outrider makes short work of the traffic and Taj arrives at the turn for the Beausejour Stadium at 9.20 a.m. Ten minutes to go. A long drive leads up to the stadium building; the setting is magnificent. Sponsors' flags fly, schoolchildren wave signs with fours and sixes on them and Indian fans, some wearing traditional dress, walk up to the stadium, which is hugged by lush green hills. The sparkling Caribbean Sea is only a mile away. The sun shines. The sky is cloudless. It is the perfect backdrop to a televised world debut.

As Taj pulls up at the stadium his tribulations are not over. How much can one man take? Ten years of no salary, a sacking, a reinstatement, threats, coups, violence and now this. The liaison officer has forgotten his pass and security won't let him into the stadium.

He pleads with the guards, while hurried phone calls are made and people dash around trying to find his pass. Five minutes until the anthem. He tells the security guards he is the assistant coach and he must be let in.

Three minutes to go.

Finally his pass arrives. He rushes upstairs, strips off his T-shirt, puts on a sleeveless blue Afghan training shirt and joins the team. He has made it – unbelievable.

Before the anthem a group of children, dressed in cricket whites, carry the two country's flags onto the pitch. As they do, Vangelis' 'Conquest of Paradise' booms through the speakers. Deep, moody and atmospheric, the music rebounds around the stadium, which at this time in the morning is still only a quarter full.

Next are the anthems. The moment the first note is struck, the tears start to trickle down Taj's face. There have been so many moments of extreme emotion since he arrived back in Afghanistan in 2001 – some of happiness, many of anger, frustration and disappointment – but this is one of joy, pure and simple.

The teams line up. On one side the Indians: among them MS Dhoni, Yuvraj Singh, Virender Sehwag, Yusuf Pathan and Harbhajan Singh. They are millionaires, household names and between them veterans of hundreds of televised games. On the other side the Afghans: Karim Saddiq, Hamid Hassan, Mohammed Nabi, Mohammed Sherzad, Noor Ali, Raees Ahmadzai and Asghar Stanikzai and the others. They have only just started getting paid and are pocketing no more than US$800 a month, they are virtual unknowns and they have never played in a match like this before. In the press conference the day before, Dhoni, the Indian captain, admitted he couldn't name a single Afghan player. The Afghans cannot only name the whole Indian team but can reel off statistics for each player.

Afghanistan lose the toss and are put in to bat. Opening the batting are Noor Ali Zadran and Karim Saddiq, Taj's younger brother. Karim Saddiq doesn't really walk to the crease; he swaggers. Once again though, Karim's innate unshakeable confidence projects from his short frame and his presence fills the stadium.

Karim isn't nervous, he doesn't 'do' nervous, and besides, he is where he has always believed he belongs... on the world stage. His only concern is the bat he has to use. A friend in London had acquired it from a manu-facturer – they have promised him £1,000 if he scores

50 runs. The bat they have given him though is rubbish. He has scoured St Lucia's sports shops trying to find the sponsor's stickers, he thought he'd just put them on his old bat, but he couldn't find any. He is stuck using the new bat. Still £1,000 is £1,000.

Karim might not be nervous but Noor Ali, who shuffles onto the pitch ahead of him, certainly is. He swings his bat over his shoulder in a windmill and wiggles his body from side to side, partly to warm up and partly to rid himself of his nerves.

To clear his mind and rid himself of some of the tingling nerves, he leans down and touches the grass, looks towards the heavens and then utters a prayer:

In the name of Allah, the Beneficent, the Merciful,
Show us the straight path.
The path of those whom Thou hast favoured;
Not the path of those who earn Thine anger
Nor of those who go astray.

At least, he thinks, he has his faith. With faith comes strength and self-belief and he draws on it today more than ever before. He also made sure to follow his superstition of dressing right side first.

This is it, he thinks to himself. This is everything I have dreamed of. He can show all those who said he was a waster, who said cricket would never get him anywhere, just how wrong they were – including many of his relatives. It is always his brother, the bus driver in Walthamstow in

London who'd sent part of his salary back to Afghanistan to support his family, that they praised. Noor Ali, who has only just started being paid to play cricket and had dropped out of law school to follow his passion, was always ridiculed. They thought cricket was just a ridiculous game, worse than that it was a foreign game. He'd let his intellect go to waste on frivolous, vainglorious pursuits. Today he will show them.

Under his helmet he wears a red and blue headband. He'd fashioned it by cutting a strip out of the leg of his tracksuit bottoms. By the time he gets on the pitch his bandana is already wet with sweat. It isn't the heat – Khost in Afghanistan, where he learnt the game and still lives, gets hotter than the 29 degrees it is on this day – it is a nervous sweat. As if he needs a further reminder of the magnitude of the day, when he looks to his right the stadium screen, looming large by the steel band, is broadcasting his image to the world.

For comfort he looks down at his bat and sees, scrawled in red biro, the word 'Ricky', reminding him of his cricketing hero – the indomitable Ricky Ponting. He doesn't want to let him down.

These two players with very different demeanours make it to the crease. They have shared the extraordinary journey of the Afghan cricket team from trials on a scrub pitch surrounded by burnt-out shells of military helicopters to this glorious moment beamed to 181 countries.

From the boundary Taj watches his brother and pinches himself. In his wildest dreams this was what he saw, an Afghan team playing a top Test nation with television cameras, a huge crowd and the world watching. Afghanistan has achieved many unique feats to get from that battle-scarred ground in Kabul to the Beausejour Stadium in St Lucia. Without doubt, though, the most remarkable aspect of their momentous, unrivalled sprint to prominence is that at home; while the team has battling with bat and ball thousands of miles away, their country was being torn apart by war. It is a country considered one of the most dangerous and poverty-stricken in the world. There's not even a proper cricket pitch to be found there. They have had amazing obstacles to overcome to get here. Rarely in human sport has the courage and determination of a team been so apparent.

But back at the beginning Taj knew something no one else knew, he knew that his team, his guys, the boys he had known all his life, wanted this more than anyone had ever wanted anything, and they believed. Not only that, but they had talent, real talent. They were, he thought, some of the most gifted cricketers he had ever seen. With talent and belief, anything was possible.

As Taj remembers the dark places they have been, Kumar, the Indian fast bowler, approaches the crease and lets fly an outswinging delivery. It's pitching outside off stump. Noor Ali raises his bat. Two years ago he would have tried to thump it out of the ground. He lets the ball zip safely past his wicket. With that Afghanistan cricket takes its hard-won place on the world stage.

Afterword

Getting to the World Twenty20 was not a flash in the pan for the Afghan team. In January 2011 they are ranked 14th in the world. Aside from the ten Test nations only the Netherlands, Ireland and Kenya are above them. In 2001, when the team first started, they were bottom of the pile – 90th in the world. To say it has been a remarkable rise is not doing justice to the Afghans and their journey. Afghanistan has the 13th lowest GDP of any nation in the world; this is despite the investment of billions of dollars of aid since 2001. In early 2011 the country still doesn't have a national academy or a stadium. The academy the Olympic Committee provided that was used in the early days was reclaimed when the Afghan Cricket Board was formed and all funds from the ICC and ACC stopped going through the Olympic Committee's bank account. The team now trains in Sharjah or at Hasti's private academy in Jalalabad. The foundation stone was laid in

Kabul in November 2010 for the Kabul National Cricket Stadium and work is due to finish in July 2011. There are also plans to build another eight stadiums.

Though they lost both their games at the World Twenty20 tournament, there was no shame in their performances. They showed talent and tenacity in all aspects of their game. Noor Ali scored a superb half-century in their seven-wicket defeat against India, putting on a 68-run stand for the fourth wicket with Asghar. They lost to South Africa by 59 runs but not before Hamid bowled superbly to take three for 21.

Later that same month, 24 teams from Afghanistan's 34 provinces took part in a 50-over domestic tournament. It was the largest tournament ever held in Afghanistan and was televised live across the country. At the end of September and start of October, 24 provinces took part in a regional Twenty20 tournament.

In July 2010, the Afghan team finished third in the ICC Division One – the same performance in South Africa in 2009 would have taken them to the World Cup.

In October the ICC announced that from 2015 the World Cup would be a ten-team tournament, open only to the top ten Test nations. This decision means that for Afghanistan and other non-Test nations, the highest they can get is the 20-over version. Considering how much the ICC has done to help cricket grow in Afghanistan it seems a ludicrous decision. Why would they spend so much money helping cricket grow outside of the top nations and then deny them the chance to appear in the sport's premier tournament?

Afghanistan didn't let the disappointment stop them winning. In November 2010 cricket debuted at the Asian Games in Guangzhou, China. Afghanistan took the silver medal and the notable scalp of Pakistan along the way, before losing to Bangladesh in the final.

On 6 December 2010, Afghanistan won the final of the Intercontinental Cup, the premier non-Test competition that included the Netherlands, Ireland, Scotland, Canada and a Zimbabwe XI.

There have also been numerous changes in personnel along the way. After a game in Scotland, Kabir accused the board of interference – apparently they had been critical of him for not enforcing the follow-on despite the fact that the team went on to win by 229 runs. He texted the chairman objecting to the meddling from the board only to hear two days later in a press release issued by the board that his 'resignation' had been accepted. It was a shameful way to treat someone who had given so much to the team and taken them so far in such a short space of time. Rashid Latif, another Pakistani Test player, who had been assisting Kabir, became the new coach. Kabir is now back coaching the United Arab Emirates.

For most of the players that Kabir nurtured and got the best out of, life has been much improved by their involvement with the team. Hasti Gul has left his cricketing days behind him but is now the technical manager on the board. He also runs an academy in Jalalabad and there is talk that he may become the team's full-time bowling coach. Ahmad Shah has been appointed chief selector.

Raees Ahmadzai, who retired during the West Indies competition, was not rewarded with a position on the cricket board, despite years of dedicated service. He runs a charity that organises cricket camps in Afghanistan. During 2010, along with the charity Afghan Connection, they held ten cricket camps for over 600 boys and girls. At one camp 12,000 spectators turned up to watch. His work is supported by MCC. Dawlat Ahmadzai has been appointed Domestic Development Manager and is now working for the Afghan Cricket Board.

Hamid, Nabi, Gulbadeen, Sharpour, Nowroz, Sherzad, Sami, Noor Ali, Mirwais and Asghar continue to play for the national team. The players now, finally, receive a salary of around US$800 a month. Allah Dad Noori is involved in local cricket but is no longer involved in the national team. His brother Khaliq Dad, however, still plays for the national team on occasions.

Taj quit as assistant coach after the World Twenty20 because of a dispute about bonuses; he was later appointed coach of the A team and still holds that position. His contribution and personal odyssey from cricket fanatic to 'Father of Afghan Cricket' is one of the most remarkable stories in modern sport.

Acknowledgments

First and foremost I would like to thank Taj Malik Alam, who generously allowed me to follow the team. Taj never asked for anything in return except that I tell the story faithfully I hope I haven't let him down. Kabir Khan, who replaced Taj, was equally welcoming and gracious, and without him I wouldn't have been able to continue the story. I would also like to thank members of the Afghan Cricket Board who welcomed me and encouraged the project. Allah Dad Noori, who persuaded the Taliban to allow cricket and set up the first Afghan team, Sherzada Massoud, Bashir Stanikzai and everyone else in cricket in Afghanistan deserves recognition for what they have done, it's incredible.

Above all though I thank the team. I wouldn't have had a story without them and each and every one welcomed me like I was a player. They took me to their homes, shared their food with me and made me feel welcome. I can't thank them enough. It was an amazing privilege and one I will never forget. They made me realise how much one can achieve if one believes in oneself and it is a lesson I will never forget. I think about what you guys have achieved often and I'm still amazed by it.

This project started as a documentary film (www. outoftheashes.tv) that was screened on the BBC. Leslie Knott and Lucy Martens, my partners in that project, have offered their memories and help with the book. Without them this would have never happened. I owe both of you a huge debt of gratitude. I spent two years travelling the world and watching cricket with you and it was a lot of fun.

Without Ed Faulkner at Virgin Books, this book would never have got off the ground, he commissioned it. From the first moment I met Ed I knew he was the right person to do this book. He helped and encouraged me more than I thought possible. He was always at the end of the phone or email with a constructive thought and a kind word. Thanks Ed for making the project as painless as possible.

At Virgin I also owe a great deal of thanks to Clare Wallis whose enthusiasm for the project was infectious. Simon and Martin Toseland have helped shape this book and have aided it greatly. Julian Flanders, with his deep knowledge of cricket and critical but kind eye, also helped immeasurably.

I'd also like to thank Matthew Hamilton, my agent, who saw a magazine piece I'd written on the team, got in touch and encouraged me to write a book. For a Spurs fan you're not a bad guy.

Many people kindly helped me with translation and context. Emal Passerly, one of the finest journalists I have met, went above and beyond the call of duty in his help. He was always available and willing to answer a question or clear something up. Thank you Emal.

Ahmad Wali, Ilham Yassini, Hilal Yassini, Adnan Rashid, Khalil Khan, Ali Ahmad, Hashim Shakour, Bilal Sarwary, Sulaiman Khan, Azam Shah, Inam ur Rahman, Raess

Ahmadzai, Atiq Zafry, Roohullah Janat and Mohammad Ismael all helped more than they needed to.

Martin Fletcher at *The Times* suggested back in 2005 that I write an article on cricket in Afghanistan. Without that suggestion it is unlikely this book would have been commissioned.

The following each played a special part in the development of Afghan cricket and gave freely of their time and memories: Iqbal Sikander, Andrew Banks, William Reeve, Stuart Bentham, John Stephenson, Mark Scrase-Dickins, Peter Frawley, Robin Marlar, Sarah Fane and her children and Paul Carroll.

I would also like to thank Debbie Moore and Matthew Fleming at Marylebone Cricket Club.

Huge thanks to Romaine Lancaster who helped with research.

Aryn Baker, Alice Fordham, Yvonne Hutchison, Nick Schifrin, Jerome Starkey and particularly Julius Cavendish and Mike Popham all read parts of the book and gave me feedback. It helped more than you can imagine. Christina Lamb and Jon Lee Anderson have also given time and great advice.

At the International Cricket Council, Chris Hurst deserves special thanks for all the help he gave me. Aarti Dabas and Lucy Benjamin were also very encouraging of this project.

At the Asian Cricket Council Shahriar Khan was a huge help.

I'd also like to thank: Ben Keeling, Juliet Love, Sam Mendes, Julie Blumenthal, Nick Fraser from Storyville, Greg Sanderson from BBC, Tom Roberts, Gregor Lyon, Ethan Mitchell, Nikolaus Gruebeck, Sophie Toumazis and Suzie Schilling at

TPR Media, Izzy and Francis Haydon, John Butt, Claire Billet, George Chignell, Belinda Bowling, Graeme Smith, Miles Amoore, Alex Strick van Linschoten, Felix Kuehn, Oliver Englehart, Richard Beeston, Mark Hudson, Tom Coghlan, Anthony Loyd, Sam Kiley, Lesley Thorne, Zygmun Jablonski, Michael Friedman, Grandma Nora and Maurice, Auntie Kim, Uncle Allen, George Morris, Briony Morris, Auntie Sheena and Uncle Ian, Rob Hurst, Sarah Hurst, Phillip Welch, John Williams, Morgan Williams, Nadene Ghouri, Neill and Milly Ghosh, Gemma Hyde, Joseph O'Neill, Andy Bull, Ed Smith, Nick Lockwood, His Excellency Homayoun Tandar and Rachel Wexler, Jez Lewis and Rebecca Day at Bungalow Town productions.

Thanks to Georgia Hardinge for her generosity in lending me her flat in Portugal to write in, it was a real sanctuary. Martin and all the Shelley family have offered me support and encouragement above and beyond, thank you.

A special thanks to Mike Atherton for writing the foreword.

I'd like to thank my dad for getting me interested in cricket and travel and inspiring me to go to Afghanistan in the first place. I know if you were still here you would have loved the Afghan team. My mum supported this crazy venture from the start and I couldn't have done it without her. To my brother, Charlie, and sister, Liz, for being my best friends. Everything in life is so much easier when I know you guys are there for me.

To Victoria Shelley, without you this wouldn't have happened. You inspire me and amaze me. Thank you.

The Road to
the World Cup

MATCH RESULTS AND SCORECARDS

ICC WORLD CRICKET LEAGUE, DIVISION 5, JERSEY, MAY 2008

AFGHANISTAN v JAPAN

50-over match played at Victoria College, 23 May, Group B – Afghanistan won by 92 runs

Match details: Toss: Afghanistan **Man of the Match:** Karim Sadiq: **Points Awarded:** Afghanistan 2, Japan 0

Afghanistan: 179 all out (35.4 overs)

Batsman		Bowler	Runs	Balls	4s	6s
Nowroz Mangal*		b Giles-Jones	22	20	3	1
Karim Sadiq+	c Beath	b Matsubara	47	46	10	0
Asghar Stanikzai	c Irie	b Hagihara	14	21	3	0
Ahmad Shah	lbw	b Hagihara	28	38	3	1
Mohammad Nabi	c Giles-Jones	b Matsubara	22	15	2	1
Raees Ahmadzai	lbw	b Hagihara	1	7	0	0
Samiullah Shinwari		b Hagihara	0	5	0	0
Gulbadeen Naib	not out		22	30	2	1
Hasti Gul	lbw	b Beath	1	2	0	0
Dawlat Ahmadzai		b Beath	0	8	0	0
Hamid Hassan		b Hagihara	7	22	0	0
Extras		(lb1 w14)	15			
TOTAL		**10 wickets for**	**179**			

Bowling	O	M	R	W	Wd	Nb
PJ Giles-Jones	7	0	46	1	1	0
NA Miyaji	10	1	61	0	5	0
Y Matsubara	6	0	33	2	3	0
T Hagihara	7.4	0	25	5	3	0
GB Beath	5	1	13	2	2	0

Fall of wickets: 1-33 (Nowroz Mangal); 2-90 (Karim Sadiq); 3-94 (Asghar Stanikzai); 4-137 (Mohammad Nabi); 5-141 (Ahmad Shah); 6-142 (Samiullah Shenwari); 7-143 (Raees Ahmadzai); 8-144 (Hasti Gul); 9-146 (Dawlat Ahmadzai); 10-179 (Hamid Hassan)

Japan: 87 all out (40.2 overs)

Batsman		Bowler	Runs	Balls	4s	6s
T Chino+	c Karim Sadiq	b Dawlat Ahmadzai	0	3		
GB Beath	c Karim Sadiq	b Hamid Hassan	5	38		
M Kobayashi		c&b Hasti Gul	10	35		
K Irie*	lbw	b Hasti Gul	0	3		
CP Jones	c Karim Sadiq	b Hasti Gul	0	17		
Munir Ahmed	c Asghar Stanikzai	b Ahmad Shah	18	37		
PJ Giles-Jones	c Mohammad Nabi	b Hamid Hassan	4	30		
NA Miyaji	not out		19	54		
Y Matsubara	c Karim Sadiq	b Nowroz Mangal	1	12		
T Hagihara		b Ahmad Shah	1	13		
S Nakano	run out		0	3		
Extras		(b2 lb4 w19 nb4)	29			
TOTAL		**10 wickets for**	**87**			

Bowling	O	M	R	W	Wd	Nb
Dawlat Ahmadzai	7.1	3	6	1	2	0
Hasti Gul	10	1	22	3	3	1
Hamid Hassan	10	3	18	2	2	3
Gulbaddeen Naib	4	1	20	0	5	0
Ahmad Shah	4	0	9	2	1	0
Nowroz Mangal	2	0	4	1	1	0
Asghar Stanikzai	1.5	0	2	0	1	0
Mohammad Nabi	1	1	0	0	0	0
Samiullah Shinwari	0.2	0	0	0	0	0

Fall of wickets: 1-0 (Chino); 2-19 (Kobayashi); 3-19 (Irie); 4-21 (Beath); 5-25 (Jones); 6-66 (Munir Ahmed); 7-66 (Giles-Jones); 8-78 (Matsubara); 9-87 (Hagihara); 10-87 (Nakano)

AFGHANISTAN v BAHAMAS

50-over match played at Les Quennevais 1, 24 May, Group B – Afghanistan won by 5 wickets

Match details: Toss: Afghanistan **Man of the Match:** Gulbadeen Naib

Points Awarded: Bahamas 0, Afghanistan 2

Bahamas: 46 all out (24 overs)

Batsman		Bowler	Runs	Balls	4s	6s
GT Taylor	c Asghar Stanikzai	b Dawlat Ahmadzai	1	4	0	0
DG Weakley	lbw	b Dawlat Ahmadzai	0	11	0	0
D Morrison	c Karim Sadiq	b Hamid Hassan	7	42	0	0
JR Barry	run out		8	39	1	0
RA Tappin	lbw	b Hamid Hassan	2	12	0	0
NH Ekanayake+	c Karim Sadiq	b Gulbadeen Naib	1	7	0	0
WN Atkinson*	not out		2	16	0	0
ML Ford	lbw	b Gulbadeen Naib	4	7	1	0
LF Melville		b Gulbadeen Naib	3	6	0	0
AR Ford		b Gulbadeen Naib	0	1	0	0
RP Mitchell		b Gulbadeen Naib	0	1	0	0
Extras		(b2 lb5 w10 nb1)	18			
TOTAL		**10 wickets for**	**46**			

Bowling	O	M	R	W	Wd	Nb
Dawlat Ahmadzai	6	1	14	2	2	1
Hasti Gul	8	5	6	0	2	0
Hamid Hassan	6	0	12	2	4	0
Gulbadeen Naib	4	1	7	5	2	0

Fall of wickets: 1-4 (Taylor); 2-6 (Weakley); 3-29 (Barry); 4-29 (Morrison); 5-31 (Ekanayake); 6-35 (Tappin); 7-42 (Ford); 8-46 (Melville); 9-46 (Ford); 10-46 (Mitchell)

Afghanistan: 49 for 5 (6.3 overs)

Batsman		Bowler	Runs	Balls	4s	6s
Nowroz Mangal*	c Mitchell	b Weakley	18	10	2	1
Karim Sadiq+	lbw	b ML Ford	11	6	2	0
Mohammad Nabi	c Taylor	b Weakley	7	7	1	0
Asghar Stanikzai	c Atkinson	b ML Ford	4	4	1	0
Noor Ali	not out		7	5	1	0
Raees Ahmadzai	c Atkinson	b ML Ford	2	6	0	0
Ahmad Shah	not out		0	1	0	0
Hamid Hassan	did not bat		-			
Gulbadeen Naib	did not bat		-			
Hasti Gul	did not bat		-			
Dawlat Ahmadzai	did not bat		-			
Extras			0			
TOTAL		**5 wickets for**	**49i**			

Bowling	O	M	R	W	Wd	Nb
RP Mitchell	1	0	12	0	0	0
LF Melville	1	0	15	0	0	0
DG Weakley	2.3	0	17	2	0	0
ML Ford	2	0	5	3	0	0

Fall of wickets: 1-28 (Nowroz Mangal); 2-32 (Karim Sadiq); 3-36 (Asghar Stanikzai); 4-40 (Mohammad Nabi); 5-43 (Raees Ahmadzai)

AFGHANISTAN v BOTSWANA

50-over match played at Les Quennevais 2, 26 May, Group B – Afganistan won by 7 wickets

Match details: Toss: Afghanistan **Man of the Match:** Karim Sadiq **Points Awarded:** Botswana 0, Afghanistan 2

Botswana: 128 all out (34.4 overs)

Batsman		Bowler	Runs	Balls	4s	6s
Shahzaib Khan		b Dawlat Ahmadzai	9	28	1	0
S Mohiyuddin	c Nowroz Mangal	b Mohammad Nabi	36	77	3	0
ARM Patel*		c&b Mohammad Nabi	30	50	0	0
K Modise	run out		4	10	0	0
K Kapoor	st Karim Sadiq	b Ahmad Shah	14	26	1	0
JWN Moses		b Hamid Hassan	6	8	0	1
MA Ali		b Hamid Hassan	2	8	0	0
DK Sequeira+		b Hamid Hassan	0	1	0	0
N Tajbhay	st Karim Sadiq	b Mohammad Nabi	0	4	0	0
M Gaolekwe	not out		0	0	0	0
M Barot		b Mohammad Nabi	0	2	0	0
Extras		(b9 lb4 w8 nb6)	27			
TOTAL		10 wickets for	128			

Bowling	O	M	R	W	Wd	Nb
Dawlat Ahmadzai	6	0	19	1	1	1
Hasti Gul	4	0	18	0	0	1
Gulbadeen Naib	1	0	4	0	3	0
Ahmad Shah	8	0	20	1	0	0
Hamid Hassan	7	0	19	3	1	4
Mohammad Nabi	5.4	1	20	4	0	0
Nowroz Mangal	3	0	15	0	1	0

Fall of wickets: 1-35 (Shahzaib Khan); 2-79 (Mohiyuddin); 3-90 (Modise); 4-109 (Patel); 5-121 (Moses); 6-126 (Ali); 7-126 (Sequeira); 8-128 (Kapoor); 9-128 (Tajbhay); 10-128 (Barot)

Afghanistan: 129 for 3 (19.5 overs)

Batsman		Bowler	Runs	Balls	4s	6s
Nowroz Mangal*	lbw	b Gaolekwe	1	2	0	0
Karim Sadiq+	c Gaolekwe	b Modise	62	71	6	0
Noor Ali	not out		48	40	6	0
Mohammad Nabi		b Moses	5	4	1	0
Asghar Stanikzai	not out		3	2	0	0
Raees Ahmadzai	did not bat		-			
Dawlat Ahmadzai	did not bat		-			
Ahmad Shah	did not bat		-			
Hasti Gul	did not bat		-			
Hamid Hassan	did not bat		-			
Gulbadeen Naib	did not bat		-			
Extras		(b1 w8 nb1)	10			
TOTAL		3 wickets for	129			

Bowling	O	M	R	W	Wd	Nb
MA Ali	2	0	15	0	0	0
M Gaolekwe	2	0	19	1	1	0
ARM Patel	1	0	8	0	2	0
JWN Moses	1.5	0	12	1	2	0
M Barot	4	0	19	0	1	0
K Kapoor	3	0	16	0	0	0
Shahzaib Khan	3	0	24	0	1	1
K Modise	3	0	15	1	1	0

Fall of wickets: 1-5 (Nowroz Mangal); 2-117 (Karim Sadiq); 3-122 (Mohammad Nabi)

AFGHANISTAN v SINGAPORE

50-over match played at FB Fields, 27 May, Group B – Singapore won by 69 runs

Match details: Toss: Afghanistan **Man of the Match:** Christopher Janik

Points Awarded: Singapore 2, Afghanistan 0

Singapore: 145 all out (29.3 overs)

Batsman		Bowler	Runs	Balls	4s	6s
CR Suryawanshi	c Karim Sadiq	b Dawlat Ahmadzai	26	41	2	1
YOB Mendis	c Mohammad Nabi	b Hasti Gul	0	3	0	0
Syed Ali	c Karim Sadiq	b Mohammad Nabi	21	25	1	1
CR Kumarage*	c Nowroz Mangal	b Mohammad Nabi	32	45	3	0
AE Param		b Hamid Hassan	3	2	0	0
C Janik	c Dawlat Ahmadzai	b Mohammad Nabi	27	27	0	2
B Narender Reddy	c Mohammad Nabi	b Ahmad Shah	6	13	0	0
JK Muruthi	lbw	b Hamid Hassan	3	8	0	0
Shoaib Razak	run out (Gulbadeen Naib)		2	5	0	0
Z Renchum+	c Noor Ali	b Ahmad Shah	0	4	0	0
Rizwan Madakia	not out		6	7	1	0
Extras		(b4 lb6 w7 nb2)	19			
TOTAL		**10 wickets for**	**145**			

Bowling	O	M	R	W	Wd	Nb
Dawlat Ahmadzai	6	2	16	1	0	0
Hasti Gul	6	1	26	1	1	1
Hamid Hassan	6	0	34	2	0	1
Mohammad Nabi	4	0	23	3	1	0
Gulbadeen Naib	2	0	20	0	1	0
Ahmad Shah	5.3	0	16	2	0	0

Fall of wickets: 1-0 (Mendis); 2-33 (Suryawanshi); 3-58 (Syed Ali); 4-61 (Param); 5-125 (Janik); 6-127 (Kumarage); 7-136 (Muruthi); 8-138 (Narender Reddy); 9-138 (Renchum); 10-145 (Shoaib Razak)

Afghanistan: 76 all out (20.2 overs)

Batsman		Bowler	Runs	Balls	4s	6s
Nowroz Mangal*		b Razak	5	29	1	0
Karim Sadiq+	c Narender Reddy	b Param	22	21	5	0
Noor Ali		b Param	0	4	0	0
Asghar Stanikzai	lbw	b Shoaib Razak	0	1	0	0
Gulbadeen Naib	c Renchum	b Janik	7	24	1	0
Mohammad Nabi	c Syed Ali	b Janik	24	24	3	0
Raees Ahmadzai	c Syed Ali	b Janik	3	8	0	0
Ahmad Shah	c Rizwan Madakia	b Janik	3	5	0	0
Hasti Gul		b Param	0	1	0	0
Dawlat Ahmadzai		b C Janik	0	6	0	0
Hamid Hassan	not out		0	1	0	0
Extras		(w11 nb1)	12			
TOTAL		**10 wickets for**	**76**			

Bowling	O	M	R	W	Wd	Nb
Syed Ali	4	1	10	0	0	1
CR Kumarage	3	0	17	0	2	0
AE Param	5	1	15	3	1	0
Shoaib Razak	3	1	12	2	3	0
C Janik	3.2	0	9	5	0	0
Rizwan Madakia	1	0	11	0	0	0
B Narender Reddy	1	0	2	0	0	0

Fall of wickets: 1-31 (Karim Sadiq); 2-33 (Nowroz Mangal); 3-34 (Asghar Stanikzai); 4-39 (Noor Ali); 5-66 (Mohammad Nabi); 6-70 (Gulbadeen Naib); 7-74 (Ahmad Shah); 8-76 (Hasti Gul); 9-76 (Raees Ahmadzai); 10-76 (Dawlat Ahmadzai)

GROUP B – POINTS TABLE

Team	P	W	L	T	N/R	NRR	Pts
Jersey	5	4	0	0	1	+2.46	9
Afghanistan	5	3	1	0	1	+1.63	7
Singapore	5	2	1	0	1	+0.24	7
Botswana	5	1	3	0	1	-0.75	3
Japan	5	0	3	1	1	-1.35	2
Bahamas	5	0	3	1	1	-2.65	2

Jersey and Afghanistan through to the semi-finals.

AFGHANISTAN v NEPAL

50-over match played at Grainville, 30 May, Semi-Final – Afghanistan won by 37 runs

Match details: **Toss:** Afghanistan **Man of the Match:** Mohammad Nabi

Afghanistan: 142 all out (49.3 overs)

Batsman		Bowler	Runs	Balls	4s	6s
Karim Sadiq+		b Das	18	30	1	0
Ahmad Shah		b Das	10	39	0	0
Noor Ali	lbw	b Alam	0	1	0	0
Nowroz Mangal*	c Alam	b Gauchan	7	37	0	0
Asghar Stanikzai	c Khadka	b Regmi	18	55	1	0
Mohammad Nabi	c Regmi	b Pradhan	48	64	3	1
Raees Ahmadzai	c Malla	b Gauchan	22	46	0	1
Samiullah Shinwari	st Chhetri	b Regmi	11	19	0	0
Hasti Gul	c Regmi	b Gauchan	1	4	0	0
Dawlat Ahmadzai	not out		1	2	0	0
Hamid Hassan		b Regmi	0	1	0	0
Extras		(b1 lb2 w2 nb1)	6			
TOTAL		**10 wickets for**	**142**			

Bowling	O	M	R	W	Wd	Nb
M Alam	8	2	13	1	0	0
BK Das	8	3	22	2	0	1
SP Gauchan	8	3	12	3	0	0
P Khadka	7	1	19	0	1	0
B Regmi	8.3	0	30	3	1	0
RK Pradhan	8	0	30	1	0	0
S Regmi	2	0	13	0	0	0

Fall of wickets: 1-26 (Karim Sadiq); 2-29 (Noor Ali); 3-29 (Ahmad Shah); 4-40 (Nowroz Mangal); 5-83 (Asghar Stanikzai); 6-119 (Mohammad Nabi); 7-135 (Raees Ahmadzai); 8-140 (Hasti Gul); 9-142 (Samiullah Shinwari); 10-142 (Hamid Hassan)

Nepal: 105 all out (45.5 overs)

Batsman		Bowler	Runs	Balls	4s	6s
PP Lohani		b Dawlat Ahmadzai	0	2	0	0
MK Chhetri+	c Asghar Stanikzai	b Hamid Hassan	9	66	1	0
S Vesawkar	lbw	b Hasti Gul	3	8	0	0
SP Gauchan	c Asghar Stanikzai	b Dawlat Ahmadzai	9	57	0	0
G Malla	c Mohammad Nabi	b Dawlat Ahmadzai	11	34	0	1
P Khadka		b Hamid Hassan	1	9	0	0
M Alam	c Samiullah Shinwari	b Mohammad Nabi	17	37	1	0
B Regmi		b Mohammad Nabi	10	16	2	0
BK Das*	c Raees Ahmadzai	b Hasti Gul	12	32	0	1
S Regmi	not out		5	13	0	0
RK Pradhan	st Karim Sadiq	b Ahmad Shah	1	6	0	0
Extras		(b4 lb3 w15 nb5)	27			
TOTAL		**10 wickets for**	**105**			

Bowling	O	M	R	W	Wd	Nb
Dawlat Ahmadzai	10	3	18	3	6	0
Hasti Gul	6	2	13	2	5	3
Asghar Stanikzai	2	0	6	0	0	0
Ahmad Shah	1.5	0	4	1	0	0
Hamid Hassan	10	6	12	2	1	2
Karim Sadiq	10	4	30	0	1	0
Mohammad Nabi	6	0	15	2	0	0

Fall of wickets: 1-0 (Lohani); 2-12 (Vesawkar); 3-37 (Chhetri); 4-50 (Gauchan); 5-51 (Malla); 6-55 (Khadka); 7-72 (Regmi); 8-97 (Alam); 9-103 (Das); 10-105 (Pradhan)

AFGHANISTAN v JERSEY

50-over match played at Grainville, 31 May, Final – Afghanistan won by 2 wickets

Match details: **Toss:** Jersey **Man of the Match:** Hasti Gul **Comment:** Both teams qualify for Division 4

Jersey: 80 all out (39.5 overs)

Batsman		Bowler	Runs	Balls	4s	6s
PW Gough		b Hasti Gul	5	22	0	0
SR Carlyon	c Karim Sadiq	b Mohammad Nabi	17	84	1	0
MR Hague*	c Karim Sadiq	b Hasti Gul	0	6	0	0
RC Driver	c Asghar Stanikzai	b Dawlat Ahmadzai	1	5	0	0
ASJ Dewhurst	c Hamid Hassan	b Hasti Gul	4	10	0	0
JM Gough		b Hamid Hassan	23	56	1	0
C Jones		b Hamid Hassan	0	17	0	0
SM Patidar		b Hamid Hassan	4	33	0	0
TP Carlyon	lbw	b Hamid Hassan	0	2	0	0
BM Vowden	run out Hasti Gul		0	0	0	0
RD Minty+	not out		1	7	0	0
Extras		(b2 lb2 w17 nb4)	25			
TOTAL		10 wickets for	80			

Bowling	O	M	R	W	Wd	Nb
Dawlat Ahmadzai	10	3	17	1	4	0
Hasti Gul	10	3	17	3	2	0
Hamid Hassan	9.5	1	27	4	5	4
Mohammad Nabi	7	3	9	1	0	0
Ahmad Shah	3	0	6	0	1	0

Fall of wickets: 1-13 (Gough); 2-13 (Hague); 3-17 (Driver); 4-25 (Dewhurst); 5-67 (Carlyon); 6-71 (Gough); 7-74 (Jones); 8-78 (Carlyon); 9-78 (Vowden); 10-80 (Patidar)

Afghanistan: 81 for 8 (37.4 overs)

Batsman		Bowler	Runs	Balls	4s	6s
Karim Sadiq+	run out (Carlyon)		3	3	0	0
Ahmad Shah	c Minty	b Driver	8	34	1	0
Noor Ali	c Patidar	b Driver	0	2	0	0
Nowroz Mangal*	c Minty	b Carlyon	14	33	1	0
Asghar Stanikzai	lbw	b Hague	10	65	0	0
Mohammad Nabi		b Driver	2	12	0	0
Samiullah Shinwari	lbw	b Driver	0	3	0	0
Raees Ahmadzai	c Minty	b Carlyon	2	18	0	0
Hasti Gul	not out		29	40	2	2
Dawlat Ahmadzai	not out		3	16	0	0
Hamid Hassan	did not bat		-			
Extras		(lb1 w9)	10			
TOTAL		8 wickets for	81			

Bowling	O	M	R	W	Wd	Nb
RC Driver	10	2	26	4	5	0
C Jones	6	1	19	0	1	0
TP Carlyon	10	4	13	2	1	0
MR Hague	9	6	8	1	1	0
ASJ Dewhurst	1	0	11	0	0	0
SR Carlyon	1.4	0	3	0	0	0

Fall of wickets: 1-11 (Karim Khan); 2-11 (Noor Ali); 3-28 (Nowroz Mangal); 4-28 (Ahmad Shah); 5-38 (Mohammad Nabi); 6-38 (Samiullah Shinwari); 7-42 (Raees Ahmadzai); 8-62 (Asghar Stanikzai);

Both finalist progress to Division 4.

ICC WORLD CRICKET LEAGUE, DIVISION 4, TANZANIA, OCTOBER 2008

AFGHANISTAN v FIJI

50-over match played at Leaders Club, Kinondoni, 4 October – Afghanistan won by 81 runs, D/L method

Match details: Toss: Fiji **Man of the Match:** Hamid Hassan

Comment: Match reduced to 36 overs a side. Fiji set a revised target of 134 **Points Awarded:** Afghanistan 2, Fiji 0

Afghanistan: 132 all out (35.3 overs)

Batsman		Bowler	Runs	Balls	4s	6s
Karim Sadiq+		b Tavo	21	24	2	1
Ahmad Shah		b Cakacaka	34	43	3	1
Nowroz Mangal*		b Tukana	9	51	0	0
Mohammad Nabi	c Bulabulavu	b Cakacaka	12	16	0	0
Asghar Stanikzai	run out (Tukana/Cakacaka)		2	6	0	0
Raees Ahmadzai		b Cakacaka	0	3	0	0
Shafiqullah Shinwari	lbw	b Tukana	3	5	0	0
Samiullah Shinwari	lbw	b Jepson	28	43	5	0
Dawlat Ahmadzai	c Browne	b Jepson	8	17	0	0
Hasti Gul	not out		3	3	0	0
Hamid Hassan		b Lomani	4	5	0	0
Extras		(w5 nb3)	8			
TOTAL		10 wickets for	132			

Bowling	O	M	R	W	Wd	Nb
KSB Tavo	7	1	22	1	0	0
SR Lomani	4.3	0	35	1	2	2
J Seuvou	7	1	13	0	0	1
I Cakacaka	8	1	26	3	2	0
W Tukana	5	2	16	2	0	0
J Bulabulavu	2	0	10	0	0	0
S Jepson	2	0	10	2	1	0

Fall of wickets: 1-34 (Karim Sadiq); 2-54 (Ahmad Shah); 3-72 (Mohammad Nabi); 4-82 (Asghar Stanikzai); 5-89 (Raees Ahmadzai); 6-101(Nowroz Mangal); 7-105 (Shafiqullah Shinwari); 8-122 (Dawlat Ahmadzai); 9-127 (Samiullah Shinwari); 10-132 (Hamid Hassan)

Fiji: 52 all out (20.4 overs)

Batsman		Bowler	Runs	Balls	4s	6s
JF Rika	c Shafiqullah Shinwari	b Dawlat Ahmadzai	3	10	0	0
J Bulabulavu	lbw	b Dawlat Ahmadzai	0	13	0	0
W Tukana	c Samiullah Shinwari	b Hasti Gul	7	22	0	0
CD Rika*+	not out		5	45	0	0
S Jepson	lbw	b Ahmad Shah	8	5	0	1
J Dabea		b Hamid Hassan	7	11	0	0
I Cakacaka		b Hamid Hassan	0	1	0	0
G Browne		b Ahmad Shah	0	4	0	0
KSB Tavo	lbw	b Hamid Hassan	0	3	0	0
J Seuvou		b Hamid Hassan	0	2	0	0
SR Lomani	st Karim Sadiq	b Mohammad Nabi	9	9	2	0
Extras		(b1 lb4 w7 nb1)	13			
TOTAL		10 wickets for	52			

Bowling	O	M	R	W	Wd	Nb
Dawlat Ahmadzai	6	2	14	2	1	0
Hasti Gul	6	1	7	1	0	0
Ahmad Shah	4	3	3	2	0	0
Hamid Hassan	4	0	22	4	2	1
Mohammad Nabi	0.4	0	1	1	0	0

Fall of wickets: 1-3 (Rika); 2-10 (Bulabulavu); 3-12 (Tukana); 4-25 (Jepson); 5-32 (Dabea); 6-32 (Cakacaka); 7-34 (Browne); 8-40 (Tavo); 9-40 (Seuvou); 10-52 (Lomani)

AFGHANISTAN V JERSEY

50-over match played at University of Dar-es-Salaam Ground, 5 October – Afghanistan won by 122 runs

Match details: Toss: Afghanistan **Man of the Match:** Karim Sadiq **Points Awarded:** Afghanistan 2, Jersey 0

Afghanistan: 203 for 9 (50 overs)

Batsman		Bowler	Runs	Balls	4s	6s
Karim Sadiq+	c Driver	b SSJ Dewhurst	60	106	3	1
Ahmad Shah	c Gough	b Stevens	14	41	0	0
Nowroz Mangal*	c Driver	b Gough	21	28	3	0
Mohammad Nabi	run out		19	14	1	1
Asghar Stanikzai	c Gough	b SSJ Dewhurst	12	38	0	0
Raees Ahmadzai	st Minty	b TP Carlyon	22	28	1	0
Shafiqullah Shinwari	run out		27	24	3	1
Samiullah Shinwari	c Hague	b Kay	2	6	0	0
Hasti Gul	lbw	b Driver	13	9	2	0
Dawlat Ahmadzai	not out		2	2	0	0
Hamid Hassan	not out		2	3	0	0
Extras		(b1 lb2 w6)	9			
TOTAL		9 wickets for	203			

Bowling	O	M	R	W	Wd	Nb
RC Driver	10	2	52	1	4	0
AW Kay	10	2	28	1	1	0
MR Hague	3	0	15	0	0	0
BD Stevens	10	2	35	1	1	0
PW Gough	10	1	36	1	0	0
SSJ Dewhurst	5	0	26	2	0	0
TP Carlyon	2	0	8	1	0	0

Fall of wickets: 1-39 (Ahmad Shah); 2-73 (Nowroz Mangal); 3-97 (Mohammad Nabi); 4-130 (Karim Sadiq); 5-149 (Asghar Stanikzai); 6-166 (Raees Ahmadzai); 7-173 (Samiullah Shinwari); 8-194 (Hasti Gul); 9-200 (Shafiqullah Shinwari)

Jersey: 81 all out (35.5 overs)

Batsman		Bowler	Runs	Balls	4s	6s
PW Gough	c Mohammad Nabi	b Hasti Gul	5	35	0	0
SR Carlyon	c Shafiqullah Shinwari	b Hasti Gul	17	34	0	0
MR Hague*	c Shafiqullah Shinwari	b Hasti Gul	7	25	0	0
RC Driver	c Raees Ahmadzai	b Mohammad Nabi	15	27	2	0
JM Gough		b Hamid Hassan	0	2	0	0
ASJ Dewhurst	c Shafiqullah Shinwari	b Samiullah Shinwari	12	28	0	0
AW Kay	lbw	b Hamid Hassan	4	19	0	0
TP Carlyon	lbw	b Ahmad Shah	2	21	0	0
SSJ Dewhurst	c Nowroz Mangal	b Samiullah Shinwari	1	10	0	0
RD Minty+	not out		2	10	0	0
BD Stevens	lbw	b Hamid Hassan	0	1	0	0
Extras		(b4 lb6 w6)	16			
TOTAL		10 wickets for	81			

Bowling	O	M	R	W	Wd	Nb
Dawlat Ahmadzai	6	0	15	0	1	0
Hasti Gul	10	1	20	3	1	0
Hamid Hassan	8.5	0	17	3	2	0
Mohammad Nabi	3	1	9	1	0	0
Samiullah Shinwari	6	2	8	2	0	0
Ahmad Shah	2	1	2	1	2	0

Fall of wickets: 1-20 (Gough); 2-29 (SR Carlyon); 3-43 (Hague); 4-49 (Gough); 5-55 (ASJ Dewhurst); 6-62 (Driver); 7-76 (TP Carlyon); 8-76 (SSJ Dewhurst); 9-76 (Kay); 10-81 (Stevens)

AFGHANISTAN v TANZANIA

50-over match played at Anadil Burhani, 7 October – Afghanistan won by 8 runs, D/L method

Match details: Toss: Afghanistan **Man of the Match:** Mohammad Nabi **Comment:** Tanzania were set a revised target of 139 from 46 overs after rain stopped play at 27.3 overs with the score at 71-5

Points Awarded: Afghanistan 2, Tanzania 0

Afghanistan: 143 all out (46.3 overs)

Batsman		Bowler	Runs	Balls	4s	6s
Karim Sadiq+	c Kikasi	b Rehemtulla	0	8	0	0
Ahmad Shah		b Kakonzi	12	41	1	0
Nowroz Mangal*	c Abdallah	b Rehemtulla	13	13	3	0
Mohammad Nabi	run out (Damji/Kikasi)		7	10	1	0
Asghar Stanikzai	c Shaheed Dhanani	b Nassoro	13	31	1	0
Raees Ahmadzai	c Shaheed Dhanani	b Kakonzi	11	37	0	0
Dawlat Ahmadzai	c Abdallah	b Nassoro	14	45	1	0
Shafiqullah Shinwari	c Patel	b Nassoro	25	49	3	0
Samiullah Shinwari	c Kikasi	b Mwita	7	23	0	0
Hasti Gul	c Mwita	b Abdallah	15	22	2	0
Hamid Hassan	not out		0	0	0	0
Extras		(lb2 w24)	26			
TOTAL		**10 wickets for**	**143**			

Bowling	O	M	R	W	Wd	Nb
KZ Rehemtulla	10	0	30	2	11	0
H Abdallah	3	0	25	1	2	0
B Mwita	8.3	2	17	1	2	0
A Kakonzi	7	0	23	2	2	0
R Kiseto	8	1	22	0	3	0
K Nassoro	10	2	24	3	1	0

Fall of wickets: 1-9 (Karim Sadiq); 2-27 (Nowroz Mangal); 3-36 (Mohammad Nabi); 4-50 (Ahmad Shah); 5-69 (Raees Ahmadzai); 6-74 (Asghar Stanikzai); 7-112 (Shafiqullah Shafaq); 8-118 (Dawlat Ahmadzai); 9-143 (Hasti Gul); 10-143 (Samiullah Shinwari)

Tanzania: 130 all out (44.2 overs)

Batsman		Bowler	Runs	Balls	4s	6s
RD Patel	c Asghar Stanikzai	b Mohammad Nabi	13	60	1	0
AR Patwa	lbw	b Hasti Gul	15	20	2	0
Shaheed Dhanani	lbw	b Ahmad Shah	7	8	1	0
H Abdallah*		b Hamid Hassan	6	27	0	0
A Kakonzi		b Mohammad Nabi	26	68	0	0
I Kikasi+	c Raees Ahmadzai	b Hamid Hassan	0	6	0	0
B Mwita	c Asghar Stanikzai	b Hasti Gul	37	54	4	0
K Nassoro	c Karim Sadiq	b Hasti Gul	1	3	0	0
HM Damji		b Hamid Hassan	0	1	0	0
KZ Rehemtulla	not out		2	11	0	0
R Kiseto	c Karim Sadiq	b Mohammad Nabi	1	9	0	0
Extras		(b5 lb6 w10 nb1)	22			
TOTAL		**10 wickets for**	**130**			

Bowling	O	M	R	W	Wd	Nb
Dawlat Ahmadzai	5	2	12	0	1	0
Hasti Gul	9	2	29	3	2	0
Ahmad Shah	9	2	14	1	1	0
Hamid Hassan	10	1	37	3	4	1
Mohammad Nabi	7.2	1	12	3	0	0
Samiullah Shinwari	4	1	15	0	0	0

Fall of wickets: 1-25 (Patwa); 2-32 (Shaheed Dhanani); 3-46 (Abdallah); 4-52 (Patel); 5-56 (Kikasi); 6-112 (Mwita); 7-114 (Nassoro); 8-115 (Damji); 9-126 (Kakonzi); 10-130 (Kiseto)

AFGHANISTAN v HONG KONG

50-over match played at Anadil Burhani, 8 October – Afghanistan won by 4 wickets

Match details: Toss: Hong Kong **Man of the Match:** Mohammad Nabi

Points Awarded: Hong Kong 0, Afghanistan 2

Hong Kong: 206 for 9 (50 overs)

Batsman		Bowler	Runs	Balls	4s	6s
Tabarak Dar*	c Karim Sadiq	b Hasti Gul	5	21	1	0
JPR Lamsam		b Hamid Hassan	35	46	6	0
Zain Abbas		b Mohammad Nabi	69	119	5	0
Butt Hussain	run out (Samiullah Shinwari)		34	60	0	1
Moner Ahmed	c Hasti Gul	b Mohammad Nabi	6	12	0	0
Ilyas Gul	c Shafiqullah Shinwari	b Mohammad Nabi	10	20	0	0
Najeeb Amar	c Raees Ahmadzai	b Hamid Hassan	4	2	1	0
Irfan Ahmed	st Karim Sadiq	b Mohammad Nabi	6	7	1	0
Skhawat Ali	c Shafiqullah Shinwari	b Mohammad Nabi	4	4	0	0
Waqas Barkat+	not out		12	8	0	1
Nadeem Ahmed	not out		6	3	1	0
Extras		(b4 lb6 w3 nb2)	15			
TOTAL		**9 wickets for**	**206**			

Bowling	O	M	R	W	Wd	Nb
Hasti Gul	8	3	37	1	0	1
Sharpour Zadran	8	1	50	0	1	1
Ahmad Shah	10	1	28	0	0	0
Mohammad Nabi	9	0	32	5	0	0
Hamid Hassan	10	3	26	2	0	0
Nowroz Mangal	2	0	7	0	1	0
Samiullah Shinwari	3	0	16	0	0	0

Fall of wickets: 1-25 (Tabarak Dar); 2-68 (Lamsam); 3-152 (Zain Abbas); 4-158 (Butt Hussain); 5-165 (Moner Ahmed); 6-170 (Najeeb Amar); 7-176 (Irfan Ahmed); 8-182 (Skhawat Ali); 9-188 (Ilyas Gul)

Afghanistan: 209 for 6 (49.4 overs)

Batsman		Bowler	Runs	Balls	4s	6s
Karim Sadiq+		b Nadeem Ahmed	20	13	5	0
Ahmad Shah	c Zain Abbas	b Moner Ahmed	7	46	0	0
Asghar Stanikzai	run out		18	51	2	0
Nowroz Mangal*	st Waqas Barkat	b Moner Ahmed	50	65	6	0
Mohammad Nabi	c Skhawat Ali	b Irfan Ahmed	70	78	2	3
Raees Ahmadzai	not out		14	41	1	0
Shafiqullah Shinwari	c Waqas Barkat	b Irfan Ahmed	6	4	1	0
Samiullah Shinwari	not out		4	1	1	0
Hasti Gul	did not bat		-			
Sharpour Zadran	did not bat		-			
Hamid Hassan	did not bat		-			
Extras		(b9 lb2 w8 nb1)	20			
TOTAL		**6 wickets for**	**209**			

Bowling	O	M	R	W	Wd	Nb
Irfan Ahmed	8.4	2	59	2	2	1
Najeeb Amar	10	2	22	0	0	0
Nadeem Ahmed	10	1	49	1	0	0
Moner Ahmed	10	2	27	2	0	0
Ilyas Gul	10	1	33	0	1	0
Zain Abbas	1	0	8	0	0	0

Fall of wickets: 1-23 (Karim Sadiq); 2-47 (Ahmad Shah); 3-48 (Asghar Stanikzai); 4-153 (Nowroz Mangal); 5-193 (Mohammad Nabi); 6-204 (Shafiqullah Shinwari)

AFGHANISTAN v ITALY

50-over match played at Leaders Club Kinondoni, 10 October – Afghanistan won by 93 runs

Match details: **Toss:** Afghanistan **Man of the Match:** Raees Ahmadzai **Points Awarded:** Afghanistan 2, Italy 0

Afghanistan: 234 all out (50 overs)

Batsman		Bowler	Runs	Balls	4s	6s
Karim Sadiq+	lbw	b AlaudDin	3	8	0	0
Ahmad Shah	lbw	b Jayasena	54	99	5	1
Asghar Stanikzai	lbw	b AlaudDin	33	31	3	2
Nowroz Mangal*		b Munasinghe	15	34	2	0
Mohammad Nabi	c Munasinghe	b Pennazza	32	49	0	1
Raees Ahmadzai	run out (A Northcote)		68	63	7	2
Shafiqullah Shinwari		b Petricola	3	7	0	0
Hasti Gul	run out		7	7	0	0
Samiullah Shinwari	c Jayasena	b Pennazza	2	3	0	0
Dawlat Ahmadzai	run out (Munasinghe)		0	0	0	0
Hamid Hassan	not out		1	1	0	0
Extras		(b3 lb6 w5 nb2)	16			
TOTAL		**10 wickets for**	**234**			

Bowling	O	M	R	W	Wd	Nb
AlaudDin	8	2	21	2	1	0
V Pennazza	9	1	61	2	0	2
GRdeS Munasinghe	8	1	27	1	1	0
HS Jayasena	10	1	38	1	3	0
A Northcote	8	0	50	0	0	0
PA Petricola	7	0	28	1	0	0

Fall of wickets: 1-8 (Karim Sadiq); 2-47 (Asghar Stanikzai); 3-86 (Nowroz Mangal); 4-125 (Ahmad Shah); 5-194 (Mohammad Nabi); 6-206 (Shafiqullah Shinwari); 7-217 (Hasti Gul); 8-230 (Samiullah Shinwari); 9-231 (Raees Ahmadzai); 10-232 (Dawlat Ahmadzai)

Italy: 141 all out (44.4 overs)

Batsman		Bowler	Runs	Balls	4s	6s
A Northcote	run out (Raees Ahmadzai)		29	48	3	0
TA Kurukulasuriya		b Dawlat Ahmadzai	0	1	0	0
MN Northcote+	c Raees Ahmadzai	b Hamid Hassan	35	91	3	0
JC Scuderi*	run out (Hamid Hassan)		20	27	3	0
PA Petricola		c&b Nowroz Mangal	1	11	0	0
HS Jayasena	run out Mohammad Nabi		0	0	0	0
S Ketipe	lbw	b Hamid Hassan	15	24	3	0
V Pennazza		b Hamid Hassan	14	29	1	0
N Puccio	not out		9	29	0	0
GRdeS Munasinghe	run out		3	5	0	0
AlaudDin	c Mohammad Nabi	b Ahmad Shah	3	16	0	0
Extras		(lb3 w6 nb3)	12			
TOTAL		**10 wickets for**	**141**			

Bowling	O	M	R	W	Wd	Nb
Dawlat Ahmadzai	10	0	33	1	0	0
Hasti Gul	7	1	29	0	1	1
Ahmad Shah	7.4	3	22	1	2	0
Hamid Hassan	8	1	19	3	0	2
Nowroz Mangal	3	1	7	1	1	0
Samiullah Shinwari	7	0	16	0	1	0
Mohammad Nabi	2	0	12	0	0	0

Fall of wickets: 1-1 (Kurukulasuriya); 2-62 (A Northcote); 3-89 (MN Northcote); 4-89 (Scuderi); 5-89 (Jayasena); 6-91 (Petricola); 7-123 (Pennazza); 8-124 (Ketipe); 9-135 (Munasinghe); 10-141 (AlaudDin)

DIVISION 4 – FINAL TABLE

Team	P	W	L	T	N/R	NRR	Pts
Afghanistan	5	5	0	0	0	+1.33	10
Hong Kong	5	4	1	0	0	+1.67	8
Italy	5	3	2	0	0	+0.91	6
Tanzania	5	1	4	0	0	-0.66	2
Jersey	5	1	4	0	0	-0.91	2
Fiji	5	1	4	0	0	-2.38	2

Top two teams progress to Division 3.

AFGHANISTAN v HONG KONG

50-over match played at Anadil Burhani, 11 October, Final – Afghanistan won by 57 runs

Match details: **Toss:** Afghanistan **Man of the Match:** Raees Ahmadzai

Comment: Both teams qualify for Division 3

Afghanistan: 179 all out (49.4 overs)

Batsman		Bowler	Runs	Balls	4s	6s
Karim Sadiq+	c Waqas Barkat	b Irfan Ahmed	4	17	0	0
Ahmad Shah	c Zain Abbas	b Nadeem Ahmed	14	43	1	0
Asghar Stanikzai		c&b Irfan Ahmed	11	18	2	0
Nowroz Mangal*	c Tabarak Dar	b Nadeem Ahmed	40	75	4	0
Mohammad Nabi	c Tabarak Dar	b Najeeb Amar	14	24	2	0
Raees Ahmadzai	c Moner Ahmed	b Nizakat Khan	49	69	2	3
Samiullah Shinwari	st Waqas Barkat	b Najeeb Amar	23	35	0	0
Shafiqullah Shinwari	c Irfan Ahmed	b Nizakat Khan	5	6	1	0
Hasti Gul	c Moner Ahmed	b Nizakat Khan	5	7	0	0
Dawlat Ahmadzai	st Waqas Barkat	b Nizakat Khan	2	3	0	0
Hamid Hassan	not out		0	1	0	0
Extras		(b2 lb3 w7)	12			
TOTAL		10 wickets for	179			

Bowling	O	M	R	W	Wd	Nb
Irfan Ahmed	6	2	12	2	0	0
Ilyas Gul	9	2	23	0	2	0
Nadeem Ahmed	10	1	42	2	0	0
Moner Ahmed	6	0	21	0	0	0
Najeeb Amar	9	1	33	2	0	0
Nizakat Khan	7.4	0	29	4	4	0
Zain Abbas	2	0	14	0	0	0

Fall of wickets: 1-6 (Karim Sadiq); 2-28 (Asghar Stanikzai); 3-31 (Ahmad Shah); 4-59 (Mohammad Nabi); 5-125 (Nowroz Mangal); 6-162 (Raees Ahmadzai); 7-167 (Shafiqullah Shinwari); 8-174 Samiullah Shinwari); 9-178 (Dawlat Ahmadzai); 10-179 (Hasti Gul)

Hong Kong: 122 all out (45 overs)

Batsman		Bowler	Runs	Balls	4s	6s
Nadeem Ahmed	lbw	b Hasti Gul	14	19	1	1
Tabarak Dar*		b Hamid Hassan	33	106	2	0
Zain Abbas	c Ahmad Shah	b Hasti Gul	4	30	0	0
Butt Hussain		b Mohammad Nabi	17	48	0	1
Ilyas Gul	run out		2	13	0	0
Najeeb Amar	c Hamid Hassan	b Mohammad Nabi	1	5	0	0
Skhawat Ali	c Nowroz Mangal	b Samiullah Shinwari	8	19	1	0
Moner Ahmed		b Mohammad Nabi	9	8	2	0
Irfan Ahmed	not out		14	20	2	0
Waqas Barkat+		b Hamid Hassan	0	1	0	0
Nizakat Khan	c Raees Ahmadzai	b Mohammad Nabi	0	4	0	0
Extras		(b3 lb8 w6 nb3)	20			
TOTAL		10 wickets for	122			

Bowling	O	M	R	W	Wd	Nb
Dawlat Ahmadzai	4	0	18	0	0	1
Hasti Gul	10	3	23	2	2	0
Ahmad Shah	7	3	14	0	0	0
Nowroz Mangal	5	1	10	0	1	0
Hamid Hassan	7	0	28	2	1	2
Mohammad Nabi	9	3	9	4	0	0
Samiullah Shinwari	3	0	9	1	0	0

Fall of wickets: 1-20 (Nadeem Ahmed); 2-32 (Tabarak Dar); 3-69 (Butt Hussain); 4-79 (Ilyas Gul); 5-80 (Najeeb Amar); 6-95 (Skhawat Ali); 7-106 (Moner Ahmed); 8-108 (Tabarak Dar); 9-108 (Waqas Barkat); 10-122 (Nizakat Khan)

ICC WORLD CRICKET LEAGUE, DIVISION 3, ARGENTINA, JANUARY 2009

AFGHANISTAN v UGANDA

50-over match played at Corimayo, Buenos Aires, 24 January, Round 1
– Uganda won by 14 runs

Match details: **Toss:** Uganda **Man of the Match:** Kenneth Kamyuka **Points Awarded:** Uganda 2, Afghanistan 0

Uganda: 216 for 8 (50 overs)

Batsman		Bowler	Runs	Balls	4s	6s
R Mukasa+		b Ahmad Shah	38	48	5	0
AS Kyobe	c Shafiqullah Shinwari	b Nowroz Mangal	50	100	5	1
NKJ Bibodi		b Mohammad Nabi	7	27	1	0
MA Baig	run out (Mohammad Nabi)		12	30	1	0
J Olwemy		c&b Samiullah Shinwari	11	19	1	0
JZ Kwebiiha*	c Samiullah Shinwari	b Mohammad Nabi	10	11	1	0
F Nsubuga	c Ahmad Shah	b Samiullah Shinwari	62	44	7	3
K Kamyuka	c Nowroz Mangal	b Samiullah Shinwari	1	7	0	0
B Musoke	not out		8	18	0	0
D Ruyange	not out		0	1	0	0
DK Arinaitwe	did not bat		-			
Extras		(b5 lb2 w5 nb5)	17			
TOTAL		8 wickets for	216			

Bowling	O	M	R	W	Wd	Nb
Dawlat Ahmadzai	7	1	27	0	2	0
Hasti Gul	8	1	20	0	1	0
Ahmad Shah	5	0	23	1	0	0
Hamid Hassan	10	2	54	0	1	5
Mohammad Nabi	9	2	41	2	2	0
Nowroz Mangal	3	0	12	1	1	0
Samiullah Shinwari	8	1	32	3	-	-

Fall of wickets: 1-65 (Mukasa); 2-98 (Bibodi); 3-112 (Kyobe); 4-124 (Baig); 5-129 (Olwemy); 6-149 (Kwebiiha); 7-169 (Kamyuka); 8-214 (Nsubuga);

Afghanistan: 202 all out (49.3 overs)

Batsman		Bowler	Runs	Balls	4s	6s
Shafiqullah Shinwari	c Ruyange	b Kamyuka	18	25	2	1
Ahmad Shah		b Kamyuka	1	9	0	0
Asghar Stanikzai		b Ruyange	3	13	0	0
Nowroz Mangal*	c Mukasa	b Ruyange	0	7	0	0
Mohammad Nabi		b Kamyuka	0	5	0	0
Karim Sadiq+		b Nsubuga	17	23	3	0
Raees Ahmadzai	c Mukasa	b Kamyuka	78	100	6	3
Samiullah Shinwari	c Arinaitwe	b Kamyuka	52	93	5	0
Hasti Gul	c Musoke	b Olwemy	11	8	2	0
Dawlat Ahmadzai	not out		13	9	0	1
Hamid Hassan	run out (Kamyuka)		2	5	0	0
Extras		(b1 lb2 w4)	7			
TOTAL		10 wickets for	202			

Bowling	O	M	R	W	Wd	Nb
K Kamyuka	9.3	0	36	5	1	0
D Ruyange	10	2	24	2	0	0
JZ Kwebiiha	1	0	10	0	1	0
F Nsubuga	10	3	29	1	0	0
DK Arinaitwe	5	0	28	0	2	0
NKJ Bibodi	10	1	39	0	0	0
J Olwemy	4	0	33	1	0	0

Fall of wickets: 1-3 (Ahmad Shah); 2-12 (Asghar Stanikzai); 3-23 (Shafiqullah Shinwari); 4-23 (Nowroz Mangal); 5-23 (Mohammad Nabi); 6-53 (Karim Sadiq); 7-174 (Rais Ahmadzai); 8-189 (Samiullah Shinwari); 9-190 (Hasti Gul); 10-202 (Hamid Hassan)

AFGHANISTAN v HONG KONG

50-over match played at the Belgrano Club, Buenos Aires, 25 January,
Round 2 – Afghanistan won by 13 runs

Match details: Toss: Hong Kong **Man of the Match:** Mohammad Nabi

Points Awarded: Afghanistan 2, Hong Kong 0

Afghanistan: 201 all out (49.5 overs)

Batsman		Bowler	Runs	Balls	4s	6s
Karim Sadiq+		b Najeeb Amar	36	50	6	0
Shafiqullah Shinwari	c Atkinson	b Nadeem Ahmed	24	34	1	2
Asghar Stanikzai		b Nadeem Ahmed	9	21	1	0
Nowroz Mangal*	c Nadeem Ahmed	b Irfan Ahmed	35	68	5	0
Mohammad Nabi	c Atkinson	b Lamsam	40	44	3	2
Dawlat Ahmadzai	c Butt Hussain	b Lamsam	0	10	0	0
Raees Ahmadzai	c Nadeem Ahmed	b Lamsam	7	16	0	0
Samiullah Shinwari	c Atkinson	b Najeeb Amar	25	39	1	1
Hasti Gul	c Skhawat Ali	b Irfan Ahmed	2	14	0	0
Mirwais Ashraf		b Irfan Ahmed	4	5	1	0
Hamid Hassan	not out		0	0	0	0
Extras		(b1 lb4 w12 nb2)	19			
TOTAL		**10 wickets for**	**201**			

Bowling	O	M	R	W	Wd	Nb
Irfan Ahmed	9.5	0	62	3	7	2
JPR Lamsam	10	1	33	3	0	0
Najeeb Amar	10	2	35	2	0	0
Nadeem Ahmed	8	1	23	2	1	0
Moner Ahmed	10	2	32	0	0	0
Ilyas Gull	2	0	11	0	0	0

Fall of wickets: 1-72 (Shafiqullah Shinwari); 2-72 (Karim Sadiq); 3-98 (Asghar Stanikzai); 4-146 (Nowroz Mangal); 5-151 (Dawlat Ahmadzai); 6-162 (Mohammad Nabi); 7-167 (Raees Ahmadzai); 8-188 (Hasti Gul); 9-197 (Samiullah Shinwari); 10-201 (Mirwais Ashraf)

Hong Kong: 188 all out (48.2 overs)

Batsman		Bowler	Runs	Balls	4s	6s
JPR Lamsam		b Hasti Gul	14	33	2	0
Irfan Ahmed		b Dawlat Ahmadzai	4	6	1	0
Zain Abbas	c Karim Sadiq	b Hamid Hassan	13	54	1	0
Butt Hussain	c Asghar Stanikzai	b Mirwais Ashraf	16	44	2	0
Tabarak Dar*	c Nowroz Mangal	b Mirwais Ashraf	19	28	4	0
Najeeb Amar	run out (Mirwais Ashraf)		1	7	0	0
Skhawat Ali	c Karim Sadiq	b Hasti Gul	7	15	1	0
JJ Atkinson+	lbw	b Mohammad Nabi	3	6	0	0
Moner Ahmed		b Samiullah Shinwari	49	39	2	4
Ilyas Gull	not out		11	44	0	0
Nadeem Ahmed	c Mirwais Ashraf	b Mohammad Nabi	27	18	5	0
Extras		(b1 lb6 w14 nb3)	24			
TOTAL		**10 wickets for**	**188**			

Bowling	O	M	R	W	Wd	Nb
Dawlat Ahmadzai	9	1	27	1	1	0
Hasti Gul	10	0	31	2	3	3
Mirwais Ashraf	10	3	32	2	5	0
Hamid Hassan	10	2	35	1	3	0
Mohammad Nabi	6.2	1	38	2	1	0
Samiullah Shinwari	3	0	18	1	1	0

Fall of wickets: 1-6 (Irfan Ahmed); 2-27 (Lamsam); 3-47 (Zain Abbas); 4-60 (Butt Hussain); 5-72 (Najeeb Amar); 6-81 (Tabarak Dar); 7-88 (Skhawat Ali); 8-90 (Atkinson); 9-152 (Moner Ahmed); 10-188 (Nadeem Ahmed)

AFGHANISTAN v ARGENTINA

50-over match played at the Hurlingham Club Ground, Buenos Aires, 27 January,
Round 3 – Afghanistan won by 19 runs

Match details: Toss: Afghanistan **Man of the Match:** Ahmad Shah **Points Awarded:** Afghanistan 2, Argentina 0

Afghanistan: 164 all out (47.4 overs)

Batsman		Bowler	Runs	Balls	4s	6s
Karim Sadiq*+	c MJ Paterlini	b Savage	7	14	1	0
Shafiqullah Shinwari	c Siri	b Casime	29	21	3	1
Ahmad Shah	st A Ferguson	b Barton	44	93	3	0
Asghar Stanikzai	c LM Paterlini	b Lord	11	17	2	0
Mohammad Nabi	c P Ferguson	b Lord	17	26	1	1
Raees Ahmadzai	run out (Siri/A Ferguson)		7	10	1	0
Samiullah Shinwari	c P Ferguson	b Barton	22	45	2	0
Hasti Gul	c LM Paterlini	b Barton	2	22	0	0
Mirwais Ashraf	not out		3	12	0	0
Dawlat Ahmadzai	c MJ Paterlini	b LM Paterlini	10	26	1	0
Hamid Hassan	run out (Savage/LM Paterlini)		0	2	0	0
Extras		(lb2 w8 nb2)	12			
TOTAL		10 wickets for	164			

Bowling	O	M	R	W	Wd	Nb
GJ Savage	7	1	21	1	1	0
AL Casime	6	1	29	1	0	0
LM Paterlini	7.4	1	23	1	0	1
DM Lord	7	0	43	2	1	1
E MacDermott	10	1	34	0	0	0
HD Barton	10	5	12	3	0	0

Fall of wickets: 1-31 (Karim Sadiq); 2-39 (Shafiqullah Shinwari); 3-61 (Asghar Stanikzai); 4-91 (Mohammad Nabi); 5-117 (Raees Ahmadzai); 6-127 (Ahmad Shah); 7-145 (Hasti Gul); 8-148 (Samiullah Shinwari); 9-164 (Dawlat Ahmadzai); 10-164 (Hamid Hassan)

Argentina: 145 all out (overs 46.4)

Batsman		Bowler	Runs	Balls	4s	6s
HD Barton		b Ahmad Shah	33	36	7	0
LM Paterlini	c Samiullah Shinwari	b Mohammad Nabi	35	55	6	0
MJ Paterlini	c Karim Sadiq	b Hamid Hassan	6	28	0	0
RM Siri	lbw	b Mohammad Nabi	2	20	0	0
A Ferguson+	c Ahmad Shah	b Samiullah Shinwari	10	29	1	0
GJ Savage	run out (Samiullah Shinwari)		7	13	0	0
D Forrester	lbw	b Samiullah Shinwari	2	13	0	0
P Ferguson		b Hamid Hassan	14	50	1	0
E MacDermott*		b Ahmad Shah	13	19	1	0
DM Lord	run out		17	16	1	0
AL Casime	not out		1	2	0	0
Extras		(b1 lb1 w2 nb1)	5			
TOTAL		10 wickets for	145			

Bowling	O	M	R	W	Wd	Nb
Dawlat Ahmadzai	4	0	25	0	0	1
Hamid Hassan	10	1	26	2	2	0
Mohammad Nabi	8	1	24	2	0	0
Hasti Gul	5	0	19	0	0	0
Ahmad Shah	10	5	21	2	0	0
Samiullah Shinwari	9.4	1	28	2	0	0

Fall of wickets: 1-56 (Barton); 2-74 (MJ Paterlini); 3-76 (LM Paterlini); 4-78 (Siri); 5-95 (Savage); 6-95 (Ferguson); 7-105 (Forrester); 8-122 (MacDermott); 9-142 (Ferguson); 10-145 (Lord)

AFGHANISTAN v PAPUA NEW GUINEA

50-over match played at the Hurlingham Club Ground, Buenos Aires, 28 January,
Round 4 – Afghanistan won by 8 wickets

Match details: Toss: Papua New Guinea **Man of the Match:** Karim Sadiq

Points Awarded: Papua New Guinea 0, Afghanistan 2

Papua New Guinea: 93 all out (31 overs)

Batsman		Bowler	Runs	Balls	4s	6s
VV Morea	c Karim Sadiq	b Dawlat Ahmadzai	0	2	0	0
CR Amini	c Karim Sadiq	b Mirwais Ashraf	15	30	2	0
J Ovia	c Karim Sadiq	b Hamid Hassan	15	51	1	0
A Vala	run out (Raees Ahmadzai)		4	8	0	0
P Moide	c Karim Sadiq	b Dawlat Ahmadzai	0	5	0	0
JL Brazier		c&b Ahmad Shah	22	18	3	0
M Dai	c Assadullah Khan	b Mohammad Nabi	5	14	1	0
R Dikana*	c Karim Sadiq	b Hamid Hassan	9	12	2	0
I Morea+	c Karim Sadiq	b Samiullah Shinwari	8	22	0	0
L Nou	not out		5	19	0	0
WT Gavera		b Hamid Hassan	6	6	1	0
Extras		(lb2 w1 nb1)	4			
TOTAL		10 wickets for	93			

Bowling	O	M	R	W	Wd	Nb
Dawlat Ahmadzai	9	2	27	2	0	1
Mirwais Ashraf	7	2	22	1	1	0
Ahmad Shah	3	1	9	1	0	0
Hamid Hassan	7	1	26	3	0	0
Mohammad Nabi	3	2	4	1	0	0
Samiullah Shinwari	2	0	3	1	0	0

Fall of wickets: 1-0 (Morea); 2-23 (Amini); 3-28 (Vala); 4-29 (Moide); 5-58 (Brazier); 6-60 (Ovia); 7-66 (Dai); 8-74 (Dikana); 9-84 (Morea); 10-93 (Gavera)

Afghanistan: 94 for 2 (15.4 overs)

Batsman		Bowler	Runs	Balls	4s	6s
Karim Sadiq*+	c Vala	b Brazier	50	43	8	0
Shafiqullah Shinwari	run out		20	32	2	0
Mohammad Nabi	not out		19	16	3	1
Raees Ahmadzai	not out		2	3	0	0
Asghar Stanikzai	did not bat		-			
Assadullah Khan	did not bat		-			
Ahmad Shah	did not bat		-			
Mirwais Ashraf	did not bat		-			
Samiullah Shinwari	did not bat		-			
Dawlat Ahmadzai	did not bat		-			
Hamid Hassan	did not bat		-			
Extras		(w2 nb1)	3			
TOTAL		2 wickets for	94			

Bowling	O	M	R	W	Wd	Nb
WT Gavera	2.4	0	8	0	0	0
L Nou	2	0	19	0	2	0
R Dikana	6	1	29	0	0	1
JL Brazier	5	0	38	1	0	0

Fall of wickets: 1-63 (Shafiqullah Shinwari); 2-73 (Karim Sadiq)

AFGHANISTAN v CAYMAN ISLANDS

50-over match played at Corimayo, Buenos Aires, 30 January, Round 5 – No result

Match details: **Toss:** Cayman Islands **Comment:** Match reduced to 20 overs: Cayman Islands target 63

Points Awarded: None, match to be replayed

Afghanistan: 68 for 5, innings closed (31 overs)

Batsman		Bowler	Runs	Balls	4s	6s
Karim Sadiq+	c Roach	b Bovell	3	16	0	0
Shafiqullah Shinwari	c Hall	b Tulloch	13	8	3	0
Ahmad Shah	c Irving	b Tulloch	5	39	0	0
Nowroz Mangal*	not out		26	73	2	0
Raees Ahmadzai		b Mohamed	3	17	0	0
Mohammad Nabi	st Hall	b Mohamed	0	3	0	0
Asghar Stanikzai	not out		11	31	1	0
Samiullah Shinwari	did not bat		-			
Dawlat Ahmadzai	did not bat					
Mirwais Ashraf	did not bat		-			
Hamid Hassan	did not bat		-			
Extras		(lb4 w2 nb1)	7			
TOTAL		**5 wickets for**	**68**			

Bowling	O	M	R	W	Wd	Nb
KG Tulloch	10	2	24	2	1	1
RD Bovell	9	2	17	1	1	0
SA Mohamed	7	2	10	2	0	0
A Morris	4	1	9	0	0	0
KF Bazil	1	0	4	0	0	0

Fall of wickets: 1-17 (Shafiqullah Shinwari); 2-17 (Karim Sadiq); 3-36 (Ahmad Shah); 4-47 (Raees Ahmadzai); 5-47 (Mohammad Nabi)

Cayman Islands: 35 for 2, innings abandoned (7 overs)

Batsman		Bowler	Runs	Balls	4s	6s
AE Hall+		b Dawlat Ahmadzai	4	4	1	0
RA Sealy	c Raees Ahmadzai	b Dawlat Ahmadzai	1	15	0	0
KD Irving	not out		18	16	3	0
SC Gordon*	not out		10	7	2	0
SA Mohamed	did not bat		-			
RN Roach	did not bat		-			
A Morris	did not bat		-			
KG Tulloch	did not bat		-			
OR Willis	did not bat		-			
KF Bazil	did not bat		-			
RD Bovell	did not bat		-			
Extras		(lb1 w1)	2			
TOTAL		**2 wickets for**	**35**			

Bowling	O	M	R	W	Wd	Nb
Dawlat Ahmadzai	4	2	8	2	0	0
Hamid Hassan	2	0	14	0	1	0
Mirwais Ashraf	1	0	12	0	0	0

Fall of wickets: 1-4 (Hall); 2-18 (Sealy)

AFGHANISTAN v CAYMAN ISLANDS

50-over match played at Corimayo, Buenos Aires, 31 January, Round 5 (rescheduled) – Afghanistan won by 82 runs

Match details: Toss: Cayman Islands **Man of the Match:** Nowroz Mangal **Points Awarded:** Afghanistan 2, Cayman Islands 0. **Comment:** Afghanistan finish top of the table and are declared winners of Division 3. They advance to Division 1 along with runners-up Uganda

Afghanistan: 230 for 8 (50 overs)

Batsman		Bowler	Runs	Balls	4s	6s
Karim Sadiq+	c Hall	b Tulloch	4	23	0	0
Shafiqullah Shinwari	c Sealy	b Bazil	39	83	3	1
Ahmad Shah	c Hall	b Bovell	1	9	0	0
Nowroz Mangal*	c Hall	b Bovell	70	89	7	0
Asghar Stanikzai	not out		66	62	7	1
Mohammad Nabi	c Sealy	b Mohamed	3	9	0	0
Raees Ahmadzai	c Hall	b Bovell	13	13	1	0
Samiullah Shinwari	lbw	b Tulloch	14	8	2	0
Hasti Gul	run out (Bazil/Mohamed)		1	3	0	0
Dawlat Ahmadzai	not out		1	1	0	0
Hamid Hassan	did not bat		-			
Extras		(b6 lb5 w7)	18			
TOTAL		8 wickets for	230			

Bowling	O	M	R	W	Wd	Nb
KG Tulloch	10	1	55	2	3	0
RD Bovell	10	1	55	3	1	0
SA Mohamed	10	1	47	1	1	0
A Morris	10	3	31	0	1	0
KF Bazil	10	2	31	1	0	0

Fall of wickets: 1-23 (Karim Sadiq); 2-28 (Ahmad Shah); 3-97 (Shafiqullah Shinwari); 4-132 (Nowroz Mangal); 5-160 (Mohammad Nabi); 6-196 (Raees Ahmadzai); 7-217 (Samiullah Shinwari); 8-220 (Hasti Gul)

Cayman Islands: 148 all out (45 overs)

Batsman		Bowler	Runs	Balls	4s	6s
AE Hall+	c Karim Sadiq	b Hasti Gul	11	23	1	0
RA Sealy		b Mohammad Nabi	14	36	0	0
KD Irving	lbw	b Mohammad Nabi	12	29	2	0
SC Gordon	c Asghar Stanikzai	b Hamid Hassan	20	41	2	0
SA Mohamed	lbw	b Nowroz Mangal	9	31	0	0
RN Roach		b Hamid Hassan	5	21	1	0
PI Best*		b Hamid Hassan	0	2	0	0
RD Bovell	run out		29	37	4	0
KF Bazil	not out		14	34	0	1
A Morris		b Mohammad Nabi	4	8	1	0
KG Tulloch	c Dawlat Ahmadzai	b Mohammad Nabi	1	8	0	0
Extras		(b3 lb13 w13)	29			
TOTAL		10 wickets for	148			

Bowling	O	M	R	W	Wd	Nb
Dawlat Ahmadzai	7	1	17	0	1	0
Hasti Gul	10	2	28	1	0	0
Mohammad Nabi	9	1	23	4	1	0
Hamid Hassan	8	0	16	3	3	0
Nowroz Mangal	4	0	16	1	1	0
Samiullah Shinwari	6	1	28	0	1	0
Ahmad Shah	1	0	4	0	1	0

Fall of wickets: 1-22 (Hall); 2-40 (Sealy); 3-41 (Irving); 4-79 (Mohamed); 5-82 (Gordon); 6-82 (Best); 7-92 (Roach); 8-139 (Bovell); 9-144 (Morris); 10-148 (Tulloch)

DIVISION 3 – FINAL TABLE

Team	P	W	L	T	N/R	NRR	Pts
Afghanistan	5	4	1	0	0	+0.971	8
Uganda	5	4	1	0	0	+0.768	8
Papua New Guinea	5	4	1	0	0	+0.665	8
Hong Kong	5	2	3	0	0	-0.005	4
Cayman Islands	5	1	4	0	0	-1.384	2
Argentina	5	0	5	0	0	-1.031	0

Top two teams progress to World Cup Qualifer.

ICC WORLD CUP QUALIFIER, DIVISION 1, SOUTH AFRICA, APRIL 2009

AFGHANISTAN v DENMARK

50-over match played at Vaal University Ground, 1 April,
Group B – Afghanistan won by 5 wickets

Match details: Toss: Afghanistan **Man of the Match:** Karim Sadiq **Points Awarded:** Denmark 0, Afghanistan 2

Denmark: 204 for 9 (50 overs)

Batsman		Bowler	Runs	Balls	4s	6s
F Klokker*+	c Raees Ahmadzai	b Mohammad Nabi	26	36	2	0
M Pedersen	c Karim Sadiq	b Hasti Gul	15	39	2	0
C Pedersen	lbw	b Karim Sadiq	46	69	6	0
S Vestergaard		b Karim Sadiq	39	64	3	0
M Lund		b Karim Sadiq	2	7	0	0
M Overgaard	not out		22	46	0	0
M Andersen	lbw	b Karim Sadiq	4	9	0	0
T Hansen	run out		4	8	0	0
A Chawla	st Mohammed Sherzad	b Mohammad Nabi	0	2	0	0
D Borchersen	c Samiullah Shinwari	b Hamid Hassan	16	17	1	1
H Hansen	not out		7	4	1	0
Extras		(b1 lb2 w19 nb1)	15			
TOTAL		**9 wickets for**	**204**			

Bowling	O	M	R	W	Wd	Nb
Dawlat Ahmadzai	5	0	37	0	4	1
Hasti Gul	9	0	28	1	3	0
Nowroz Mangal	1	0	8	0	0	0
Mohammad Nabi	10	1	34	2	3	0
Samiullah Shinwari	10	0	43	0	4	0
Hamid Hassan	7	0	24	1	2	0
Karim Sadiq	8	0	27	4	2	0

Fall of wickets: 1-42 (M Pedersen); 2-68 (Klokker); 3-133 (C Pedersen); 4-138 (Lund); 5-150 (Vestergaard); 6-158 (Andersen); 7-165 (Hansen); 8-167 (Chawla); 9-190 (Borchersen)

Afghanistan: 205 for 5 (46.2 overs)

Batsman		Bowler	Runs	Balls	4s	6s
Shafiqullah Shinwari	c Hansen	b Borchersen	6	17	0	0
Karim Sadiq	lbw	b Hansen	39	40	7	0
Noor Ali	c sub	b Hansen	1	15	0	0
Nowroz Mangal*		b M Pedersen	13	35	1	0
Mohammed Sherzad+	not out		55	94	5	1
Mohammad Nabi	c Overgaard	b Hansen	47	51	4	0
Raees Ahmadzai	not out		13	29	2	0
Samiullah Shinwari						
Hasti Gul						
Dawlat Ahmadzai						
Hamid Hassan						
Extras		(b0 lb6 w22 nb3)	31			
TOTAL		**5 wickets for**	**205**			

Bowling	O	M	R	W	Wd	Nb
T Hansen	7	0	46	1	5	0
D Borchersen	10	1	31	1	4	0
H Hansen	10	1	43	2	3	2
M Andersen	4.2	0	29	0	2	1
A Chawla	7	0	29	0	0	0
M Pedersen	8	0	21	1	2	0

Fall of wickets: 1-22 (Shafiqullah Shinwari); 2-44 (Noor Ali); 3-73 (Karim Sadiq); 4-88 (Nowroz Mangal); 5-166 (Mohammad Nabi)

AFGHANISTAN v BERMUDA

50-over match played at Senwes Park, Potchefstroom 2 April,
Group B – Afghanistan won by 60 runs

Match details: Toss: Afghanistan **Man of the Match:** Nowroz Mangal

Points Awarded: Afghanistan 2, Bermuda 0

Afghanistan: 239 for 9 (50 overs)

Batsman		Bowler	Runs	Balls	4s	6s
Shafiqullah Shinwari	c Edness	b O'Brien	2	8	0	0
Karim Sadiq	c Outerbridge	b Tucker	83	103	10	0
Noor Ali	c Hemp	b Leverock	38	69	2	0
Nowroz Mangal*	run out (Hemp/O'Brien)		71	77	6	2
Mohammed Sherzad+	c Hemp	b Trott	0	3	0	0
Mohammad Nabi	c Leverock	b Tucker	1	3	0	0
Raees Ahmadzai		c&b Trott	1	11	0	0
Samiullah Shinwari	run out (Romaine/Trott)		9	9	1	0
Hasti Gul		b O'Brien	9	9	1	0
Dawlat Ahmadzai	not out		11	9	1	0
Hamid Hassan	did not bat		-			
Extras		(lb3 w10 nb1)	14			
TOTAL		**9 wickets for**	**239**			

Bowling	O	M	R	W	Wd	Nb
GH O'Brien	9	1	53	2	1	0
SKW Kelly	6	0	35	0	1	1
JJ Tucker	9	0	44	2	0	0
SD Outerbridge	3	0	23	0	0	0
RDM Leverock	10	1	33	1	0	0
RJ Trott	10	0	33	2	1	0
IH Romaine	3	1	15	0	0	0

Fall of wickets: 1-26 (Shafiqullah Shinwari); 2-128 (Asghar Stanikzai); 3-147 (Karim Sadiq); 4-147 (Mohammed Sherzad); 5-150 (Mohammad Nabi); 6-157 (Raees Ahmadzai); 7-174 (Samiullah Shinwari); 8-190 (Hasti Gul); 9-239 (Nowroz Mangal)

Bermuda: 179 all out (49.3 overs)

Batsman		Bowler	Runs	Balls	4s	6s
J Edness+	c Mohammed Sherzad	b Hasti Gul	1	13	0	0
LOB Cann		B Dawlat Ahmadzai	0	1	0	0
G Blakeney		b Mohammad Nabi	68	104	7	1
SD Outerbridge	c Nowroz Mangal	b Samiullah Shinwari	62	103	6	0
JJ Tucker	st Mohammed Sherzad	b Samiullah Shinwari	3	8	0	0
DL Hemp		b Samiullah Shinwari	4	7	0	0
IH Romaine*	c Mohammed Sherzad	b Samiullah Shinwari	9	9	2	0
RJ Trott		b Hamid Hassan	2	8	0	0
GH O'Brien		b Hamid Hassan	12	6	1	1
RDM Leverock	not out		2	19	0	0
SKW Kelly	lbw	b Karim Sadiq	3	18	0	0
Extras		(lb6 w7)	13			
TOTAL		**10 wickets for**	**179**			

Bowling	O	M	R	W	Wd	Nb
Dawlat Ahmadzai	5	3	5	1	0	0
Hasti Gul	7	0	34	1	0	0
Mohammad Nabi	8	2	24	1	0	0
Karim Sadiq	4.3	0	16	1	1	0
Nowroz Mangal	7	0	27	0	0	0
Raees Ahmadzai	6	0	21	0	1	0
Samiullah Shinwari	7	1	28	4	1	0
Hamid Hassan	5	0	18	2	2	0

Fall of wickets: 1-1 (Lob Cann); 2-7 (Edness); 3-125 (Blakeney); 4-128 (Tucker); 5-134 (Hemp); 6-148 (Romaine); 7-151 (Trott); 8-167 (O'Brien); 9-174 (Outerbridge); 10-179 (Kelly)

AFGHANISTAN v KENYA

50-over match played at Fanie du Toit, Potchesfstroom, 4 April, Group B – Kenya won by 107 runs

Match details: **Toss:** Afghanistan **Man of the Match:** KO Otieno **Points Awarded:** Afghanistan 0, Kenya 2

Kenya: 204 for 9 (50 overs)

Batsman		Bowler	Runs	Balls	4s	6s
MA Ouma+	c Mohammed Sherzad	b Samiullah Shinwari	35	59	3	1
KO Otieno	not out		109	138	11	1
AO Obanda		c&b Nowroz Mangal	60	62	6	1
SO Tikolo*	c Samiullah Shinwari	b Karim Sadiq	28	21	3	1
CO Obuya	run out (Mohammed Sherzad)		18	16	1	1
JK Kamande	c Raees Ahmadzai	b Mohammad Nabi	0	1	0	0
TM Odoyo	not out		16	6	1	1
N Odhiambo	did not bat					
LN Onyango	did not bat					
HA Varaiya	did not bat					
PJ Ongondo	did not bat					
Extras		(b1 lb7 w5 nb3)	16			
TOTAL		**5 wickets for**	**282**			

Bowling	O	M	R	W	Wd	Nb
Dawlat Ahmadzai	9	1	23	0	1	1
Khaliq Dad	3	0	29	0	0	0
Asghar Stanikzai	6	0	30	0	0	0
Hamid Hassan	9	1	67	0	1	2
Samiullah Shinwari	9	0	36	1	0	0
Mohammad Nabi	7	0	36	1	0	0
Karim Sadiq	3	0	23	1	1	0
Nowroz Mangal	4	0	30	1	1	0

Fall of wickets: 1-87 (Ouma); 2-175 (Obanda); 3-217 (Tikolo); 4-264 (Obuya); 5-264 (Kamande)

Afghanistan: 175 all out (47 overs)

Batsman		Bowler	Runs	Balls	4s	6s
Shafiqullah Shinwari	lbw	b Odoyo	25	33	2	1
Karim Sadiq	c Otieno	b Ongondo	8	9	1	0
Mohammed Sherzad+		b Odoyo	4	8	1	0
Nowroz Mangal*	c Ouma	b Odoyo	10	14	2	0
Asghar Stanikzai	c Ouma	b Odhiambo	6	15	1	0
Mohammad Nabi	lbw	b Varalya	56	71	2	2
Raees Ahmadzai		b Tikolo	19	28	3	0
Samiullah Shinwari	c Ongondo	b Varalya	25	53	2	0
Dawlat Ahmadzai	not out		10	31	0	0
Khaliq Dad		c&b Kamande	3	17	0	0
Hamid Hassan	c Kamande	b Obuya	0	4	0	0
Extras		(b1 w7 nb1)	9			
TOTAL		**10 wickets for**	**175**			

Bowling	O	M	R	W	Wd	Nb
TM Odoyo	6	2	29	3	2	0
PJ Ongondo	7	1	25	1	0	0
LN Onyango	7	0	22	0	3	1
N Odhiambo	2.4	0	18	1	0	0
SO Tikolo	3.2	1	16	1	0	0
HA Varalya	10	0	29	2	1	0
JK Kamande	10	0	33	1	0	0
CO Obuya	1	0	2	1	1	0

Fall of wickets: 1-20 (Shafiqullah Shinwari); 2-31 (Karim Sadiq); 3-49 (Nowroz Mangal); 4-50 (Mohammed Sherzed); 5-62 (Asghar Stanikzai); 6-96 (Raees Ahmadzai); 7-153 (Mohammad Nabi); 8-160 (Samiullah Shinwari); 9-173 (Khaliq Dad); 10-175 (Hamid Hassan)

AFGHANISTAN v NETHERLANDS

50-over match played at Vaal University Ground, Vanderbiljipark, 6 April,
Group B – Netherlands won by 5 wickets

Match details: Toss: Netherlands **Man of the Match:** Daan van Bunge

Points Awarded: Afghanistan 0, Netherlands 2

Afghanistan: 239 for 9 (50 overs)

Batsman		Bowler	Runs	Balls	4s	6s
Shafiqullah Shinwari	c Smits	b ten Doeschate	9	8	1	0
Karim Sadiq	c Szwarcznski	b Seelaar	72	101	6	0
Noor Ali	c van Bunge	b ten Doeschate	14	22	2	0
Nowroz Mangal*	c Kervezee	b Schiferli	0	1	0	0
Mohammed Sherzad+	lbw	b Seelaar	8	28	0	0
Asghar Stanikzai	c Smits	b Bukhari	18	47	0	0
Mohammad Nabi	c Kervezee	b Bukhari	36	42	3	0
Samiullah Shinwari		b Bukhari	18	24	0	0
Hasti Gul	c van Bunge	b ten Doeschate	10	16	1	0
Dawlat Ahmadzai	not out		5	10	0	0
Hamid Hassan	not out		2	1	0	0
Extras		(lb5 w7)	12			
TOTAL		9 wickets for	204			

Bowling	O	M	R	W	Wd	Nb
E Schiferli	10	0	39	1	0	0
RN ten Doeschate	10	0	50	3	0	0
M Bukhari	10	0	41	3	5	0
DJ Reekers	7	3	16	0	1	0
PM Seelaar	10	0	39	2	1	0
DLS van Bunge	3	0	14	0	0	0

Fall of wickets: 15-1 (Shafiqullah Shinwari); 43-2 (Noor Ali); 44-3 (Nowroz Mangal); 75-4 (Mohammed Sherzad); 126-5 (Karim Sadiq); 130-6 (Asghar Stanzai); 186-7 (Mohammad Nabi); 186-8 (Samiullah Shinwari); 201-9 (Hasti Gul)

Netherlands: 208 for 5 (46.2 overs)

Batsman		Bowler	Runs	Balls	4s	6s
AN Kervezee	c Mohammed Sherzad	b Mohammad Nabi	21	47	2	0
DJ Reekers	lbw	b Hasti Gul	23	18	4	1
ES Szwarczynski	st Mohammed Sherzad	b Mohammad Nabi	16	18	2	0
RN ten Doeschate	run out (Samiullah Shinwari)		13	26	1	0
DLS van Bunge	not out		65	87	4	2
B Zuiderent	run out (Samiullah Shinwari)		30	59	1	0
TN de Grooth	not out		25	23	3	0
J Smits*+	did not bat					
E Schiferli	did not bat					
PM Seelaar	did not bat					
M Bukhari	did not bat					
Extras		(lb3 w12)	15			
TOTAL		5 wickets for	208			

Bowling	O	M	R	W	Wd	Nb
Dawlat Ahmadzai	8	0	35	0	0	0
Hasti Gul	5	0	31	1	4	0
Mohammad Nabi	10	1	31	2	1	0
Hamid Hassan	7	0	30	0	1	0
Samiullah Shinwari	9	1	49	0	1	0
Karim Sadiq	7.2	1	29	0	2	0

Fall of wickets: 1-33 (Reekers); 2-65 (Kervezee); 3-66 (Szwarczynski); 4-80 (ten Doeschate); 5-146 (Zuiderent)

AFGHANISTAN v UNITED ARAB EMIRATES

50-over match played at Isak Steyl Stadium, Vanderbijlpark, 8 April,
Group B – United Arab Emirates won by 5 wickets

Match details: **Toss:** United Arab Emirates **Man of the Match:** N Gopal

Points Awarded: Afghanistan 0, United Arab Emirates 2

Afghanistan: 251 for 8 (50 overs)

Batsman		Bowler	Runs	Balls	4s	6s
Shafiqullah Shinwari		b Aman Ali	0	7	0	0
Noor Ali	c Arshad Ali	b Amjad Javed	5	10	1	0
Mohammed Sherzad+		b Zahid Shah	30	26	4	1
Asghar Stanikzai	c Gopal	b Zahid Shah	69	107	4	0
Nowroz Mangal*		b Zahid Shah	46	101	1	0
Mohammad Nabi	c Saqib Ali	b Arshad Ali	26	18	4	0
Raees Ahmadzai		b Zahid Shah	18	12	2	0
Samiullah Shinwari	not out		31	18	4	0
Sharpour Zadran	run out (Khurram Khan)		0	1	0	0
Dawlat Ahmadzai	not out		4	3	0	0
Hamid Hassan	did not bat					
Extras		(b4 lb6 w9 nb3)	22			
TOTAL		**8 wickets for**	**251**			

Bowling	O	M	R	W	Wd	Nb
Amjad Javed	4	0	31	1	1	0
Aman Ali	3	0	13	1	2	1
Zahid Shah	10	1	59	4	3	2
N Gopal	8	0	34	0	2	0
Fayyaz Ahmed	10	1	27	0	0	0
Arshad Ali	10	0	53	1	1	0
Khurram Khan	5	0	24	0	0	0

Fall of wickets: 1-3 (Shafiqullah Shinwari); 2-7 (Noor Ali); 3-58 (Mohammed Sherzad); 4-160 (Nowroz Mangal); 5-169 (Asghar Stanikzai); 6-212 (Mohammad Nabi); 7-218 (Raees Ahmadzai); 8-218 (Sharpour Zadran)

United Arab Emirates: 257 for 5 (47.2 overs)

Batsman		Bowler	Runs	Balls	4s	6s
Amjad Javed		b Sharpour Zadran	0	1	0	0
Arshad Ali	run out (Shafiqullah Shinwari)		41	70	2	0
N Gopal	c Mohammed Sherzad	b Hamid Hassan	81	99	6	0
Saqib Ali	c Hamid Hassan	b Noor Ali	69	64	7	0
Khurram Khan*		c&b Mohammad Nabi	8	8	1	0
Naeemuddin Aslam+	not out		47	42	6	1
Fayyaz Ahmed	not out		0	0	0	0
S Nayak	did not bat					
Owais Hameed	did not bat					
Zahid Shah	did not bat					
Aman Ali	did not bat					
Extras		(lb1 w10)	11			
TOTAL		**5 wickets for**	**257**			

Bowling	O	M	R	W	Wd	Nb
Sharpour Zadran	3	1	9	1	2	0
Hamid Hassan	10	1	53	1	4	0
Dawlat Ahmadzai	10	0	61	0	3	0
Mohammad Nabi	10	0	55	1	1	0
Asghar Stanikzai	2	0	9	0	0	0
Samiullah Shinwari	9	0	50	0	0	0
Nowroz Mangal	3	0	13	0	0	0
Noor Ali	0.2	0	6	1	0	0

Fall of wickets: 1-0 (Amjad Javed); 2-117 (Arshad Ali); 3-150 (Gopal); 4-160 (Khurram Khan); 5-251 (Saqib Ali)

GROUP B – FINAL TABLE

Team	P	W	L	T	N/R	NRR	Pts
Kenya	5	4	1	0	0	+1.683	8
Netherlands	5	4	1	0	0	+0.557	8
United Arab Emirates	5	4	1	0	0	–0.131	8
Afghanistan	5	2	3	0	0	–0.278	4
Bermuda	5	1	4	0	0	–0.441	2
Denmark	5	0	5	0	0	–1.341	0

Top four teams progress to the Super Eight.

AFGHANISTAN v IRELAND

50-over match played at Stan Friedman Oval, Krugersdorp, 11 April,
Super Eights – Afghanistan won by 22 runs

Match details: Toss: Ireland **Man of the Match:** Hamid Hassan **Points Awarded:** Afghanistan 2, Ireland 0

Afghanistan: 218 for 7 (50 overs)

Batsman		Bowler	Runs	Balls	4s	6s
Noor Ali	lbw	b Mooney	18	27	3	0
Karim Sadiq	c Mooney	b Connell	6	19	1	0
Mohammed Sherzad+	run out (Cussack/NJ O'Brien)		46	64	8	0
Nowroz Mangal*	c Wilson	b White	23	39	3	0
Asghar Stanikzai	c&b Cusack		47	78	3	1
Mohammad Nabi	c&b White		0	2	0	0
Raees Ahmadzai	not out		50	65	4	0
Samiullah Shinwari	b Connell		14	13	2	0
Khaliq Dad	not out		1	3	0	0
Hamid Hassan	did not bat					
Nasratullah	did not bat					
Extras		(b6 lb4 w3)	13			
TOTAL		7 wickets for	251			

Bowling	O	M	R	W	Wd	Nb
P Connell	7	1	36	2	1	0
WB Rankin	7	0	37	0	1	0
JF Mooney	8	1	38	1	0	0
AR Cusack	6	0	30	1	1	0
RM West	10	2	35	0	0	0
AR White	10	0	27	2	0	0
EJG Morgan	2	0	5	0	0	0

Fall of wickets: 1-9 (Karim Sadiq); 2-46 (Noor Ali); 3-84 (Mohammed Sherzad); 4-101 (Nowroz Mangal); 5-101 (Mohammad Nabi); 6-190 (Asghar Stanikzai); 7-212 (Samiullah Shinwari)

Ireland: 196 all out (47.3 overs)

Batsman		Bowler	Runs	Balls	4s	6s
WTS Porterfield*		b Hamid Hassan	4	10	1	0
GC Wilson		b Khaliq Dad	1	9	0	0
EJG Morgan		b Karim Sadiq	20	41	2	0
NJ O'Brien+	run out (Raees Ahmadzai)		29	43	2	0
AR Cusack	st Mohammed Sherzad	b Samiullah Shinwari	14	39	1	0
AR White		b Hamid Hassan	56	64	6	0
KJ O'Brien		b Hamid Hassan	52	66	2	3
JF Mooney		b Mohammad Nabi	4	9	0	0
RM West	c Mohammed Sherzad	b Hamid Hassan	0	2	0	0
P Connell		b Hamid Hassan	1	2	0	0
WB Rankin	not out		0	0	0	0
Extras		(b1 lb3 w11)	15			
TOTAL		10 wickets for	196			

Bowling	O	M	R	W	Wd	Nb
Hamid Hassan	9	2	23	5	2	0
Khaliq Dad	5	1	20	1	0	0
Mohammad Nabi	9.3	1	30	1	1	0
Karim Sadiq	7	0	35	1	0	0
Samiullah Shinwari	8	0	45	1	4	0
Nasratullah	9	0	39	0	4	0

Fall of wickets: 1-4 (Porterfield); 2-6 (Wilson); 3-40 (Morgan); 4-62 (NJ O'Brien); 5-73 (Cusack); 6-186 (White); 7-194 (KJ O'Brien); 8-194 (West); 9-196 (Connell); 10-196 (Mooney)

AFGHANISTAN v CANADA

50-over match played at LC de Villiers Oval, Pretoria, 13 April,
Super Eights – Canada won by 6 wickets

Match details: Toss: Canada **Man of the Match:** IS Billcliff **Points Awarded:** Afghanistan 0, Canada 2

Afghanistan: 265 for 8 (50 overs)

Batsman		Bowler	Runs	Balls	4s	6s
Noor Ali	run out (Rizwan Cheema)		122	140	8	1
Karim Sadiq	c Bagai	b Khurram Chohan	13	23	2	0
Mohammed Sherzad+	c Bagai	b Rizwan Cheema	10	18	2	0
Nowroz Mangal*	c Bagai	b Rizwan Cheema	49	69	3	1
Asghar Stanikzai	run out (Billcliff)		0	3	0	0
Mohammad Nabi	lbw	b Rizwan Cheema	0	5	0	0
Raees Ahmadzai	lbw	b Khurram Chohan	18	23	2	0
Samiullah Shinwari		b Osinde	15	8	0	1
Khaliq Dad	not out		8	9	1	0
Sharpour Zadran	not out		3	2	0	
Hamid Hassan	did not bat					
Extras		(lb14 w13)	27			
TOTAL		8 wickets for	265			

Bowling	O	M	R	W	Wd	Nb
U Bhatti	6	0	31	0	0	0
H Osinde	8	0	37	1	6	0
Khurram Chohan	10	0	56	2	1	0
Rizwan Cheema	10	1	41	3	2	0
S Dhaniram	3	0	24	0	0	0
HS Baidwan	10	0	42	0	0	0
S Jyoti	3	0	20	0	0	0

Fall of wickets: 1-39 (Karim Sadiq); 2-69 (Mohammed Sherzad); 3-187 (Nowroz Mangal); 4-187 (Asghar Stanikzai); 5-189 (Mohammad Nabi); 6-233 (Noor Ali); 7-238 (Raees Ahmadzai); 8-261 (Samiullah Shinwari)

Canada: 268 for 4 (48.3 overs)

Batsman		Bowler	Runs	Balls	4s	6s
GEF Barnett		b Samiullah Shinwari	19	28	2	0
Rizwan Cheema	c Hamid Hassan	b Mohammad Nabi	46	23	8	2
AA Mulla	lbw	b Khaliq Dad	16	18	1	1
IS Billcliff	not out		96	134	8	2
A Bagai*+		b Hamid Hassan	68	82	3	1
S Dhaniram	not out		15	6	1	1
S Joyri	did not bat					
U Bhatti	did not bat					
HS Baidwan	did not bat					
Khurram Chohan	did not bat					
H Osinde	did not bat					
Extras		(lb5 w3)	8			
TOTAL		4 wickets for	268			

Bowling	O	M	R	W	Wd	Nb
Sharpour Zadran	10	1	53	0	1	0
Hamid Hassan	9.3	0	76	1	2	0
Nowroz Mangal	2	0	19	0	0	0
Mohammad Nabi	10	0	43	1	0	0
Samiullah Shinwari	7	1	26	1	0	0
Khaliq Dad	7	0	22	1	0	0
Karim Sadiq	3	0	24	0	0	0

Fall of wickets: 1-67 (Barnett); 2-67 (Rizwan Cheema); 3-96 (Mulla); 4-244 (Bagai)

AFGHANISTAN v SCOTLAND

50-over match played at Willowmoore Park, Benoni, 15 April,
Super Eights – Afghanistan won by 42 runs

Match details: **Toss:** Scotland **Man of the Match:** Karim Sadiq **Points Awarded:** Afghanistan 2, Scotland 0

Afghanistan: 279 all out (50 overs)

Batsman		Bowler	Runs	Balls	4s	6s
Noor Ali	c Smith	b Stander	24	42	2	0
Karim Sadiq	run out (Stander)		92	101	10	2
Mohammed Sherzad+		b Wright	22	26	4	0
Nowroz Mangal*	c McCallum	b Blain	72	70	7	1
Asghar Stanikzai	c Stander	b Wright	0	5	0	0
Mohammad Nabi	c Poonia	b Haq	2	2	0	0
Raees Ahmadzai	c Watson	b Nel	16	28	2	0
Samiullah Shinwari	c Poonia	b Blain	22	11	2	1
Khaliq Dad	c Smith	b Nel	5	7	0	0
Sharpour Zadran	st Smith	b Haq	9	5	0	1
Hamid Hassan	not out		4	3	0	0
Extras		(lb3 w8)	11			
TOTAL		**10 wickets for**	**279**			

Bowling	O	M	R	W	Wd	Nb
JAR Blain	10	1	54	2	1	0
JD Nel	10	0	52	2	2	0
CM Wright	10	2	41	2	1	0
JH Stander	10	0	67	1	2	0
RM Haq	9	0	55	2	1	0
RR Watson	1	0	7	0	0	0

Fall of wickets: 1-57 (Noor Ali); 2-105 (Mohammed Sherzad; 3-177 (Karim Sadiq); 4-179 (Asghar Stanikzai); 5-181 (Mohammad Nabi); 6-216 (Raees Ahmadzai); 7-257 (Samiullah Shinwari); 8-261 (Nowroz Mangal); 9-273 (Sharpour Zadran); 10-279 (Khaliq Dad)

Scotland: 237 all out (47.1 overs)

Batsman		Bowler	Runs	Balls	4s	6s
RR Watson*		b Khaliq Dad	13	34	1	0
RM Haq	c Mohammed Sherzad	b Sharpour Zadran	1	8	0	0
KJ Coetzer	c Mohammad Nabi	b Karim Sadiq	91	127	10	1
GM Hamilton	c Hamid Hassan	b Karim Sadiq	71	75	3	2
NFI McCallum	c Raees Ahmadzai	b Samiullah Shinwari	5	3	1	0
NS Poonia		b Hamid Hassan	17	15	1	0
JH Stander	c Raees Ahmadzai	b Hamid Hassan	2	7	0	0
CJO Smith+	run out (Mohammed Sherzad)		11	9	0	0
CM Wright	c Samiullah Shinwari	b Sharpour Zadran	0	1	0	0
JAR Blain		b Sharpour Zadran	5	3	1	0
JD Nel	not out		0	1	0	0
Extras		(b1 lb9 w11)	21			
TOTAL		**10 wickets for**	**237**			

Bowling	O	M	R	W	Wd	Nb
Sharpour Zadran	9.1	2	36	3	2	0
Hamid Hassan	9	1	45	2	0	0
Khaliq Dad	9	1	43	1	3	0
Mohammad Nabi	8	0	30	0	0	0
Karim Sadiq	7	0	44	2	1	0
Samiullah Shinwari	5	0	29	1	1	0

Fall of wickets: 1-1 (Haq); 2-54 (Watson); 3-187 (Coetzer); 4-200 (McCallum); 5-200 (Hamilton); 6-208 (Stander); 7-231 (Smith); 8-231 (Wright); 9-237 (Poonia); 10-237 (Blain)

AFGHANISTAN v NAMIBIA

50-over match played at Stan Friedman Oval, Krugersdorp, 17 April,
Super Eights – Afghanistan won by 21 runs

Match details: Toss: Afghanistan **Man of the Match:** Nowroz Mangal

Points Awarded: Afghanistan 2, Namibia 0

Afghanistan: 243 for 7 (50 overs)

Batsman		Bowler	Runs	Balls	4s	6s
Noor Ali	lbw	Klazinga	2	18	0	0
Karim Sadiq		b SF Burger	14	23	2	0
Mohammed Sherzad+	c van de Westhuizen	b DB Kotze	73	99	12	0
Nowroz Mangal*	run out (DB Kotze/Snyman)		78	106	5	1
Asghar Stanikzai	c BL Kotze	b Scholtz	27	39	2	1
Mohammad Nabi	c Scholtz	b van der Westhuizen	10	5	1	1
Sharpour Zadran	run out (van Schoor)		10	9	0	1
Raees Ahmadzai	not out		0	0	0	0
Samiullah Shinwari	not out		8	2	2	0
Hamid Hassan	did not bat					
Nasratullah	did not bat					
Extras		(b5 lb6 w9 nb1)	21			
TOTAL		7 wickets for	243			

Bowling	O	M	R	W	Wd	Nb
G Snyman	7	2	41	0	1	0
L Klazinga	5	0	21	1	2	0
SF Burger	5	1	11	1	2	0
DB Kotze	10	0	27	1	1	0
BL Kotze	1	0	12	0	1	1
LJ Burger	4	0	24	0	0	0
LP van der Westhuizen	10	0	49	1	1	0
NRP Scholtz	6	0	38	1	0	0
AJ Burger	2	0	9	0	0	0

Fall of wickets: 1-15 (Noor Ali); 2-51 (Karim Sadiq); 3-138 (Mohammed Sherzad); 4-186 (Asghar Stanikzai); 5-205 (Mohammad Nabi); 6-235 (Nowroz Mangal); 7-235 (Sharpour Zadran)

Namibia: 222 all out (48.3 overs)

Batsman		Bowler	Runs	Balls	4s	6s
R van Schoor+	run out (Nasratullah/Samiullah Shinwari)		14	34	1	0
AJ Burger	c Mohammad Nabi	b Sharpour Zadran	0	2	0	0
SF Burger		b Hamid Hassan	16	25	1	1
CG Williams		b Mohammad Nabi	25	31	3	0
G Snyman		b Hamid Hassan	54	93	2	1
LJ Burger*	lbw	b Nasratullah	6	14	1	0
NRP Scholtz	c Mohammed Sherzad	b Karim Sadiq	33	36	4	1
DB Kotze	lbw	b Sharpour Zadran	19	23	1	0
LP van der Westhuizen		b Karim Sadiq	12	12	2	0
BL Kotze		b Hamid Hassan	10	19	2	0
L Klazinga	not out		3	3	0	0
Extras		(b4 lb6 w10 nb1)	21			
TOTAL		10 wickets for	222			

Bowling	O	M	R	W	Wd	Nb
Sharpour Zadran	6	0	27	2	0	1
Hamid Hassan	9.3	1	37	3	0	0
Samiullah Shinwari	6	0	39	0	1	0
Mohammad Nabi	10	1	28	1	3	0
Nasratullah	7	1	30	1	0	0
Karim Sadiq	9	1	43	2	3	0
Nowroz Mangal	1	0	8	0	0	0

Fall of wickets: 1-1 (AJ Burger); 2-21 (SF Burger); 3-40 (van Schoor); 4-67 (Williams); 5-79 (LJ Burger); 6-157 (Scholtz); 7-166 (Snyman); 8-186 (van der Westhuizen); 9-214 (DB Kotze); 10-222 (BL Kotze)

SUPER EIGHTS – FINAL TABLE

Team qualifies for 2011 Cricket World Cup and gains/retains ODI status							
Team gains/retains ODI status							
Team plays in the 7th place playoff							
Team	**P**	**W**	**L**	**T**	**N/R**	**NRR**	**Pts**
Ireland	7	5	2	0	0	+0.689	10
Canada	7	4	3	0	0	+0.687	8
Kenya	7	4	3	0	0	+0.035	8
Netherlands	7	4	3	0	0	+0.025	8
Scotland	7	3	4	0	0	−0.140	6
Afghanistan	7	3	4	0	0	−0.209	6
United Arab Emirates	7	3	4	0	0	−1.080	6
Namibia	7	2	5	0	0	−0.079	4

Top four progress to the World Cup, top six secure One Day International status.

AFGHANISTAN v SCOTLAND

50-over match played at Willowmoore Park, Benoni, 19 April,
5th Place Playoff – Afghanistan won by 89 runs

Match details: **Toss:** Afghanistan **Man of the Match:** Mohammad Nabi

Points Awarded: Afghanistan 2, Scotland 0

Afghanistan: 295 for 8 (50 overs)

Batsman		Bowler	Runs	Balls	4s	6s
Noor Ali	c Coetzer	b Stander	45	28	9	0
Karim Sadiq+	lbw	b Stander	2	22	1	2
Mohammad Nabi	c Hamilton	b Iqbal	58	64	3	3
Nowroz Mangal*	run out (MacLeod/Smith)		32	47	3	0
Asghar Stanikzai	lbw	b Iqbal	9	25	0	0
Raees Ahmadzai	c&b Blain		39	43	5	0
Samiullah Shinwari	c Drummond	b Blain	52	57	6	0
Hasti Gul	not out		23	11	2	1
Khaliq Dad	c Coetzer	b Blain	0	1	0	0
Hamid Hassan	not out		0	2	0	0
Dawlat Ahmadzai	did not bat					
Extras		(b 2 lb3 w12)	17			
TOTAL		**8 wickets for**	**295**			

Bowling	O	M	R	W	Wd	Nb
JAR Blain	9	0	62	3	0	0
CS MacLeod	8	0	63	0	2	0
JH Stander	5	1	25	2	2	0
GD Drummond	10	1	48	0	1	0
RM Haq	9	1	46	0	2	0
MM Iqbal	9	0	46	2	1	0

Fall of wickets: 1-55 (Karim Sadiq); 2-83 (Noor Ali); 3-136 (Nowroz Mangal); 4-176 (Mohammad Nabi); 5-176 (Asghar Stanikzai); 6-262 (Raees Ahmadzai); 7-278 (Samiullah Shinwari); 8-281 (Khaliq Dad)

Scotland: 206 all out (40 overs)

Batsman		Bowler	Runs	Balls	4s	6s
GM Hamilton	c Noor Ali	b Dawlat Ahmadzai	8	11	1	0
RM Haq	lbw	b Hasti Gul	1	10	0	0
KJ Coetzer	c Noor Ali	b Hamid Hassan	44	46	8	0
NFI McCallum	lbw	b Khaliq Dad	36	33	8	0
RR Watson*	c Raees Ahmadzai	b Hasti Gul	6	10	1	0
CJO Smith+		b Khaliq Dad	15	13	2	0
JH Stander		b Hamid Hassan	0	6	0	0
MM Iqbal	run out (Nowroz Mangal)		15	25	2	0
JAR Blain		b Nowroz Mangal	41	56	3	0
CS MacLeod	lbw	b Hamid Hassan	0	4	0	0
GD Drummond	not out		25	27	3	0
Extras		(b4 lb5 w5 nb1)	15			
TOTAL		**10 wickets for**	**206**			

Bowling	O	M	R	W	Wd	Nb
Dawlat Ahmadzai	6	0	40	1	0	0
Hasti Gul	9	1	48	2	1	1
Khaliq Dad	6	0	25	2	0	0
Hamid Hassan	8	1	33	3	1	0
Mohammad Nabi	8	0	41	0	2	0
Samiullah Shinwari	2	0	8	0	1	0
Nowroz Mangal	1	0	2	1	0	0

Fall of wickets: 1-10 (Hamilton); 2-11 (Haq); 3-72 (McCallum); 4-83 (Watson); 5-114 (Coetzer); 6-116 (Smith); 7-117 (Stander); 8-140 (Iqbal); 9-143 (MacLeod); 10-206 (Blain)

2010 ICC WORLD TWENTY20 QUALIFIERS, UNITED ARAB EMIRATES, FEBRUARY 2010

AFGHANISTAN v IRELAND

Played at Dubai International Cricket Stadium, 9 February, Group A – Afghanistan won by 13 runs

Match details: Toss: Ireland **Man of the Match:** Mohammad Nabi **Points Awarded:** Afghanistan 2, Ireland 0

Afghanistan: 139 for 8 (20 overs)

Batsman		Bowler	Runs	Balls	4s	6s
Noor Ali	c Stirling	b Botha	42	45	5	0
Karim Sadiq		b Johnston	4	5	1	0
Shafiqullah Shinwari	c Mooney	b Johnston	3	6	0	0
Mohammed Sherzad+	run out (Mooney)		12	17	0	0
Nowroz Mangal*	st NJ O'Brien	b Dockrell	13	11	0	0
Mohammad Nabi	not out		43	25	3	2
Samiullah Shinwari	run out (Cusack/Connell)		2	4	0	0
Raees Ahmadzai	st NJ O'Brien	Botha	9	5	0	1
Mirwais Ashraf	run out (KJ O'Brien)		1	1	0	0
Hamid Hassan	not out		1	1	0	0
Sharpour Zadran	did not bat		-			
Extras		(b1 lb1 w7)	9			
TOTAL		8 wickets for	139			

Bowling	O	M	R	W	Wd	Nb
P Connell	4	0	20	0	3	0
DT Johnston	4	0	18	2	0	0
KJ O'Brien	2	0	20	0	0	0
AC Botha	4	0	25	2	2	0
GH Dockrell	3	0	31	1	1	0
AR Cusack	3	0	23	0	1	0

Fall of wickets: 1-6 (Karim Sadiq); 2-14 (Shafiqullah Shinwari); 3-61 (Mohammed Sherzad); 4-69 (Noor Ali); 5-93 (Nowroz Mangal); 6-97 (Samiullah Shinwari); 7-130 (Raees Ahmadzai); 8-131 Mirwais Ashraf)

Ireland: 126 all out (19.2 overs)

Batsman		Bowler	Runs	Balls	4s	6s
WTS Porterfield*		b Karim Sadiq	35	23	4	2
NJ O'Brien+	c Noor Ali	b Sharpour Zadran	2	6	0	0
PR Stirling	c Nowroz Mangal	b Hamid Hassan	21	23	2	0
AC Botha		b Karim Sadiq	0	2	0	0
KJ O'Brien	c Nowroz Mangal	b Karim Sadiq	7	9	0	0
AR Cusack	run out (Nowroz Mangal)		15	13	0	0
GC Wilson	c Mohammed Sherzad	b Mohammad Nabi	8	10	0	0
DT Johnston	c Samiullah Shinwari	B Mohammad Nabi	18	17	4	0
JF Mooney		b Hamid Hassan	9	13	1	0
P Connell	run out (Hamid Hassan)		0	1	0	0
GH Dockrell	not out		0	2	0	0
Extras		(b1 lb6 w3 nb1)	11			
TOTAL		10 wickets for	126			

Bowling	O	M	R	W	Wd	Nb
Sharpour Zadran	3	0	31	1	1	0
Mirwais Ashraf	4	0	20	0	0	0
Karim Sadiq	3	0	17	3	1	0
Samiullah Shinwari	2	0	7	0	0	0
Hamid Hassan	3.2	0	19	2	0	1
Mohammad Nabi	4	0	25	2	1	0

Fall of wickets: 1-22 (NJ O'Brien); 2-52 (Porterfield); 3-52 Botha); 4-63 (KJ O'Brien); 5-78 (Stirling); 6-91 (Cusack); 7-98 Wilson); 8-125 (Johnston); 9-126 (Connell); 10-126 (Mooney)

AFGHANISTAN v SCOTLAND

Played at Sheikh Zayed Stadium, Abu Dhabi, 10 February,
Group A – Afghanistan won by 14 runs

Match details: **Toss:** Scotland **Man of the Match:** Noor Ali **Points Awarded:** Afghanistan 2, Scotland 0

Afghanistan: 131 for 7 (20 overs)

Batsman		Bowler	Runs	Balls	4s	6s
Noor Ali		b Coetzer	42	37	4	1
Karim Sadiq		b Drummond	3	7	0	0
Shafiqullah Shinwari	c Stander	b Drummond	0	2	0	0
Mohammed Sherzad+	c Nel	b Coetzer	30	40	1	0
Nowroz Mangal*		b Nel	18	16	0	1
Mohammad Nabi	c Hamilton	b Coetzer	0	1	0	0
Raees Ahmadzai	not out		17	13	0	0
Samiullah Shinwari	c Hamilton	b Stander	1	2	0	0
Mirwais Ashraf	not out		8	3	0	6
Sharpour Zadran	did not bat		-			
Hamid Hassan	did not bat		-			
Extras		(b5 lb1 w6)	12			
TOTAL		**7 wickets for**	**131**			

Bowling	O	M	R	W	Wd	Nb
JD Nel	4	0	23	1	2	0
GD Drummond	4	0	14	2	0	0
RD Berrington	2	0	12	0	1	0
KM Coetzer	4	0	25	3	1	0
RM Haq	3	0	24	0	0	0
JH Stander	3	0	28	1	2	1

Fall of wickets: 1-8 (Karim Sadiq); 2-8 (Shafiqullah Shinwari); 3-79 (Noor Ali); 4-96 (Mohammed Sherzad); 5-97 (Mohammad Nabi); 6-107 (Nowroz Mangal); 7-116 (Samiullah Shinwari)

Scotland: 117 for 9 (20 overs)

Batsman		Bowler	Runs	Balls	4s	6s
KM Coetzer	c Raees Ahmadzai	b Sharpour Zadran	2	15	0	0
NS Poonia		b Mirwais Ashraf	0	2	0	0
GM Hamilton*	st Mohammed Sherzad	b Karim Sadiq	32	34	1	0
NFI McCallum	run out (Mohammad Nabi/Mohammed Sherzad)	b Khaliq Dad	38	34	3	1
JH Stander		b Hamid Hassan	4	4	0	0
DF Watts		b Hamid Hassan	12	10	0	0
RD Berrington	not out		19	12	2	0
GD Drummond	c Sharpour Zadran	b Mohammad Nabi	5	4	0	0
SJS Smith+	c Shafiquallah Shinwari	b Mohammad Nabi	0	1	0	0
RM Haq		b Hamid Hassan	1	4	0	0
JD Nel	did not bat		-			
Extras		(lb4)	4			
TOTAL		**9 wickets for**	**117**			

Bowling	O	M	R	W	Wd	Nb
Sharpour Zadran	4	2	8	1	0	0
Mirwais Ashraf	3	0	13	1	0	0
Karim Sadiq	4	0	19	1	0	0
Mohammad Nabi	3	0	27	2	0	0
Hamid Hassan	4	0	32	3	0	0
Samiullah Shinwari	2	0	14	2	0	0

Fall of wickets: 1-0 (Poonia); 2-8 (Coetzer); 3-74 (Hamilton); 4-75 (McCallum); 5-81 (Stander); 6-98 (Watts); 7-111 (Drummond); 8-111 (Smith); 9-117 (Haq)

AFGHANISTAN v UNITED STATES OF AMERICA

Played at Dubai International Cricket Stadium, 11 February,
Group A – Afghanistan won by 29 runs

Match details: Toss: Afghanistan **Man of the Match:** Hamid Hassan **Points Awarded:** Afghanistan 2, USA 0

Afghanistan: 135 for 4 (20 overs)

Batsman		Bowler	Runs	Balls	4s	6s
Noor Ali	run out (Imran Awan)		26	27	3	0
Mohammed Sherzad+	c Wright	b Cush	0	5	0	0
Nowroz Mangal*	run out (Baker)		30	27	3	0
Karim Sadiq	st Wright	b Allen	25	26	2	0
Mohammad Nabi	not out		25	18	2	1
Raees Ahmadzai	not out		26	17	2	0
Shafiqullah Shinwari	did not bat		-			
Hamid Hassan	did not bat		-			
Sharpour Zadran	did not bat		-			
Mirwais Ashraf	did not bat		-			
Samiullah Shinwari	did not bat		-			
Extras		(b2 lb1)	3			
TOTAL		**4 wickets for**	**135**			

Bowling	O	M	R	W	Wd	Nb
LJ Cush	4	0	18	1	0	0
KG Darlington	4	0	25	0	0	0
Imran Awan	3	0	25	0	0	0
Sudesh Dhaniram	4	0	19	0	0	0
TP Allen	3	0	26	1	0	0
OM Baker	2	0	19	0	0	0

Fall of wickets: 1-5 (Mohammed Sherzad); 2-38 (Noor Ali); 3-82 (Karim Sadiq); 4-89 (Nowroz Mangal)

United States of America: 108 for 7 (20 overs)

Batsman		Bowler	Runs	Balls	4s	6s
SS Nadkarni	c Nowroz Mangal	b Mirwais Ashraf	12	22	1	0
CD Wright+	Mohammad Nabi	b Hamid Hassan	28	38	2	0
LD Cush	c Nowroz Mangal	b Mohammad Nabi	7	11	0	0
Sudesh Dhaniram	c Noor Ali	b Mohammad Nabi	4	6	0	0
TP Allen		b Hamid Hassan	9	8	0	1
RA Marshall	run out (Mohammed Sherzad/Sharpour Zadran)		19	18	2	0
A Thyagarajan		b Hamid Hassan	14	11	0	1
SA Massiah*	not out		5	6	0	0
OM Baker	not out		0	1	0	0
Imran Awan	did not bat		-			
KG Darlington	did not bat		-			
Extras		(lb6 w2)	8			
TOTAL		**7 wickets for**	**108**			

Bowling	O	M	R	W	Wd	Nb
Sharpour Zadran	4	1	13	0	1	0
Mirwais Ashraf	4	0	14	1	0	0
Karim Sadiq	3	0	25	0	0	0
Samiullah Shinwari	2	0	12	0	0	0
Mohammad Nabi	3	0	22	2	1	0
Hamid Hassan	4	0	14	3	0	0

Fall of wickets: 1-28 (Nadkarni); 2-47 (Cush); 3-54 (Wright); 4-58 (Dhaniram); 5-69 (Allen); 6-95 (Thyagarajan); 7-104 (Marshall)

GROUP A – FINAL TABLE

Team	P	W	L	T	N/R	NRR	Pts
Afghanistan	3	3	0	0	0	+0.933	6
Ireland	3	2	1	0	0	+1.717	4
United States of America	3	1	2	0	0	−1.684	2
Scotland	3	0	3	0	0	−0.509	0

Top two teams progress to the Super Fours.

AFGHANISTAN v NETHERLANDS

Played at Dubai International Cricket Stadium, 12 February,
Super Fours – Netherlands won by 4 wickets

Match details: Toss: Netherlands **Man of the Match:** RN ten Doeschate

Points Awarded: Afghanistan 0, Netherlands 2

Afghanistan: 128 for 9 (20 overs)

Batsman		Bowler	Runs	Balls	4s	6s
Karim Sadiq	c Seelaar	b Jonkman	18	17	1	0
Nowroz Mangal*		b Jonkman	10	11	1	0
Mohammed Sherzad+	run out (Szwarczynski/Borren)		11	10	0	1
Mohammad Nabi	c Borren	b ten Doeschate	1	3	0	0
Raees Ahmadzai	c ten Doeschate	B Mohammad Kashif	23	23	0	0
Noor Ali	run out (Borren/Buurman)		18	25	0	0
Shafiqullah Shinwari	c Mohammad Kashif	b Seelaar	2	62	0	0
Samiullah Shinwari	run out (ten Doeschate/Buurman)		19	14	1	0
Mirwais Ashraf	run out (van Bunge/Buurman)		19	9	0	2
Hamid Hassan	not out		2	2	0	0
Sharpour Zadran	did not bat					-
Extras		(b1 lb1 w3)	5			
TOTAL		9 wickets for	128			

Bowling	O	M	R	W	Wd	Nb
Mudassar Bukhari	4	0	31	0	0	0
RN ten Doeschate	2	0	15	1	1	0
MBS Jonkman	4	0	23	2	2	0
PM Seelaar	4	0	25	1	0	0
PW Borren	4	0	24	0	0	0
Mohammad Kashif	2	0	8	1	0	0

Fall of wickets: 1-30 (Karim Sadiq); 2-31 (Nowroz Mangal);
3-32 (Mohammad Nabi); 4-51 (Mohammed Sherzad);
5-82 (Raees Ahmadzai); 6-86 (Noor Ali); 7-92 (Shafiqullah
Shinwari); 8-118 (Samiullah Shinwari); 9-128 (Mirwais
Ashraf)

Netherlands: 132 for 6 (18.5 overs)

Batsman		Bowler	Runs	Balls	4s	6s
AN Kervezee		b Mohammad Nabi	39	33	5	0
ES Szwarczynski	Mohammad Nabi	c&b Mohammad Nabi	21	24	0	1
DLS van Bunge	c Mirwais Ashraf	b Mohammad Nabi	24	22	0	1
B Zuiderent	lbw	b Samiullah Shinwari	2	3	0	0
RN ten Doeschate	not out		24	20	2	0
PW Borren*	run out (Raees Ahmadzai)		1	5	0	0
AF Buurman+		b Hamid Hassan	0	2	0	0
Mudassar Bukhari	not out		3	4	0	0
MBS Jonkman	did not bat		-			
PM Seelaar	did not bat		-			
Mohammad Kashif	did not bat		-			
Extras		(b1 lb7 w10)	18			
TOTAL		6 wickets for	132			

Bowling	O	M	R	W	Wd	Nb
Sharpour Zadran	2	0	20	0	0	0
Mirwais Ashraf	3	0	17	0	0	0
Karim Sadiq	3	0	16	0	1	0
Samiullah Shinwari	3	0	26	1	3	0
Mohammad Nabi	4	0	23	3	1	0
Hamid Hassan	3.5	0	22	1	0	0

Fall of wickets: 1-64 (Kervezee); 2-71 (Szwarczynski);
3-74 (Zuiderent); 4-109 (van Bunge); 5-113 (Borren); 6-118
(Buurman)

AFGHANISTAN v UNITED ARAB EMIRATES

Played at Dubai International Cricket Stadium, 13 February,
Super Fours – Afghanistan won by 4 wickets

Match details: Toss: United Arab Emirates **Man of the Match:** Noor Ali

Points Awarded: United Arab Emirates 0, Afghanistan 2

United Arab Emirates: 100 for 9 (20 overs)

Batsman		Bowler	Runs	Balls	4s	6s
Mohammad Iqbal		b Mirwais Ashraf	0	1	5	5
Arfan Haider	c Hamid Hassan	b Sharpour Zadran	2	6	0	0
Abdul Rehman+	lbw	b Mohammad Nabi	18	20	1	0
Khurram Khan*	c Mohammed Sherzad	b Mirwais Ashraf	1	3	0	0
Saqib Ali	lbw	b Mohammad Nabi	24	33	2	0
Naeemuddin Aslan		b Hamid Hassan	18	24	1	0
Fayyaz Ahmed		b Mohammad Nabi	9	15	0	0
EHSN Silva		b Hamid Hassan	1	2	0	0
Qadar Nawaz	st Mohammed Sherzad	b Samiullah Shinwari	4	5	0	0
Qasim Zubair	not out		6	5		
Ahmed Raza	not out		4	2		
Extras		(lb2 w6)	18			
TOTAL		**9 wickets for**	**100**			

Bowling	O	M	R	W	Wd	Nb
Sharpour Zadran	4	0	18	1	0	0
Mirwais Ashraf	4	0	15	2	1	0
Samiullah Shinwari	2	0	16	1	3	0
Mohammad Nabi	4	0	17	3	1	0
Karim Sadiq	2	0	9	0	0	0
Hamid Hassan	4	0	23	2	0	0

Fall of wickets: 1-5 (Mohammad Iqbal); 2-9 (Arfan Haider); 3-11 (Khurram Khan); 4-53 (Abdul Rehman); 5-56 (Saqib Ali); 6-77 (Fayyaz Ahmed); 7-80 (Silva); 8-85 (Qadar Nawaz); 9-91 (Naeemuddin Aslan)

Afghanistan: 101 for 6 (19.3 overs)

Batsman		Bowler	Runs	Balls	4s	6s
Karim Sadiq		b Silva	2	6	0	0
Noor Ali	not out		38	46	1	0
Mohammed Sherzad+		b Silva	9	11	0	0
Nowroz Mangal*	c Qadar Nawaz	b Fayyaz Ahmed	1	3	0	0
Asghar Stanikzai	c Qadar Nawaz	b Fayyaz Ahmed	26	32	1	2
Mohammad Nabi		b Qadar Nawaz	1	2	0	0
Samiullah Shinwari	run out (Qasim Zubair)		4	1	1	0
Raees Ahmadzai	not out		0	0	0	0
Mirwais Ashraf	did not bat		19	9	0	2
Hamid Hassan	did not bat		2	2	0	0
Sharpour Zadran	did not bat		-			
Extras		(b1 lb3 w3)	7			
TOTAL		**6 wickets for**	**101**			

Bowling	O	M	R	W	Wd	Nb
Qasim Zubair	1.3	0	6	0	0	0
EHSN Silva	4	0	14	2	1	0
Ahmed Raza	4	0	12	0	0	0
Saqib Ali	1	0	9	0	0	0
Khurram Khan	4	0	25	0	2	0
Fayyaz Ahmed	3	0	14	2	0	0
Qadar Nawaz	2	0	17	1	0	0

Fall of wickets: 1-5 (Karim Sadiq); 2-16 (Mohammed Sherzad); 3-48 (Nowroz Mangal); 4-88 (Asghar Stanikzai); 5-96 (Mohammad Nabi); 6-100 (Samiullah Shinwari)

AFGHANISTAN v IRELAND

Played at Dubai International Cricket Stadium, 13 February,
Final – Afghanistan won by 8 wickets

Match details: **Toss:** Ireland **Man of the Match:** Mohammed Sherzad **Comments:** day/night match. Afghanistan won the tournament. Both finalists proceed to 2010 World Twenty20 Finals.

Ireland: 142 for 8 (20 overs)

Batsman		Bowler	Runs	Balls	4s	6s
WTS Porterfield*	c Mirwais Ashraf	b Mohammad Nabi	20	15	3	0
NJ O'Brien+	run out (Samiullah Shinwari)		28	27	3	0
AR Cusack	st Mohammed Sherzad	b Samiullah Shinwari	28	22	1	1
KJ O'Brien	c Raees Ahmadzai	b Nowroz Mangal	2	3	0	0
GC Wilson	c Hamid Hassan	b Nowroz Mangal	5	7	1	0
NG Jones		b Nowroz Mangal	14	14	1	0
JF Mooney		b Hamid Hassan	5	9	0	0
DT Johnston	c Nowroz Mangal	b Sharpour Zadran	15	12	1	0
AR White	not out		7	9	0	0
P Connell	not out		3	4	0	0
GH Dockrell	did not bat		-			
Extras		(b1 lb7 w5 nb2)	15			
TOTAL		8 wickets for	142			

Bowling	O	M	R	W	Wd	Nb
Sharpour Zadran	3	0	25	1	1	0
Mirwais Ashraf	2	0	10	0	0	0
Karim Sadiq	2	0	17	0	1	0
Mohammad Nabi	3	0	23	1	0	0
Samiullah Shinwari	2	0	9	1	0	0
Nowroz Mangal	4	0	23	3	2	0
Hamid Hassan	4	0	27	1	1	2

Fall of wickets: 1-42 (Porterfield); 2-81 (NJ O'Brien); 3-87 (Cusack); 4-87 (KJ O'Brien); 5-97 (Wilson); 6-111 (Jones); 7-117 (Mooney); 8-137 (Johnston)

Afghanistan: 147 for 2 (17.3 overs)

Batsman		Bowler	Runs	Balls	4s	6s
Karim Sadiq	c White	b Johnston	34	17	4	1
Noor Ali	lbw	b KJ O'Brien	16	24	1	0
Mohammed Sherzad+	not out		65	46	6	1
Nowroz Mangal*	not out		21	18	3	0
Asghar Stanikzai	did not bat		-			
Mohammad Nabi	did not bat		-			
Samiullah Shinwari	did not bat		-			
Raees Ahmadzai	did not bat		-			
Mirwais Ashraf	did not bat		-			
Hamid Hassan	did not bat		-			
Sharpour Zadran	did not bat		-			
Extras		(b1 lb1 w9)	11			
TOTAL		2 wickets for	147			

Bowling	O	M	R	W	Wd	Nb
P Connell	3.3	0	46	0	1	0
DT Johnston	4	0	28	1	0	0
AR Cusack	3	0	21	0	2	0
GH Dockrell	4	0	26	0	2	0
KJ O'Brien	2	0	16	1	0	0
NG Jones	1	0	8	0	0	0

Fall of wickets: 1-37 (Karim Sadiq); 2-89 (Noor Ali)

SUPER FOURS – FINAL TABLE

Team	P	W	L	T	N/R	NRR	Pts
Ireland	3	2	1	0	0	+1.233	4
Afghanistan	3	2	1	0	0	+0.100	4
United Arab Emirates	3	1	2	0	0	−0.244	2
Netherlands	3	1	2	0	0	−1.105	2

Top two teams progress to the ICC World Twenty20.

2010 ICC WORLD TWENTY20, WEST INDIES, APRIL–MAY 2010

AFGHANISTAN v INDIA

Played at Beausejour Stadium, Gros Islet, St Lucia, 1 May, Group C – India won by 7 wickets

Match details: **Toss:** India **Man of the Match:** A Nehra **Points Awarded:** Afghanistan 0, India 2

Afghanistan: 115 for 8 (20 overs)

Batsman		Bowler	Runs	Balls	4s	6s
Noor Ali	c Dhoni	b Nehra	50	48	4	0
Karim Sadiq	c Dhoni	b Nehra	0	4	0	0
Mohammed Sherzad+	c Dhoni	b Nehra	6	5	1	0
Nowroz Mangal*	c Gambhir	b Jadeja	5	11	1	0
Asghar Stanikzai	c Khan	b Kumar	30	33	0	3
Mohammad Nabi	c Dhoni	b Kumar	0	3	0	0
Raees Ahmadzai	not out		5	5	0	0
Samiullah Shinwari	run out (Jadeja/Dhoni)		7	6	1	0
Hamid Hassan	c Nehra	b Khan	6	5	1	0
Sharpour Zadran	not out		0	0	0	0
Dawlat Ahmadzai	did not bat		-			
Extras		(lb3 w3)	6			
TOTAL		8 wickets for	115			

Bowling	O	M	R	W	Wd	Nb
P Kumar	3	0	14	2	0	0
A Nehra	4	0	19	3	0	0
Z Khan	3	0	24	1	1	0
RA Jadeja	4	1	15	1	0	0
Yuvraj Singh	1	0	4	0	0	0
Harbhajan Singh	4	0	24	0	1	0
YK Pathan	1	0	12	0	1	0

Fall of wickets: 1-6 (Karim Sadiq); 2-22 (Mohammed Sherzad); 3-29 (Nowroz Mangal); 4-97 (Noor Ali); 5-97 (Asghar Stanikzai); 6-97 (Mohammad Nabi); 7-107 (Samiullah Shinwari); 8-114 (Hamid Hassan)

India: 116 for 3 (17.5 overs)

Batsman		Bowler	Runs	Balls	4s	6s
G Gambhir	c Mohammad Nabi	b Dawlat Ahmadzai	4	6	0	0
M Vijay	c Sharpour Zadran	b Hamid Hassan	48	46	2	3
SK Raina	lbw	b Samiullah Shinwari	18	13	1	1
Yuvraj Singh	not out		23	22	0	1
MS Dhoni+	not out		15	6	0	2
YK Pathan	did not bat		-			
RA Jadeja	did not bat		-			
Harbhajan Singh	did not bat		-			
P Kumar	did not bat		-			
Z Khan	did not bat		-			
A Nehra	did not bat		-			
Extras		(b1 w3 nb4)	8			
TOTAL		3 wickets for	116			

Bowling	O	M	R	W	Wd	Nb
Dawlat Ahmadzai	2	0	21	1	0	1
Sharpour Zadran	2	0	6	0	1	0
Mohammad Nabi	3	0	33	0	0	1
Samiullah Shinwari	2	0	1	1	1	0
Karim Sadiq	2	0	22	0	1	2
Hamid Hassan	3	0	8	1	0	0
Nowroz Mangal	0.5	0	14	0	0	0

Fall of wickets: 1-19 (Gambhir); 2-46 (Raina); 3-101 (Vijay)

AFGHANISTAN v SOUTH AFRICA

Played at Kensington Oval, Bridgetown, Barbados, 5 May,
Group C – South Africa won by 59 runs

Match details: **Toss:** Afghanistan **Man of the Match:** M Morkel **Points Awarded:** South Africa 2, Afghanistan 0

South Africa: 139 for 7 (20 overs)

Batsman		Bowler	Runs	Balls	4s	6s
GC Smith*	c Nowroz Mangal	b Mohammad Nabi	27	14	4	1
LE Bosman	run out (Sharpour Zadran/Samiullah Shinwari)		0	1	0	0
JH Kallis	c Mohammed Sherzad	b Hamid Hassan	34	33	0	2
AB de Villiers	st Mohammed Sherzad	b Nowroz Mangal	17	21	1	1
JP Duminy	c Nowroz Mangal	b Hamid Hassan	25	21	0	2
MV Boucher+	lbw	b Hamid Hassan	4	6	0	0
JA Morkel	c Nowroz Mangal	b Sharpour Zadran	23	17	2	1
RE van der Merwe	not out		2	6	0	0
DW Steyne	not out		1	1	0	0
M Morkel	did not bat		-			
CK Langeveldt	did not bat		-			
Extras		(lb4 w2)	6			
TOTAL		7 wickets for	139			

Bowling	O	M	R	W	Wd	Nb
DW Steyne	3	0	6	2	3	0
CK Langeveldt	4	0	12	3	3	0
M Morkel	3	0	20	4	1	2
RE van der Merwe	4	1	21	0	1	0
JA Morkel	2	0	20	0	0	0

Fall of wickets: 1-13 (Bosman); 2-45 (Smith); 3-77 (de Villiers); 4-84 (Kallis); 5-90 (Boucher); 6-133 (Duminy); 7-137 (JA Morkel)

Afghanistan: 80 all out (16 overs)

Batsman		Bowler	Runs	Balls	4s	6s
Noor Ali	c Boucher	b Steyn	0	3	0	0
Karim Sadiq	c de Villiers	b M Morkel	2	8	0	0
Mohammed Sherzad+	c Boucher	b Steyn	2	6	0	0
Nowroz Mangal*	c Kallis	b M Morkel	1	4	0	0
Asghar Stanikzai	c Steyn	b Langeveldt	3	6	0	0
Raees Ahmadzai	c Boucher	b M Morkel	4	2	1	0
Mohammad Nabi	c Duminy	b M Morkel	0	5	0	0
Samiullah Shinwari	run out (de Villiers)		11	12	0	1
Mirwais Ashraf		b Langeveldt	23	25	1	2
Hamid Hassan	c Kallis	b Langeveldt	22	21	1	2
Sharpour Zadran	not out		1	6	0	0
Extras		(lb1 w8 nb2)	11			
TOTAL		10 wickets for	80			

Bowling	O	M	R	W	Wd	Nb
Sharpour Zadran	3	0	29	1	0	1
Mirwais Ashraf	2	0	18	0	0	0
Mohammad Nabi	4	0	33	1	0	0
Samiullah Shinwari	4	0	14	0	0	0
Nowroz Mangal	3	0	20	1	0	1
Hamid Hassan	4	0	21	3	0	0

Fall of wickets: 1-1 (Noor Ali); 2-5 (Mohammed Sherzad); 3-7 (Nowroz Mangal); 4-8 (Karim Sadiq); 5-12 (Raees Ahmadzai); 6-14 (Mohammad Nabi); 7-25 (Asghar Stanikzai); 8-32 (Samiullah Shinwari); 9-65 Mirwais Ashraf); 10-80 (Hamid Hassan)

GROUP C – FINAL TABLE

Team	P	W	L	T	N/R	NRR	Pts
India	2	2	0	0	0	+1.495	4
South Africa	2	1	1	0	0	+1.125	2
Afghanistan	2	0	2	0	0	-2.446	0

Top two teams progress to the Super Eights.

Player Profiles

Aftab Alam
Born: 30 November 1992
Place of birth: Kacha Gari refugee camp, Peshawar, Pakistan
Major teams: Afghanistan, Afghanistan Under-19s
Batting style: Right-hand bat
Bowling style: Right-arm, medium-fast
Relations: Brothers – Taj Malik Alam, Hasti Gul Abid and Karim Sadiq

Ahmad Shah
Born: 20 October 1983
Place of birth: Paktika, Afghanistan
Major teams: Afghanistan
Batting style: Left-hand bat
Bowling style: Slow left-arm, orthodox

Asghar Stanikzai
(also known as Asghar Salam Khail)
Born: 27 February 1987
Place of birth: Peshawar, Pakistan
Major teams: Afghanistan
Batting style: Right-hand bat
Bowling style: Right-arm, medium-fast

Dawlat Ahmadzai
Born: 5 September 1984
Place of birth: Peshawar, Pakistan
Major teams: Afghanistan
Batting style: Right-hand bat
Bowling style: Right-arm, fast-medium

Gulbadeen Naib
Born: 16 March 1991
Place of birth: Kacha Gari refugee camp, Peshawar, Pakistan
Major teams: Afghanistan
Batting style: Right-hand bat
Bowling style: Right-arm, medium

Hamid Hassan
Born: 1 June 1987
Place of birth: Nangarhar, Afghanistan
Major teams: Afghanistan, MCC, Pakistan Customs, Norden
Cricket Club and Skegness Cricket Club
Batting style: Right-hand bat
Bowling style: Right-arm, fast-medium

Hasti Gul Abid
Born: 1 January 1984
Place of birth: Nangarhar, Afghanistan
Major teams: Afghanistan, Sebastianites Cricket and Athletic Club
Batting style: Right-hand bat
Bowling style: Right-arm, medium
Relations: Brothers – Taj Malik Alam, Karim Sadiq and Aftab Alam

Karim Sadiq
Born: 18 February 1984
Place of birth: Nangarhar, Afghanistan
Major teams: Afghanistan
Batting style: Right-hand bat
Bowling style: Right-arm, off-break
Fielding position: Wicketkeeper
Relations: Brothers – Taj Malik Alam, Hasti Gul Abid and Aftab Alam

Khaliq Dad Noori
Born: 1 January 1984
Place of birth: Baghlan, Afghanistan
Major teams: Afghanistan
Batting style: Right-hand bat
Bowling style: Right-arm, fast-medium
Relation: Brother – Allah Dad Noori

Mirwais Ashraf
Born: 30 June 1988
Place of birth: Kunduz, Afghanistan
Major teams: Afghanistan
Batting style: Right-hand bat
Bowling style: Right-arm, fast-medium

Mohammad Nabi
Born: 7 March 1985
Place of birth: Peshawar, Pakistan
Major teams: Afghanistan, MCC, Pakistan Customs
Batting style: Right-hand bat
Bowling style: Right-arm, off-break

Mohammed Sherzad
(also known as MS Sherzad)
Born: 15 July 1991
Place of birth: Peshawar, Pakistan
Major teams: Afghanistan
Batting style: Right-hand bat
Fielding position: Wicketkeeper

Noor Ali Zadran
Born: 10 July 1988
Place of birth: Khost, Afghanistan
Major teams: Afghanistan
Batting style: Right-hand bat
Bowling style: Right-arm, medium-fast

Nowroz Mangal
Born: 28 November 1984
Place of birth: Kabul, Afghanistan
Major teams: Afghanistan
Batting style: Right-hand bat
Bowling style: Right-arm, off-break

Rahmat Wali
Born: 1980
Place of birth: Khost Province, Afghanistan
Died: 27 August 2008, Khost Province, Afghanistan
Major teams: Afghanistan
Batting style: Left-hand bat
Bowling style: Slow left-arm, orthodox

Raees Ahmadzai
Born: 3 September 1984
Place of birth: Logar, Afghanistan
Major teams: Afghanistan, Sebastianites Cricket and Athletic Club
Batting style: Right-hand bat
Bowling style: Right-arm, off-break

Samiullah Shinwari
(also known as Sami Shinwari)
Born: 31 December 1987
Place of birth: Nangarhar, Afghanistan
Major teams: Afghanistan
Batting style: Right-hand bat
Bowling style: Right arm, leg-break

Shafiqullah Shinwari
(also known as Shafiq Shafaq)
Born: 7 August 1989
Place of birth: Nangarhar Province, Afghanistan
Major teams: Afghanistan
Batting style: Right-hand bat

Sharpour Zadran
Born: 8 July 1987
Place of birth: Peshawar, Pakistan
Major teams: Afghanistan, Afghanistan Under-19
and Badureliya Sports Club
Batting style: Left-hand bat
Bowling style: Left-arm, fast-medium

Coaches and Officials

Taj Malik Alam
Born: 1975
Place of birth: Jagdalik, Nangarhar Province, Afghanistan
Major teams: Afghanistan (coach)
Batting style: Right-hand bat
Bowling style: Right-arm, leg-break (hardball), fast (tennis ball)
Relations: Brothers – Karim Sadiq, Hasti Gul Abid and Aftab Alam

Kabir Khan
Born: 12 April 1974
Place of birth: Peshawar, Pakistan
Major teams: Pakistan, Habib Bank Limited, House Building
Finance Corporation, Peshawar Cricket Association, Stirling County,
Afghanistan (coach)
Batting style: Right-hand bat
Bowling style: Left-arm, fast-medium

Allah Dad Noori
Born: 1976
Place of birth: Baghlan, Afghanistan
Major teams: Afghanistan
Batting style: Right-hand bat
Bowling style: Right-arm, fast
Relation: Brother – Khaliq Dad Noori

If after reading this book you would like to help, there are a few charities I recommend you get in touch with.

Afghan Connection

Firstly Sarah Fane, who first visited Afghanistan as a doctor during the Soviet Regime, has set up a wonderful charity that builds schools and hospital, trains doctors and provides health care. Along with MCC Sarah Fane, through her charity Afghan Connection, has also started organising cricket training camps for Afghan children. I can't speak highly enough of the work Sarah does in Afghanistan, it is inspirational. At one camp for 50 children 12,000 people turned up. There need to be more of these camps. Please check out her amazing work at www.afghanconnection.org

Another charity I would recommend looking at is the Afghan Appeal Fund. They build schools in some of the most dangerous parts of the country. You can find out more about them here: www.afghanappealfund.org.uk

If you'd like to buy some Afghan kit check out www.proudtobeanafghan. com all profits go to building schools in the villages of the Afghan players. It's a great idea set up by Leslie Knott, who I did the documentary with, and Raees Ahmadzai, a former player, on the national team. www.proudtobeanafghan.com